God in an Open Universe

God in an Open Universe

Science, Metaphysics, and Open Theism

Edited by
WILLIAM HASKER, THOMAS JAY OORD,
and DEAN ZIMMERMAN

PICKWICK *Publications* · Eugene, Oregon

GOD IN AN OPEN UNIVERSE
Science, Metaphysics, and Open Theism

Pickwick Publications
An Imprint of Wipf and Stock Publishers
199 W. 8th Ave., Suite 3
Eugene, OR 97401

www.wipfandstock.com

ISBN 13: 978-1-60899-743-5

Cataloguing-in-Publication data:

    God in an open universe : science, metaphysics, and open theism / edited by William Hasker, Thomas Jay Oord, and Dean Zimmerman.

    viii + 206 p. ; 23 cm. —Includes index.

    ISBN 13: 978-1-60899-743-5

    1. Open theism. 2. God — Attributes — Biblical teaching. 3. Religion and science. I. Hasker, William, 1935–. II. Oord, Thomas Jay. III. Zimmerman, Dean W. Title.

BL240.3 .G65 2011

Manufactured in the U.S.A.

Contents

Contributors

David Basinger, PhD, is Professor of Philosophy and Ethics, Roberts Wesleyan College

Robin Collins, PhD, is Professor and Chair of the Department of Philosophy, Messiah College

William Hasker, PhD, is Professor Emeritus of Philosophy, Huntington University

Jeffrey Koperski, PhD, is Professor of Philosophy, Saginaw Valley State University

Thomas Jay Oord, PhD, is Professor of Theology and Philosophy, Northwest Nazarene University

Alan R. Rhoda, PhD, is Adjunct Associate Professor of Philosophy, University of Notre Dame

David Woodruff, PhD, is Professor of Philosophy, Azusa Pacific University

Dean Zimmerman, PhD, is Professor in the Philosophy Department, Rutgers, The State University of New Jersey

Introduction

Open Theism and the Challenge of Science

OPEN THEISM IS A style of theology whose fundamental commitment is to the relational character of God. God according to open theism *need not* have been related to a world of creatures, for there need not have been such a world at all. In fact, however, God has graciously chosen to grant existence to a universe containing an amazingly rich profusion of phenomena, including (at least in our corner of it) creatures blessed with life, consciousness, and even with rationality and the desire and capacity to experience God and relate to him. And having created such a universe, God is not indifferent or remote from it, but cares deeply about it and involves himself in the lives of his creatures, with the loving aim of bringing them into knowledge of and fellowship with himself. In contrast with the "Unmoved Mover" of Aristotle, this God has been characterized as the "Most Moved Mover."[1]

According to open theism, God's desire to be in relation with his creatures attests to the fact that the creatures have something of their own to contribute to this relationship—that they are not mere puppets or automata, carrying out a divine plan which in every detail has been scripted for them in advance. On the contrary, they have been endowed by God with a power of self-determination, enabling them to choose and in part to create their own destinies, at best following the wise guidance of their loving Creator, but with the power to choose, tragically, to reject that guidance and set out on paths of their own, however destructive those paths may in the end turn out to be. God, however, has not left his fallen creatures to their own impoverished resources, but has reached out to them in redemptive love, through the historical encounter recounted in the Bible and culminating in the life, sacrificial death, and resurrection of the Savior, Jesus Christ. The story of the redemption in Christ is the central theme of the New Testament and of the entire Christian faith.

1. This is the title of Clark Pinnock's book, *Most Moved Mover: A Theology of God's Openness* (Grand Rapids: Baker Academic, 2001).

Many of these key themes of open theism are shared with various other strands in the history of Christian faith and thought. However, there is one conclusion drawn by open theism that places it very much in a minority position in relation to the broader theological tradition. In disagreement with most of the tradition (but in agreement with some strands in the biblical text), open theism holds that if humans are to be genuinely free and self-determining, then the future must itself be "open" in the sense of containing genuine *alternative possibilities*—different ways that things can turn out, depending on the different ways in which humans can choose to shape their own lives. The future is not open in an absolute, unqualified sense, because God retains ultimate control and his designs for his creation will not in the end be thwarted. Nevertheless, a great deal of control over their own lives and destinies has been entrusted to the creatures—more control, we sometimes think, than they have proved themselves able to exercise wisely and well. But the openness of the future means that in certain respects what will happen is as yet indeterminate. And what a perfectly wise and knowing being, namely God, will know concerning the future is just that—that it *is* indeterminate, together with the possibilities and probabilities concerning how things will come about, in that sphere where the self-determining creatures hold sway. It is this feature of open theism—that God knows the future in part as a realm of possibilities and probabilities, rather than of settled facts—that has proved to be by far the most controversial.

The central ideas of open theism have been affirmed by a number of theologians and philosophers, especially in the nineteenth and twentieth centuries.[2] However, open theism began to take shape as a distinct theological movement with the publication in 1994 of *The Openness of God*,[3] a jointly authored book setting out the view in terms of its relation to Scripture, to church tradition, to systematic theology, to philosophy, and to Christian practice. The book was met with sharp controversy, but also with interest by many, and with enthusiastic acceptance by a number of evangelical Christians who found in it a preferable alternative to other

---

2. John Sanders, *The God Who Risks: A Theology of Divine Providence*, rev. ed. (Downers Grove, IL: InterVarsity, 2007) 165–69, gives an extensive listing of theologians past and present who have affirmed key ideas of open theism.

3. Clark Pinnock, Richard Rice, John Sanders, William Hasker, and David Basinger, *The Openness of God: A Biblical Challenge to the Traditional Understanding of God* (Downers Grove, IL: InterVarsity, 1994).

versions of Christian theology to which they had been exposed. Both trends—sharp resistance and enthusiastic acceptance—continue down to the present. On balance, it would probably be fair to say that the movement has won a place, though not by any means an uncontested place, within the broad spectrum of evangelical approaches to theology.

Much of the scholarly effort devoted to open theism has been dictated by the polemical context. Philosophically, continued effort has been devoted to the underlying framework of logical argument supporting this perspective against its competitors.[4] Theologically, much of the work has been devoted to considerations concerning the nature of God—"theology proper"—and to the doctrine of divine providence, which assumes a distinctively different form than for more traditional theologies.[5] Both theologians and philosophers have directed their attention to the problem of evil, a topic on which open theism offers significant advantages compared with its main competitors.[6] In comparison, very little work has been done to date in examining the interconnections between open theism and the natural sciences. Clearly, however, this is an area that needs to be addressed; the central place taken by the sciences in modern life and thought means that any perspective that hopes to have a broad impact needs to take account of them. Furthermore, there is reason to think that here, also, open theism may be able to make a distinctive contribution.

In an effort to address this need, a seminar was convened in the summer of 2007 at Eastern Nazarene College, sponsored by the John Templeton Foundation, and directed by Thomas Jay Oord, Clark Pinnock, and Karl Giberson. Additional participants were David Basinger, Dean Blevins, Gregory Boyd, Craig Boyd, Anna Case-Winters, Robin Collins, John Culp, William Hasker, Jeffrey Koperski, Michael Lodahl, Brint Montgomery, Alan Padgett, Alan Rhoda, Richard Rice, John Sanders, Karen Winslow, David Woodruff, and Dean Zimmerman.

---

4. See David Basinger, *The Case for Freewill Theism: A Philosophical Assessment* (Downers Grove, IL: InterVarsity, 1996), and William Hasker, *God, Time, and Knowledge* (Ithaca, NY: Cornell University Press, 1989).

5. Pinnock's *Most Moved Mover,* and Sanders' *The God Who Risks,* both cited above, are cases in point.

6. See Gregory Boyd, *Satan and the Problem of Evil: Constructing a Trinitarian Warfare Theodicy* (Downers Grove, IL: InterVarsity, 2001), and William Hasker, *Providence, Evil, and the Openness of God* (London: Routledge, 2004), and *The Triumph of God Over Evil: Theodicy for a World of Suffering* (Downers Grove, IL: InterVarsity, 2008).

At this seminar twenty philosophers and theologians spent three weeks intensively interacting with one another and with a series of visiting lecturers, including scientists, theologians, and philosophers. This same group met again in April of 2008 at Azusa Pacific University to share the results of their labors. After additional refinement, some of these results are presented here, in the form of essays by seven of the philosophers who attended the seminar. (A separate volume containing theological contributions has been published under the title *Creation Made Free: Open Theology Engaging Science,* edited by Thomas Jay Oord.[7]) We continue with brief summaries of each of the seven papers.

In the first essay, William Hasker addresses "The Need for a Bigger God." The "bigness" of God is an important issue for open theism, which has been stigmatized by some critics as "neotheism" and as a theology of "God's lesser glory." Hasker urges the need for a God who is "big enough" to account for the unimaginably vast universe that is now being revealed to us through astronomy and cosmology. He contends, however, that we should also consider the criteria of "bigness," or "greatness," that we apply in interpersonal relationships, especially as applied to rulers and those who exercise leadership roles. We do not, he argues, especially admire leaders or rulers who "micro-manage," being determined to keep all decision-making entirely in their own hands and regarding others merely as lackeys to carry out the leader's decisions. On the contrary, greatness and excellence are seen in the leader who is able to delegate authority and to allow and encourage her subordinates to make genuine, creative contributions of their own to the overall enterprise. Applying this model theologically, we reach the conclusion that a truly great God would not be obsessed with minutely controlling every aspect of the world's history, but would rather draw humans and other personal agents into the process of world-making, while providing guidance, support, and help in time of need. In this way we come to a picture of a truly great God that is very much in harmony with open theism.

This same line of thought can be extended as well to the subpersonal realm. Following suggestions made by John Haught and John Polkinghorne, Hasker proposes that such a great God might well prefer to bring the cosmos to its desired state through a gradual evolutionary process, in which subsequent advances are brought about through the exer-

7. Thomas Jay Oord, *Creation Made Free: Open Theology Engaging Science* (Eugene, OR: Pickwick, 2009).

cise of the powers divinely implanted in the immature stages of creation. This inference does not amount to a logical demonstration, but it does suggest a consonance between open theism and an evolutionary cosmology that does not exist for competing theological views. Hasker further proposes that an evolutionary cosmology lends in turn strong support to an "emergentist" model of the mind, in which consciousness and mentality are themselves the product of forces and powers divinely implanted in the ultimate constituents of the material world. If this is correct, it turns out that a trio of important conclusions—open theism, an evolutionary cosmology, and an emergentist view of the mental—are all suggested and supported by the initial way of understanding the greatness of God.

The next two essays are methodological in character, albeit in somewhat different ways. Jeffrey Koperski writes about "Metatheoretic Shaping Principles: Where Science Meets Theology." The principles in question stand on or very close to the boundary between science on the one hand, and philosophy and theology on the other. They are extremely general and resist straightforward empirical confirmation or disconfirmation, yet they are accepted as guiding constraints on scientific work, and are often put forward as defining "what science really is" in this or that area of scientific endeavor. Examples include metaphysical principles such as the uniformity of nature, realism, and the causal closure of the physical domain, as well as epistemological principles such as the demand for repeatable, intersubjective observations, explanatory virtues such as empirical adequacy, testability, and simplicity, and methodological naturalism. These principles exert a "downward" influence on what counts as acceptable science, but they also have "upward" ramifications in that they constrain what sorts of worldviews are deemed to be compatible with our advancing scientific knowledge. Thus, such principles tend to be at the heart of many theology-and-science debates.

Koperski points out that, even though MSPs may be regarded as integral to science at a particular time, they are subject to change and have in fact been changed in the past. Examples of this include the abandonment of determinism under the pressure of quantum mechanics and the shift from catastrophism to uniformitarianism in geology. This leads to a review of some of the MSPs currently favored in various branches of science, and a discussion of their compatibility with theism in general and with open theism in particular. Singled out for particular attention are naturalism (both metaphysical and methodological), reductionism, and realism. Koperski concludes that, perhaps surprisingly, "differences within the open theology camp are more relevant to these issues than open theism itself."

In his essay, "Religious Belief Formation: A Kantian Perspective Informed by Science," David Basinger raises rather a different sort of methodological question. How, he asks, should what we know scientifically about the process of belief formation influence the way in which we understand our own religious beliefs and those of others? He sets out a number of widely accepted, and evidentially supported, theses concerning the way our brains operate in processing data and arriving at, changing, or persisting in beliefs. (For instance, the claim that "The normal functioning of our brain is not to proportion belief to the totality of the evidence but rather to make judgments in specific situations apart from all of the relevant data of which we are aware.") He also puts forward a "Kantian hypothesis" concerning religious belief formation and retention, namely that "while there is an external reality, our understanding of this reality will always be shaped significantly by factors we don't control and can't totally avoid and that these factors always keep us to some extent from seeing reality as it really is." In the light of this Kantian hypothesis, Basinger discusses several examples of religious beliefs that have been widely held but are now universally rejected: one example is the belief that, because of what the Bible says about slavery, Christians today should regard slavery as a proper and justified social institution. He concludes that epistemic conflicts over divergent religious beliefs "remain unresolved because the proponents of none of the divergent perspectives are in a position to demonstrate in an objective, non-question-begging manner that their perspective is superior." In the light of this, "The best that the proponents of any perspective can do . . . is to justifiably believe (for various reasons) that this perspective is superior."

This does not mean, Basinger argues, that there is little reason for persons to assess their own religious beliefs or to encourage others to reflect on their own beliefs. Notwithstanding the "uncontrollable" factors in belief noted above, such reflection can lead to belief change with beneficial results, especially when the reflection is informed by an understanding of divergent perspectives and of the reasons others have for embracing such perspectives. Nor should we assume that we are never in a position to influence meaningfully the dominant religious perspective of a given group of individuals. (At this point he cites the introduction of open theism into the evangelical community through the publication of *The Openness of God,* and various decisions that were made that affected the subsequent influence of that viewpoint.)

However, certain conclusions do emerge if we understand religious belief in the light of this Kantian perspective. One conclusion relates to the practice of college teaching: teachers should not utilize the "debate model," in order to persuade as many students as possible to adopt the instructor's point of view. Rather, they ought to help their students understand the range of viewpoints on an issue under discussion, as well as the reasons why the divergent viewpoints are held. A second conclusion is that "encouraging belief assessment in a Kantian epistemic environment has the potential to minimize religious intolerance." Finally, Basinger states that "while I do not doubt that there is objective religious truth, my Kantian perspective . . . has led me increasingly to believe that the way I conceptualize such truth is simply one way in which this truth can be understood, a way that is in great part the product of the shaping factors noted previously. However," he adds, "I also believe that the Spirit of God can work within this context to help each of us better understand that which we are capable of understanding." These conclusions, one may observe, are especially relevant to open theism in that observing them would tend to make possible a constructive debate about that position, in contrast with a confrontational situation in which the view is stigmatized with the aim of preventing persons from giving it any serious consideration!

The next three papers are concerned with a topic that is central to the metaphysics of open theism, namely the nature of the future. We have already noted open theism's commitment to the "openness" of the future, but what precisely does that mean? According to Alan Rhoda, it means (or can mean) several distinct things. In "The Fivefold Openness of the Future," Rhoda elucidates as many senses in which the future can be said to be open. Roughly characterized they are as follows. (For more precise characterizations, see Rhoda's essay.) *Causal openness* means that there is some possible event at some future time whose existence is neither guaranteed nor precluded by the world state at present. *Alethic openness* means that there is a possible future event such that it is at present neither true that it will occur nor true that it will not occur. *Ontic openness* means that it is not the case that a complete future is in existence. *Epistemic openness* means that there is some possible future event concerning which no one knows whether or not it will occur. And *providential openness* for a particular agent (most likely, God) means that there is a possible future event such that this agent has not efficaciously ordained either the event's existence or its non-existence.

Having defined these five sorts of openness, Rhoda goes on to consider their relationships with each other. He argues that if we assume the existence of God (or, for non-theists, an ideal knower), it is plausible that we ought to conclude that if the future is open in any of these five senses it is open in all of them. This is an important conclusion, for many non-open theists reject causal determinism, thus accepting the causal openness of the future. If Rhoda is right, these theists have some explaining to do, as to why they do not accept that the future is open in the other ways enumerated, thus becoming full-fledged open theists.

The next two essays deal with one of the most pressing scientific issues concerning open theism. David Woodruff, in "Presentism and the Problem of Special Relativity," and Dean Zimmerman, in "Open Theism and the Metaphysics of the Space-Time Manifold" address this problem in somewhat different ways. But what precisely is the problem about open theism and special relativity? The core problem is that Einstein's theory of special relativity seems to deny what Rhoda has termed the "ontic openness of the future." That is to say, as standardly interpreted the theory seems to imply that the entire future *does exist,* just as much as the present exists—that is, the theory implies eternalism, what some have termed the "block theory" of time.[8] Here's how the implication comes about. The theory of special relativity notoriously asserts that "simultaneity is relative to a reference frame." That is to say that two observers, moving in relation to each other, will not in general agree on which events are simultaneous, or on which of two events precedes the other. Furthermore, there is no objective way to determine which of the two observers is "correct" in her own determination as to which events are simultaneous. (This is a consequence of the fact that the speed of light is the same in all reference frames.) But "the present" is best understood as "all events that are simultaneous with *now*"—and this means that, if there is no absolute simultaneity, there is also no "now" and no "present" in an absolute sense. What is "now," or what is "present" is relative to a speaker, marking the

8. Special relativity does not, however, imply that the future exists *now,* at the present time. For explanation of the difference between existence in the present and existence *simpliciter,* see Zimmerman's essay.

particular temporal point at which she is speaking, just as "here" is relative to a speaker, marking the spatial point at which she speaks.

If there is no absolute present moment, then the entire distinction between past, present and future has no absolute significance; that distinction is merely relative to the time at which a person speaks. But then the very idea of a fundamental difference between past and future, such that while the past is "closed" and settled the future is "open" and still-to-be-decided, disappears entirely. Indeed, "past," "present," and "future"—that is, the events that *we consider,* from a particular temporal standpoint, as past, present and future—will *all exist together,* and this is what the "block theory" of time amounts to. All this, it should by now be evident, is very bad news for open theists—as it is for all those who affirm libertarian free will, but the problem seems especially acute for open theism.

Woodruff and Zimmerman agree so far on the nature of the problem, and they agree in embracing the theory of time known as "presentism"— roughly, the view that only present things exist. (Things in the past *did* exist, but they do so no longer, and in the future there will be things that exist *then,* but that are now completely non-existent.) But how, then, deal with the problem posed by the theory of relativity? (As Zimmerman observes, rejecting a well-established scientific theory on metaphysical grounds is a "dangerous maneuver.") Some presentists have responded by embracing a "neo-Lorentzian" theory of relativity, which asserts that, in spite of Einstein (and in agreement with Isaac Newton), there is in fact an absolute space and time, and therefore a "privileged reference-frame" where the events that appear to be simultaneous *really are* simultaneous, in an absolute sense. The relativistic effects of time-dilation and change in length of measuring devices prevent us from being able to determine empirically which reference-frame is the privileged one, but this in no way implies that absolute space and time do not exist. Neo-Lorentzian relativity is empirically equivalent to the standard theory—that is, it makes the same observational predictions—so it has not been refuted empirically. Nevertheless, it is rather unpopular among scientists, and neither of our authors takes this route.

Woodruff and Zimmerman agree, then, that rather than reverting to Newtonian absolute space and time we should continue to think in terms of the Minkowski "spacetime manifold," the framework which reflects the spacetime relationships of relativity theory. (For the differences between Galileo, Newton, and Minkowski on the nature of space and time, see Zimmerman's article.) At this point, however, they begin to diverge. Woodruff proposes that the real source of the difficulty lies in treating the Minkowski spacetime manifold as a substance—as a real, concrete existing thing. This of course immediately entails the existence of the future along with the present, which is in direct conflict with presentism. Woodruff acknowledges that this was a reasonable supposition for Minkowski to make, in view of the empirical success of relativity theory; nevertheless, it is not mandated by that success. Instead, he suggests, we should view time as relational: "times are nothing more than sequential relations of things." By getting rid of the spacetime manifold as a substance, we get rid of the actually existing future, and presentists can once again breathe freely. Woodruff argues that doing away with substantival spacetime does not commit him to a non-realist or instrumentalist view of science as a whole.

Zimmerman also does not view the Minkowski spacetime manifold as an actually existing substance. However, he holds that the presentist needs to add something to the manifold. "If Minkowski space-time is a manifold consisting of the set of locations at which events could happen, the present is a sort of 'wave of becoming' that moves through this manifold. The Open Theist believes that God knows where this wave of becoming is located." Zimmerman argues that this kind of move successfully resolves the objection to presentism based on special relativity. Adding the "wave of becoming," he contends, should not count as an objectionable philosophical interference with a successful scientific theory. He points out that some versions of quantum theory also necessitate such an addition to the theory, another sort of "wave" that would arguably coincide with the wave of becoming. And he argues at length against the critics of presentism as well as against some presentists (notably William Craig) who hold that a presentist is obliged to accept a neo-Lorentzian interpretation of relativity.

It seems clear that this controversy will continue for some time to come. Evidently things are not as cut and dried as some proponents of the "STR refutes presentism" viewpoint would have us believe.[9] On the

---

9. See David Z. Albert and Rivka Galchen, "A Quantum Threat to Special Relativity," *Scientific American* (March 2009) 32–39, and Zeeya Merali, "Splitting Time from Space: Buzz about Quantum Gravity that Topples Einstein's Spacetime," *Scientific American* (December 2009) 18–21.

other hand, no presentist response to the objection has as yet won general acceptance. Future developments are awaited with interest!

The physics and metaphysics of time are important issues for open theism, but they do not account for the attraction the view possesses for many Christian believers. That attraction is due rather to the way the view harmonizes with and illuminates practical religious experience. This is true especially for the practice of prayer. Open theists believe that God is genuinely influenced by our prayers: it is up to us whether or not we pray, and God may and sometimes does act in response to our prayers in ways he would not have done had we not prayed. To be sure, this is the attitude to prayer that is taken in practice by a multitude of theists of every description. (Only a few hardy souls, such as Jonathan Edwards, have had the fortitude to deny it outright.) But there is something of a disconnect between this way of thinking about prayer and a view that holds that the future is already fixed as part of an immutable divine plan that is infallibly carried out in every detail. This has led to a sense of tension and conflict on the part of many believers; open theism, in contrast, offers an account of divine providence that does not have to be set aside while we are at our prayers.

In view of this, it is highly appropriate that prayer should be the topic of the final essay in this volume, Robin Collins' "Prayer and Open Theism: A Participatory, Co-Creator Model." Collins stipulates that prayer should be thought of as more than "consciousness-raising" in which the person praying cultivates desirable traits and attitudes in herself. He also rejects as inadequate a "naturalistic" account of prayer in which the effects of prayer are completely accounted for by the alleged fact that we have an ability to directly affect various aspects of the world through our thoughts and intentions. Nevertheless, his "co-creator model" incorporates aspects of the naturalistic account. This model starts with the assumption that "our prayers directly affect those things or persons for whom we pray," so that "the universe is constructed in some deep and subtle way to be responsive to human intentions, just as our body is responsive to our thoughts, as in the placebo effect." Divine action is involved in that "the Holy Spirit works within us not only to initiate the prayer, but to amplify its causal efficacy by cohering with our own intentions much as the way in which a laser beam gains its power by various individual light waves cohering together." Collins also proposes that "persistent, faithful prayer creates 'openings' for God to act in the world," whereas "bad intentions and unbelief create barriers for God." The upshot is that in this understanding of prayer, "we are co-creators or co-workers with God in Christ." Collins goes on to discuss in some detail the way in which this model coheres with various aspects of the New Testament teaching on prayer.

The interesting connection with science in this view comes about because of the assumption, noted above, that "the universe is constructed in some deep and subtle way to be responsive to human intentions." This would be seen by many as a *conflict* with science, a point at which science tells us that what the view asserts cannot possibly be true. Collins, however, demurs. The assumption that this is impossible, he argues, derives from a mechanistic view of the world that quantum mechanics has shown to be untenable. He appeals to the notion of "morphic fields," developed by biologist Robert Sheldrake. According to Sheldrake, such fields are responsible for directing the process of morpheogenesis, by which the cells in a developing organism differentiate into the pattern of the adult organism. Collins adds to this the claim that our intentions "can contribute to these holistic patterns of causality . . . and thereby non-locally influence the world"—a suggestion with which Sheldrake also agrees. In view of this, Collins asserts that "the co-creator model is consonant with science," though it "by no means could be said to have solid scientific evidence in its favor."

These, then, are the proposals put forward by one group of philosophers concerning some connections between open theism and the study of science. We make no claim to have answered conclusively the questions raised, or even to have provided a definitive mapping of the questions. These essays are more in the nature of explorers' reports, brought back from excursions into some largely uncharted territory. Like all such reports, they stand open to correction by those who come after. But they open up some intriguing areas for further discovery. We hope you will find them as interesting and instructive to read as we have found the exploratory journey.

The Editors
William Hasker,
Thomas Jay Oord,
and Dean Zimmerman

PART ONE

Open Theism and the Greatness of God

1

The Need for a Bigger God

IN 1953, J. B. Phillips, Anglican pastor and translator of the New Testament, published a little book entitled *Your God Is Too Small.*[1] In it Phillips set out and criticized a number of "too small" ideas of God held by some of his contemporaries, as a prelude to introducing the reader to a more adequate conception of God. Some of the divine caricatures criticized by Phillips are the "resident policeman," a god identified with one's conscience, the "parental hangover," modeled on a domineering or otherwise unsatisfactory father, the "god of one hundred percent" who demands an instant perfection that is impossible for growing human beings, and the "managing director," who is too involved in the overall management of the universe to take any interest in individual human lives.

A half century later, I believe we also are in need of a "bigger God." Whether or not we are in thrall of the various "small gods" identified by Phillips (and some of them are still very much alive), we have a need to reflect on the greatness, the *bigness,* of the God we worship. It is my hope, furthermore, that thinking about this may provide us with a clue to the best way of thinking about several key questions that confront contemporary Christian philosophy and theology.

To begin with, and at the risk of tautology, we need to recognize that God is very, very *big.* In fact, God is *enormous.* More than that, God is *re-*

1. J. B. Phillips, *Your God Is Too Small* (London: Macmillan, 1953).

ally tremendous. In traditional theology, one of the attributes of God was said to be *immensity*, and that is just right: God is truly *immense*.[2]

True enough, you may respond, but why bother saying it? Does anyone actually deny what is being said here? Perhaps not—at least, no thoughtful Christian would deny it—but it is still important to say it, because *in our imagination* (and imagination is religiously powerful) we are very likely to be entertaining a picture of God that is "too small" to meet our needs. According to theologian John Haught, "The universe has outgrown the anthropomorphic one-planet deity."[3] To be sure, those attributes and activities of God that directly concern us are limited to those that have an impact on this one planet of ours. (Only a very few of us have ventured even as far as the planet's satellite.) But a trap awaits us if we permit our religious thought and imagination to be locked in on a "one-planet deity." For contemporary science has begun to tell us of a universe that is unimaginably vast. This our earth, enormous from the perspective of any human being, is itself tiny in comparison with the sun and the larger planets in our own system. The sun, in turn, is a minor star located on one of the spiral arms of a galaxy that contains hundreds of billions of such stars. The galaxy itself is only one in a universe that contains many billions of other galaxies. The distances also are unimaginably great. The passage of light is in effect instantaneous from the standpoint of all ordinary human activities, yet the size of the known universe is measured by the distance traveled by light over billions of years! Our powers of imagination and visualization are completely defeated by such magnitudes; we can conceive of them at all only abstractly, by the device of taking known measures and adding to them large numbers of zeroes.

And now comes the trap. "Isn't it absurd," we will be asked, "to suppose that your little god—a god first worshiped by a bunch of wandering sheep-herders in the ancient Middle East—has any relation to all this vastness? Isn't it time to grow up, and admit that the real mysteries of the universe are the scientific mysteries of physics and cosmology, and not the parochial mystifications indulged in by theologians? And on the other hand, even if it should happen that there is some Cause, or Force, or perhaps Mind that is somehow the source of the entire universe, it is

2. What we tend to say most often is that God is *infinite*. This is certainly true, but I don't think it is an adequate replacement for divine immensity; infinity is too negative, and too abstract, to challenge our imagination as it needs to be challenged.

3. From a lecture delivered in Quincy, MA, on June 29, 2007.

surely nonsensical to suppose that it would have any particular concern for such a minuscule, thoroughly insignificant part of the whole as the human race."

To this we must answer, No it is not absurd or nonsensical, except perhaps in the sense that it is "God's foolishness" that is "wiser than human wisdom" (1 Cor 1:25). We really do believe that the One who creates, and sustains, and energizes the entirety of this impossibly huge universe has chosen—amazingly—to take an interest in us, to care for us, to redeem us from our sins and make us his own children. That is not to say that God's interests in the universe are limited to us! It is said of him that no sparrow falls to the ground apart from his will (Matt 10:31); the same will be true of the sparrows, or sparrow-analogues (if such there be), on a billion other planets in our own and other galaxies. We are right to be astonished at all this, but the invitation to disbelieve on that account should be firmly rejected. In order to see things in this light, however, we need to keep very much in mind, not only in our formal affirmations but also in our emotions and our imagination, that our God is a *very big* God.[4]

Divine immensity is only a first step on the way towards a "big enough" God, one who is adequate for our needs in the present moment. I propose that we should proceed by thinking of "bigness" in personal terms—that we should ask ourselves what we have in mind when we speak of a "big" human being. Here of course bigness is not primarily a matter of physical size—Shaquille O'Neal does not image the divine more adequately than the rest of us!—but rather of *personal qualities,* the qualities that lead us to say of someone that she or he is a "big person," or a "great human being." But aren't we in danger of anthropomorphism here? Perhaps there is a danger, but the doctrine that human beings are created in the "image of God" leads Christian thinkers precisely in this direction.

4. Sometimes it has been thought that the discovery that there are rational creatures on other planets would require us to give up the Christian belief in the uniqueness of Jesus Christ, as well as the claim that God the Son was incarnate in Jesus. Fortunately, there is no need to accept such a conclusion. If there are, elsewhere in the universe, other rational creatures made in the image of God (whatever their physical forms may be), it is quite possible that the eternal Son of God has been or will be incarnate on their planets as well, in whatever "flesh" exists there for him to indwell. Or God may have other ways of dealing with these fellow-creatures that do not require incarnation. We simply don't know, but we must not allow the limitations of our knowledge to become limits on the power and wisdom of God! For a brief but interesting discussion of these matters, see Alan Padgett, "Epiphany for a Small Planet: Christology, Astronomy, and Mutuality," in *Perspectives on Science and Christian Faith* 59 (2007) 110–18.

It is anthropomorphic to deny the differences between God and human beings, but it is also possible to exaggerate those differences in such a way that God becomes too abstract and impersonal to be the Christian God. In any case, the risk must be run; if we can't think of God in terms derived from the best and most admirable human beings we know we shall have very little to say about God that is religiously relevant.[5]

So what are some of the qualities that make for a "big person"? No doubt different people will have somewhat different lists, but there are certain attributes that should appear on nearly everybody's list. Such a person will be strong, wise, capable, reliable, and understanding, with wide sympathies, and generous with his or her efforts and resources. Further qualities come to mind when we think of such a person as the leader of a group or organization. (In Scripture, God is compared to a king, to a father, to the owner of an estate or a vineyard, and so on and on.) A leader who is a "big person" will establish and maintain the goals and the overall structure of the group or organization, and will inspire and motivate others to contribute to those goals to the maximum extent possible for them. A really great leader, we think, does not micro-manage her subordinates in such a way as to remove their own scope for initiative and creativity; rather, she develops these qualities in them and seeks to harness them for the greater good of the whole. At times a real leader may entrust resources and responsibilities to others even though she realizes that there is a danger of misuse and subsequent harm. (The father in the parable accedes to his younger son's request for his share of the inheritance, with full awareness that the wealth may be misspent and squandered.)

If we agree that these are indeed the qualities of a big person and a great leader, and that our understanding of the character of God should be modeled on them, then I submit that there is one particular way of conceiving of God that best fills the bill. This is the view that has recently come to be known as "open theism."[6] According to open theism, God has

5. I hope this is not what Haught had in mind when he warned us against being anthropomorphic, but I am not certain. If he did mean this, then on this point we part company.

6. See Clark Pinnock et al., *The Openness of God* (Downers Grove, IL: InterVarsity, 1994), and John Sanders, *The God Who Risks,* 2nd ed. (Downers Grove, IL: InterVarsity, 2007). I do not mean to claim that open theism is the *only* view that enables us to think of a God who is "big" in the way here described. A great many Christian thinkers from different branches of the church would agree with the main substance of what is being said here. I do believe that open theism is the *most consistent* way to conceive of such a "big" God, but the full argument for that claim can't be given here.

deliberately chosen to people his world with individuals possessing a real, though limited, independence. Rather than micro-managing their lives by determining everything for them in advance, he allows them genuine scope for making their own decisions, for good or for ill. In doing this God takes important risks. Not the risk that the overall order of his world will collapse; he is wise, powerful, and well able to prevent that. But he risks that persons will rebel against his good purposes for them, with tragic results for themselves and for others. Indeed, both Scripture and everyday life are full of examples of persons who have so rebelled; some of them, by God's grace, come to repent and to return to his fold and family, while others apparently persist in their disobedience. All this does not imply that God has a "hands-off," laissez-faire policy in relation to his creatures, though it does imply that his interaction with them is in part conditioned by their willingness to accept his gracious and restorative intervention. (The father of the prodigal does nothing so long as the son insists on remaining in the far country, but as soon as the son evinces a desire to return the father takes forceful initiatives in order to restore him to the bosom of the family.)

This of course is a mere sketch of the core ideas of open theism; a fuller elaboration would require more space than is available here. Still more space would be required if we were to compare open theism with each of the main rival views of God, in order to show why open theism best fulfills our idea of God as a "big person." It may be helpful nevertheless to set open theism alongside the view that most strikingly contrasts with it, as a way of bringing out open theism's distinctive merits. The view I have in mind here is the theological determinism espoused by Augustine, probably by Thomas Aquinas, and certainly by Calvin, Luther, Jonathan Edwards, and a host of more recent Calvinist and Thomist theologians. The deterministic God, unlike the God of open theism, insists on retaining for himself the sole prerogative of deciding everything that takes place in the world, including what goes on in the minds and hearts of his rational creatures. All the decisions they make are merely their enactment of the decisions God has eternally decided that they should make; they have no decisional independence whatsoever. And since this is so, God takes absolutely no risk in creating the world as he has; he has complete assurance that everything will take place exactly as he has intended, and in the way that is most pleasing to him. To be sure, there is much in the way the world progresses that does not at all *seem to us* as though it is the way things would have been decided by an all-determining God who is also perfectly good and loving. But the fact that things seem this way to us does not mean that this is really the case; in fact, everything is exactly as God wants it to be, and our inclination to think otherwise simply reveals the limitations of our merely human perspective. (For this reason, the problem of evil is especially intractable for theological determinists; the point of view that, according to them, would enable us to make sense of the problem is simply not available to us.)

This much needs to be kept in mind: the God of theological determinism is not in any way *more powerful* than the God of open theism. The God of open theism has all of the power of the deterministic God, but has chosen to use it differently. Nor is the *wisdom* of the deterministic God any greater than that of the God of openness. The contrast that stands out, as we compare the two, is that the deterministic God has an overwhelming *desire for total control;* it is totally unacceptable to such a deity that *any other being* should in any way have any role in determining the course of events in the world.[7] And now I have to say that such a conception of God is most certainly *not* the conception we will arrive at if we seek to model our notion of divine character on that of a great and excellent human being. We would not want either to be or to work for an employer with such an attitude, though sometimes people have no choice about that. We would not wish to be the children of such a parent, nor (I hope) to be such parents to our own children. To the determinists we must say, with full meaning and conviction: "It is *your* God—the God so obsessed with total control that he is unable or unwilling to allow any other being any role in determining what happens in the world—it is *this* God who is too small."[8]

---

7. A possible alternative would be to say that God is *unable* to create beings with libertarian free will; one way to support this claim would be to claim that the very conception of libertarian freedom is incoherent. The prospects for this move, however, are not favorable; libertarian freedom has been expounded in ways that leave little doubt that the conception is coherent and logically possible. (See Timothy O'Connor, *Persons and Causes: The Metaphysics of Free Will* [New York: Oxford University Press, 2000], and William Hasker, *The Emergent Self* [Ithaca: Cornell University Press, 1999].) If on the other hand the conception is admitted to be coherent and logically possible, and yet God is unable to create libertarian-free persons, this would seem to constitute a quite severe limitation on divine omnipotence.

8. The position of Molinism, the theory of divine middle knowledge, is equivocal on this topic. Persons are said to enjoy libertarian freedom, but God, in virtue of knowing the "counterfactuals of freedom," knows exactly what they would do under any possible

Can we push this line of thought a bit farther? Open theism is primarily concerned, in the first instance, with God's relationship with his rational creatures, in particular with human beings. But there is an analogy which might suggest that God would desire a somewhat similar, though more limited, independence to be in effect in the world of nature as well. God, we have already said is a *very big* God, and this helps us to understand the incredible vastness of the creation. But would God not desire for the sub-human creation, and not merely for men and women, to be genuinely "Other"—to possess and to exercise a measure of independence and autonomy?[9] Would he not desire to have his creation *do some things for itself*—sustained in being and energized by divine power, to be sure, but nevertheless *genuinely possessing* power of its own, power it is able to *do something with?* Put the question to yourself like this: If God were to manufacture a robot, what sort of a robot would it be? Would it be like the Robo Sapiens that can be purchased for a hundred dollars or so, in which all movements are controlled by signals from the operator or by a few simple, pre-programmed commands? I suspect "God's robot" would be a lot more like Commander Data in *Star Trek*: complex, subtle, and capable of deciding and doing a great many things for himself, sometimes to the chagrin of his superiors in the chain of command.

---

set of circumstances. Thus, the decisions actually made are precisely those God has planned for them to make; indeed, God himself has brought about (weakly actualized) those decisions by placing those persons in precisely those situations. This eliminates all risk on God's part, but it also greatly minimizes the genuine and spontaneous contribution of created persons to the course of events. ("Mommy, mommy: look at the picture I have made!" "Of course, dear, I planned and set things up on purpose so you would make a picture just exactly like I planned for you to make.") Process theism, on the other hand, is like open theism in that persons make spontaneous contributions to the course of events that are not the result of divine planning or manipulation. For process theism, however, this is not something God chooses to do because it is better for the creatures or more loving on God's part; rather, it represents a metaphysical limitation on God's action concerning which God has no choice.

9. According to John Haught, "The doctrine of grace claims that God loves the world and all of its various elements fully and unconditionally. By definition, however, love does not absorb, annihilate, or force itself on the beloved. Instead it longs for the beloved to become more and more 'other' or differentiated. . . . [If] God loves the world with unbounded love, then God's 'grace' must also mean 'letting the world be itself'" (John Haught, *God After Darwin: A Theology of Evolution* [Boulder, CO: Westview, 2000] 39–40). Similar ideas have been expressed by John Polkinghorne; see his *Science and Providence: God's Interaction with the World* (London: SPCK, 1989) ch. 5.

Thinking along these lines, and supposing that God would desire for the world of nature to have a genuine though limited autonomy of its own, leads us to the following conclusion: the conception of God supported by open theism lends itself very readily to an *evolutionary* understanding of the cosmos and of life on this our earth![10] An evolutionary universe is in a real sense *self-creative*; it utilizes the powers with which it has been endowed to become something distinctively its own. To be sure, the concepts of cosmic and biological evolution are not to be found in the Bible; the biblical peoples were lacking the scientific conceptualities that would have made such notions possible for them. However, Michael Lodahl has pointed out that the idea of the "creation as creative" is strongly suggested in the creation narrative in Genesis 1. He writes, "There is even an apparently playful punning in the Hebrew that may well reinforce this idea of creation's creativity: the earth is called upon by God to "put forth" (*tadshe*) vegetation (*deshe*) and the waters are called upon to "bring forth" (*yishretsu*) swarming creatures of the sea (*sherets*). *Tadshe Deshe*—the earth, we might say, is called upon to produce produce, to implant itself with plants. *Yishretsu Sherets*—the seas, we could say, are called upon to swarm with swarms of swimmers. Creaturely elements are invited to contribute their distinctive energies and capacities to what God is doing in the labor of creation."[11]

To be sure, these suggestions taken by themselves might well be insufficient to carry the day. The argument by analogy from God's treatment of his human creatures to the world of nature is suggestive, but only that; it is hardly compelling in its own right. And the language from Genesis is again merely suggestive; it certainly does not state or necessitate a full-fledged evolutionary conception. As we all know very well, a good many of our fellow-Christians have been and are strongly resistant to an evolutionary worldview, and it is not to be expected that they will be persuaded by arguments such as these. What proves decisive, in the end, is nothing more nor less than the *empirical evidence* that provides over-

---

10. To avoid all possibility of misunderstanding, let me say that I am *not* advocating a view according to which an expansive conception of evolution replaces the biblical story of sin and salvation. Evolution helps to set the stage on which the drama of redemption is played out, but evolution is not the Redeemer.

11. Michael Lodahl, *Claiming Abraham: Reading the Bible and Qur'an Side by Side* (Grand Rapids: Brazos, 2010) 47–48. My thanks to Michael Lodahl for permitting me to use this draft of work in progress.

whelmingly strong support for both cosmic and biological evolution. By now we have enough of earth history securely available to us that we can begin to perceive its inherent wonder. The majesty of the Grand Canyon, for instance, is greatly enhanced by the recognition of the hundreds of millions of years of geological history recorded in its successive strata. In this "golden age of cosmology" who can help but marvel at the story of the unfolding, since the Big Bang, of the astronomical structures of which our universe is composed? And ever since Darwin there has been the story, still far from complete but continually enriched with new discoveries, of the development of life on this our earth. So what I have to say to our anti-evolutionary brethren is this: It's understandable that you don't *like* the idea of evolution and would prefer that it not be true. But there is an enormous and ever-increasing body of evidence that shows that God *does* like the idea of an evolutionary cosmos, and has deliberately chosen to create a world like that! So wouldn't we be better advised to "get with God's program," and try to make Christian sense of evolution, rather than using huge amounts of time and energy trying to explain away the evidence?

I am not proposing, then, that an evolutionary cosmology should be accepted solely because there is an argument for such a cosmology based on open theism. The evolutionary conception of the universe, and of the history of life on earth, needs to be accepted based on solid scientific evidence, evidence that is available in plentiful and ever-increasing quantities. Nor am I suggesting that only an open theist can reasonably accept such a cosmology and harmonize it with her theological position. What I do say, however, is this: someone who is both an evolutionist and an open theist will find a consilience, an inherent affinity, between the two that is lacking for more traditional conceptions of God. For theological determinists God certainly has the power to bring about either an "all-at-once" specially created universe, or an evolutionary universe. But since God's motives in creating are almost entirely opaque to us, there is nothing in the deterministic view that argues more in favor of one than the other does.[12] Open theists, on the other hand, have all of the reasons discussed

12. On this topic, the adherents of divine middle knowledge are very much in the same situation as the determinists: the affirmation of the moral freedom of rational creatures, which is the main difference between the views, does not have application to the pre-human creation. For process theists, on the other hand, God is metaphysically incapable of bringing about a completed universe "all in one go," so the occurrence of evolution represents a metaphysical necessity rather than a choice based on divine grace.

above to welcome an evolutionary cosmology and to see in it a continuation and confirmation of the basic idea of their theological system.

In our quest for a "big enough" conception of God, a third topic suggests itself as a companion to open theism and an evolutionary cosmology. This is the topic of the nature of human beings, more specifically the nature and origin of the "soul." The soul, in Christian discourse, is the focus of personality, the seat of reason, emotion, and consciousness; in particular, it is that aspect of human beings in virtue of which we are related to God. The traditional view is that the soul is an immaterial substance, immediately created by God and united with a particular human body. An alternative view, which gains some credibility in the context of contemporary philosophy and science, is that the soul is "emergent"—that is, it is something that makes its appearance in consequence of a particular functional configuration of the brain and nervous system of a living organism. So we may ask, do our reflections to this point give us any reason to prefer one of these accounts to the other?

If the considerations listed above in support of an evolutionary cosmology are sound, it would seem that they also tend to support an emergentist view of the "soul," that is of the human person. We have supposed that God would be interested in creating the world of nature in such a way as to make it genuinely Other than God, which means that he would wish to endow it with powers enabling it to grow and develop from within, using its own resources. These considerations receive additional support from the apparent fact that God has indeed created an evolutionary cosmos. But if we suppose that created persons, as the "images of God," represent the fullest and highest expressions of creation, it would seem that God would wish so far as possible to bring the production of personhood also within the scope of the natural powers inherent in creation itself. There are, furthermore, additional reasons in support of this conclusion deriving specifically from evolution. Note first of all that, if we attribute divinely created souls to human beings, we shall have to do the same in the case of at least the higher animals as well. (We can't possibly accept Descartes's view, according to which all non-human animals are automata, lacking any sort of conscious experience.) But this raises the question, how are these divinely created souls to be incorporated into the evolutionary narrative? It turns out to be very difficult to give a sensible answer to that question. "Higher," more evolved animals will require more complex souls, with a more extensive array of powers; so at least one would think. Does God wait until a more advanced organism has evolved through natural selection, and only then create a higher-grade soul to take advantage of the superior neural circuitry? In that case it is difficult to see how the improved circuitry would be preserved by natural selection, since by hypothesis it is useless without the corresponding high-grade soul. Or does the more powerful soul come first, and assist in the evolutionary development? Does the soul have the power to identify the needed changes in the genetic code and modify the germline DNA accordingly, in order to secure the needed neural improvements? I believe that a little reflection on such options will suffice us to convince us that an emergentist theory of the mind/soul is far more congenial to an evolutionary account.[13]

More needs to be said, however, about the nature of the emergent self/soul. What exactly is it that emerges? At a minimum, *conscious experience* emerges; given the right physical processes in the nervous system, we have subjective awareness, feeling, and conscious thought—things that (so far as we can tell) simply do not exist in the inanimate physical world. But—and this is an important question—*what difference does this make* in the *physical processes and activities* that go on in the world, and in particular in the living body and brain? According to standard materialist and physicalist views—views that are very widely held among contemporary philosophers and scientists—the correct answer is, "No difference at all." The standard view on this is that the physical domain is "causally closed"—that every physical process or event that occurs, including events in the brain and nervous system of a living animal or human being, has a *complete causal explanation* in previous physical events. These processes do not operate any differently because some of them are accompanied by conscious experience; each stage in the process is purely the consequence of earlier stages in the same physical process, and each stage is predictable in terms of those earlier stages, given the fundamental laws of physics which are the final explanation for everything that ever happens in the world.[14] The conscious experiences are themselves simply a consequence

---

13. No doubt it is conceivable that God could directly bring about the genetic modification, and at the same time create a more advanced soul to match the genetic changes. But this in effect gives up the idea of evolution as a natural process, and because of that it conflicts with the reasons given for the acceptance of evolution in the first place.

14. Allowance must be made for an element of randomness that seems to be called for by quantum mechanics. But this randomness is purely a matter of chance; it does not reflect, nor is it influenced by, any kind of non-physical causation.

of the neural firings; we have the experiences we do because, and only because, of the way our brains are working. (This is required by the assumption of many physicists that it will be possible for physics to discover a "theory of everything"—a theory of the "final physics" which will provide the ultimate explanation of everything that ever happens.[15])

Now, I think there are some very good reasons why this view cannot possibly be correct. For one thing, it immediately rules out free will, in the sense that it is really in one's power to choose which of two or more alternative courses of action one will follow. The neurons in one's brain fire off in the way they are determined to fire by previous brain-states as governed by the laws of neuroscience, and one's mental state is simply a consequence of these neural firings. There may in some sense be alternative courses of action that could be taken *if* one were so to choose—but which choice will actually be made is determined by the physical causes; the other options were never real possibilities, even if they may have seemed so to the agent at the time.

But there is more. It seems clear that this physicalist theory of the mind is unable to account for a type of mental process that is absolutely crucial for our arriving at reasonable and correct conclusions in science itself—namely, the process of logical reasoning. In logical reasoning (assuming things go as they should) we arrive at certain conclusions because, and only because, we see that they are supported by the evidence, by other things we know or believe to be true. But this conflicts with the physicalist view that says that we arrive at conclusions in our reasoning because, and only because, of the way the neurological processes in our brains work out. That simply is not the same thing! It would be a colossal accident if it were always, or almost always, to come about that the result produced by those neural processes (which have no end at all in view, and certainly not the end of arriving at logically warranted beliefs) were to coincide with the result demanded by the principles of sound reasoning. On the physicalist view, the fact that we are able to reason, and to arrive at conclusions because they are supported by the evidence, is completely mysterious and without explanation.[16]

15. See Steven Weinberg, *Dreams of a Final Theory* (New York: Pantheon, 1992).

16. Many readers will be familiar with this "argument from reason" because of its occurrence in C. S. Lewis's book, *Miracles: A Preliminary Study* (New York: Macmillan, 1947; rev. ed., New York: Seabrook 1978). There is an urban legend, or perhaps I should say a campus legend, that the argument was demolished by the Catholic philosopher

More could be said along these lines, but I am going to assume at this point that the physicalist doctrine of causal closure is false and that, in consequence of the emergence of conscious experience, the self is endowed with *novel causal powers*—powers that include the capacity to seek truth and to reason logically. Furthermore, these powers involve a *modification in the ways in which certain physical processes operate*, notably the processes in a living, functioning brain. And this means that the fundamental laws of physics, even the ideal laws which will ultimately be discovered, do *not* suffice to predict the actions of a human being, and most likely not for a good many other animals as well. Some philosophers and scientists, to be sure, find this abhorrent, as a trespass on the territory that belongs by right to the physicists. But who was it that put up those "no trespassing" signs in the first place?

There is a further question to be raised concerning the ontological status of the emergent mind/soul/self. Is the emergent soul a thing in its own right—what philosophers term a "substance"—or is it merely a set of processes or functions that occur in the physical body? I believe the right answer is that the self is a real entity distinct from the body, and I will briefly suggest (though I cannot fully discuss) two reasons for saying this. One reason that ought to be especially cogent for Christians concerns the doctrine of a future life. To put it simply, if there is no soul, what is it that lives on after our bodies have decayed? "Christian materialists" are accustomed to say that this is a non-issue—that Christianity does not affirm the immortality of the soul, but rather the resurrection of the body. But this invites the question, what makes it the case that the resurrected individual is *the same identical person* as the one who formerly was born, and lived her life, and died? So far as I can see—admittedly, the point is controversial—none of the answers that have been proposed to this question is satisfactory.[17] If no good answer is available, this is a strong

---

Elizabeth Anscombe, and it is true that Anscombe forcefully criticized an early version of Lewis's argument. But Lewis himself revised the argument in order to meet her criticisms (the revised argument appears in the revised edition of *Miracles*), and a number of other philosophers have developed the argument further since then. (For an extensive discussion, see Victor Reppert, *C. S. Lewis's Dangerous Idea: A Defense of the Argument from Reason* [Downers Grove, IL: InterVarsity, 2003].) By no means did Anscombe say the final word concerning the argument from reason.

17. It seems clear that the view assumed in the New Testament is that there is an "intermediate state" between death and the final resurrection, during which persons exist without either the old earthly body or the transformed resurrection body. That

reasons for Christians to affirm the soul as a real, existent entity (though one initially "generated" by the biological organism), and not merely as a set of processes in the body. It is this soul, newly clothed in the resurrection body, that guarantees that the person who lives on is the identical individual who formerly lived and died.

The other reason focuses around this question: when a person is having a complex set of experiences, *what individual is it* that is experiencing all these things? Suppose, for instance that you are simultaneously viewing a scene, listening to music, and feeling various bodily sensations. What is it that is conscious of all this? For a materialist, the natural answer—seemingly, the only possible answer—is your body, or more specifically your brain. Your brain, however, is composed of tens of billions of individual neurons. No single neuron can be aware of the entire, complex contents of consciousness; everyone would agree with that. Is it then the case that each of vastly many neurons is conscious of some small part of the data? To say this contravenes what seems to be an obvious fact: *a complex state of consciousness cannot exist distributed among the parts of a complex object.* If each small part of your brain is conscious of some small part of the data of conscious experience, this still leaves unanswered the question, *What is it that experiences the totality of the experience, all at once, as a whole?* For it is a fact that you do experience it all at once; somehow, all of this data is simultaneously present to a single conscious subject. It begins to look as though the answer has to be something that, unlike the brain and nervous system, *exists* as a single, unified entity, and not as an assemblage of parts. And this, I want to say, is your mind or soul; it is the central core of what you as a person really are.[18]

---

this is so has been argued compellingly by philosopher John Cooper (*Body, Soul, and Life Everlasting: Biblical Anthropology and the Monism-Dualism Debate,* new ed. [Grand Rapids: Eerdmans, 2000]), and "The Bible and Dualism Once Again: A Reply to Joel B. Green and Nancey Murphy," *Philosophia Christi* 9.2 [2007] 459–69); and by New Testament scholar N. T. Wright (*The Resurrection of the Son of God* [Minneapolis: Fortress, 2003]). If this view is correct, a person's identity over time cannot consist in the identity of her body.

18. For a more extensive development of both these arguments, and an exposition and defense of the "emergent dualist" position as a whole, see William Hasker, *The Emergent Self;* also the contributions by William Hasker to Joel B. Green and Stuart Palmer, eds., *In Search of the Soul: Four Views of the Mind-Body Problem* (Downers Grove, IL: InterVarsity, 2005).

In answering the question about a "big enough" God, one who is adequate to our needs today, we have arrived at three distinct though related doctrines: open theism, an evolutionary account of the world and of life, and an emergentist account of the mind or soul. These three doctrines are not linked by logical entailment: one can consistently hold any one of the three without the other two, or any two of them without the third.[19] But each of them enjoys independent support, and in accepting all three together we find ourselves with a package of views that are individually attractive, and together form a plausible and coherent unity. "A threefold cord is not quickly broken" (Eccl 4:12).

This then is my proposal for a "big enough" conception of God, one that is worthy of our belief and is capable of sustaining us in our spiritual need. God so conceived is wise and powerful, but also gracious and compassionate. His love impels him to grant "space" and a degree of autonomy to his creation as a whole and especially to created persons. His desire to have a creation that is genuinely Other and enjoys a reality and life of its own impels him to implant in that creation the powers needed for its self-development, including the development of mind, consciousness, and "soul." He shares intimately in the pain and suffering engendered by such a creation as well as in its joys and triumphs, and we look forward to a future in which not only the overall creation but also we ourselves are brought to a completion and fulfillment of unimaginable wonder.

19. Among the various connections between the three views, I believe the tightest link is the inference from biological evolution to an emergentist view of the mind. As explained in the text, it really is very difficult to give a coherent explanation of the relationship between biological evolution and a creationist view of the soul. Still, this combination is not impossible; it has been held by some excellent thinkers, notably Richard Swinburne (see his *The Evolution of the Soul* [Oxford: Clarendon, 1986]). Ironically, Swinburne's view is (as he has acknowledged) one in which the soul is precisely what does *not* evolve!

PART TWO

Science and Open Theism

Some Methodological Insights

2

Metatheoretic Shaping Principles

Where Science Meets Theology

JEFFREY KOPERSKI

INTRODUCTION

PHILOSOPHERS OF SCIENCE HAVE seldom had much influence on academia. Thomas Kuhn was an exception. Kuhn's *The Structure of Scientific Revolutions* is widely considered to be the seminal work of postmodern conceptual relativism, the view that either there is no such thing as truth or, if there is, it is unattainable. This doctrine has been a disaster, especially in the humanities. The irony is that Kuhn himself was not a conceptual relativist. ("But I am not a Kuhnian!" he reportedly once shouted at a conference on the sociology of science.) One of the positive effects of *Structure* was to help us see that science is made up of more than observations and laws. Scientists, like the rest of us, rely on a whole host of unarticulated assumptions about the world and how it ought to be studied. Our understanding of these *metatheoretic shaping principles* (MSP) has come a long way since Kuhn. Philosophers of religion have taken interest since this is where science typically influences theology and vice versa.

In what follows we will consider different categories of MSPs, how they change over time, and their relation to theology. All this will be working its way toward what open theism has to say about science and science about open theism.

THE STRUCTURE OF SCIENCE

Any Big Picture for the whole of science must simplify things to the point of distortion. Scientific knowledge is too diverse to fit under a single organizing principle. In fact, there are enough tensions and outright inconsistencies in science to make any realist uneasy. With that caveat, let's consider a model that is useful as a first approximation.

Broadly speaking, science has three layers. Not surprisingly, we begin with observations and data—the realm of the experimentalist. Like a pyramid, this is the broadest layer in the sense that there are more data available than well-articulated theories or models to place them in. Like the CIA, there may be lots of information coming in from all kinds of sources, but good analysis is still hard to find.

The second layer is more abstract, containing theories and laws. Towards the bottom of this layer, relatively close to the data itself, are statistical correlations and phenomenological models. As statisticians repeatedly tell us, establishing a statistical correlation is not the same as discovering a cause. We know that high cholesterol is correlated with heart disease, but drugs that lower cholesterol haven't dramatically affected the rate of heart disease in America. The complete causal story appears to be more complex than "high cholesterol causes heart disease." Phenomenological models are used to replicate patterns found within data. They are built in a "bottom-up" fashion in the sense that there are no first principles or laws of nature from which to derive them. So with enough data, one can build a computer model that simulates the behavior of city traffic, even though there are no general equations governing traffic flow. Higher up in the second layer are more abstract laws of nature and mature theories: Einstein's field equations and relativity, Schrödinger's equation and quantum mechanics, and the nonlinear differential equations used in statistical mechanics, continuum mechanics, and chaos theory.

The least familiar and for our purposes most important layer is third, the level of MSPs.[1] This is the region where the philosophy of science and science proper blend into one another. There is no sharp line between the two. MSPs help determine what good theories, laws, and models look like as well as how one should proceed in their discovery and develop-

1. The name 'shaping principle' was coined by Del Ratzsch, to whom I am greatly indebted in this section of the paper. See especially ch. 9 of Ratzsch, *The Battle of the Beginnings: Why Neither Side is Winning the Creation-Evolution Debate* (Downers Grove, IL: InterVarsity, 1996).

ment. Philosophers of science have considered the role of these principles for more than a generation and there are several ways to approach the subject. I will divide them into two categories. The first are metaphysical. These include,

- *Uniformity of nature.* This is uniformity across space and time. The laws of nature are thought to be the same now as they always have been, or at least since the earliest stages of the universe. The laws of nature are the same here as they are everywhere else in the universe. If this were not so, no sound inferences could be made about astronomical data.

- *Realism.* Mature theories in science embody discovered truths about reality. Theories are not merely social constructions. It would be a miracle if science could be as successful as it has been and not be more or less true.

- *Causal closure of the physical domain.* Every physical event that has a cause has a sufficient physical cause. Hence when neurophysiologists study particular brain events, they will never trace a causal chain that takes them away from the physical and to a nonphysical cause. (This principle is a close cousin to metaphysical naturalism: the success of the natural sciences indicates that nature is all there is.)

Others are more discipline-specific, including determinism and various conservation principles.[2]

The second category of MSPs is epistemic and includes a wide variety of methodological norms.

- Reliance on repeatable, *intersubjective observations.* This is one of the principles that sets apart modern from medieval science.

- Standards of *inductive logic and mathematical rigor.* This includes the proper use of statistical methods and blind studies.

- *Explanatory virtues.* These are desiderata for good explanations including empirical adequacy, simplicity, testability, internal and external coherence, fruitfulness for future research, wide scope, and elegance.

2. As historian Charles Gillispie puts it, "[N]o one has ever discovered conservation (of whatever) in some experiment. Rather conservation has always been assumed as a condition of objective science." Gillispie, *The Edge of Objectivity* (Princeton: Princeton University Press, 1960) 385.

- *Methodological naturalism* (MN). There are two ways of under-standing this principle. Following Del Ratzsch, MN says that re-searchers must proceed *as if* metaphysical naturalism were true, regardless of whether it actually reflects their ontology. According to Alan Padgett, MN is the view that in "*natural* science, [one must] explain physical phenomena only on the basis of physical laws, principles, and properties."[3]

- *Conservatism.* There are several related principles here, but the main one has to do with theory change. Conservatism says that as new discoveries are made, scientific theories should change as little as needed in order to accommodate them.

Few of these principles are exclusive to science. Conservatism, for example, is a general principle of change in any body of knowledge. One reason John Polkinghorne rejects panentheism is that it is a more radical change than is needed to correct the problems of Augustinian-Calvinist thought. That's an expression of conservatism.

MSPs lie at the heart of many theology-and-science debates. Realism is at issue for young earth creationists. Modern cosmology, geology, and evolutionary biology all imply that the earth is far older than 20,000 years. Hence, creationists cannot take those theories in a fully realistic way. (Some possible anti-realist strategies will be discussed below.) And few seem to appreciate the central role of MSPs in the debate over Intelligent Design. Why are so many theists and relatively few nontheists attracted to ID? The best explanation, once again, is conservatism. If one already has an intelligence in one's ontology that can play the role of designer, then ID-based science is not a radical move. For an atheist, making ontological room for a supernatural designer requires a greatly expanded metaphysic. Because of this, the controversy will never be solved merely by appeal to the data or to what theory biologists currently believe.

Each of the shaping principles mentioned above is found in mod-ern science. There are many others that have been diminished or set aside. One is that nature works only by contact forces, like the gears in a clock. Scientific explanations should therefore describe the mechanism responsible for the phenomena. This principle entails the rejection of Aristotelian causes other than efficient causation. It was also the one that

3. Alan G. Padgett, *Science and the Study of God* (Grand Rapids: Eerdmans, 2003) 79.

Newton transgressed with his theory of universal gravitation. By giving a law without a mechanism behind it, Newtonian gravity was long faulted for relying on action-at-a-distance, something akin to telekinesis. Another diminished MSP is the Baconian view that laws must be inferred by enumerative induction from empirical observations. It is now clear that laws are often derived in a top-down fashion from first principles rather than exclusively from bottom-up generalizations.

These historical cases illustrate an important fact: MSPs are not set in stone but rather change over time, much like theories themselves. Some of the most interesting conflicts in science arise over which principles one might challenge. One famous example is the Bohr-Einstein dispute over quantum mechanics. According to Bohr's Copenhagen interpretation of quantum mechanics, nature is fundamentally random. The Heisenberg Uncertainty Principle is not merely a limitation on our knowledge; it is ontic—the way things really are. Einstein played the role of old-guard classicist in this dispute. He argued that Heisenberg uncertainty may put a strict limit on prediction, but our inability to predict does not mean there is no fact-of-the-matter about the position and momentum of a particle. To Einstein, Bohr was advocating the overthrow of law-governed causal regularities as they had been understood from the beginning of the scientific revolution. History sees Bohr as the winner in this dispute, in part because Bohmian mechanics, which is fully deterministic, has failed to catch on. (One wonders how all this would have turned out if Bohm's theory had been formulated in 1925, ahead of Schrödinger and Heisenberg.)

A more obscure example from the eighteenth century involved mathematician/physicists Leonhard Euler and Jean le Rond d'Alembert.[4] Like Descartes before him, d'Alembert believed that mathematics was a highly specialized tool and that most of what we observe in the physical world is beyond its resources. Mathematics, he maintained, can only describe very simple systems. Even a plucked string was thought to be beyond the domain of differential equations. Euler was less strict. He argued that the mathematics of differential equations should be relaxed on occasion, even if it meant ignoring a fundamental metaphysical rule, Leibniz's Law of Continuity. The Law of Continuity says that "nature makes no leaps"; the

---

4. This episode has been well documented by mathematician/historian Clifford Truesdell and philosopher Mark Wilson. Clifford Truesdell, *An Idiot's Fugitive Essays on Science* (New York: Springer, 1984) 80–83; Mark Wilson, "The Unreasonable Uncooperativeness of Mathematics in the Natural Sciences," *The Monist* 83 (2000) 298–301.

change from one system state to the next is always continuous. Leibniz himself took this principle to be foundational for the development of mechanics, arguing that "continuity [is] a necessary prerequisite or a distinctive character of the true laws of the communication of motion. [Can] we doubt that all phenomena are subject to it . . . ?"[5] Nonetheless, Euler ignored Leibniz's law in his analysis of a plucked string and mathematical physics has successfully followed his lead ever since.

Another eighteenth–nineteenth century debate over shaping principles is relevant to today's controversy about Intelligent Design. Geology in the 1700s was founded on *catastrophism*, the view that most geological structures are the result of large scale, system-changing events such as floods and earthquakes. Both the temperature and surface of the earth were thought to have changed dramatically over time in the wake of these special events, including the Great Flood in Genesis. Among the supporters of catastrophism was Georges Cuvier, the founder of comparative anatomy and vertebrate paleontology. A rival view, *uniformitarianism,* is attributed to Scottish geologist James Hutton and later entrenched by Charles Lyell in his *Principles of Geology* (1830). They taught that geological data should be understood in terms of ongoing forces and mechanisms such as the slow rise of mountains, underground cooling of magma, rain, erosion, runoff, and sedimentation. They then posited the continuous action of the same mechanisms back through time. In his *Theory of the Earth* (1795), Hutton stated, "In examining things present, we have data from which to reason with regard to what has been; and, from what has actually been, we have data for concluding with regard to that which is to happen thereafter."

There were two key motivations behind the change from catastrophism to uniformitarianism. One had to do with the discovery of fossils. The similarity between fossilized and living creatures supported continuity between the past and the present. Gradual sedimentation also seemed to be a good explanation for the correlation between types of fossils within specific geological strata. The second came from other shaping principles that had taken hold in the sciences. In particular, catastrophists were faulted for violating Baconian inductivism.[6] Unlike the slow, ongoing

5. Quoted in Timothy Crockett, "Continuity in Leibniz's Mature Metaphysics," *Philosophical Studies* 94 (1999) 120.

6. Del Ratzsch, *The Battle of the Beginnings* (Downers Grove, IL: InterVarsity, 1996) 13–16.

processes of Hutton and Lyell, ancient catastrophes were unobservable and thought to be beyond the reach of proper science. (Ironically, Walter Alvarez and David M. Raup, the leading supporters of the asteroid impact hypothesis as a major cause of mass extinction, attribute the stiff resistance they faced in the 1970s to uniformitarianism.[7])

There are two important conclusions to be drawn from all this. First, like everything else in science, MSPs can be trumped in particular circumstances and sometimes rejected outright.[8] Second, MSPs both influence the development of theories and are themselves influenced from below. In fact, influences flow from each of the three layers of the pyramid structure to every other layer. New observations and anomalies obviously force changes to theories. And although too much can be made of the theory-ladenness of observations, it is also true that theories affect the way one evaluates new data. Whether an observation is significant depends on what theories one already accepts. Finally as we saw in the Einstein-Bohr debate, both observations and theories can put pressure on MSPs.[9] Unlike textbook introductions of the so-called scientific method, there is no royal road to knowledge, scientific or otherwise. And even if there were, one could not use such a method in order to *derive* the right shaping principles. Any candidate for *the* scientific method rests on some notion of what it is to be good science, a notion that is itself grounded in MSPs.

MSPS AND THEISM

One of the distortions of the three-layer model is that it appears to be self-contained. Science of course influences and is influenced by many domains of study. MSPs in particular are subject to pressures from metaphysics and epistemology, which are themselves influenced by the-

7. David M. Raup, *The Nemesis Affair* (New York: Norton) ch. 2.

8. Treating them as inviolable principles as Judge Jones did in the Dover, Pennsylvania, Intelligent Design case is false in terms of the history and philosophy of science. For more on this, see section 3 of my "Two Bad Ways to Attack Intelligent Design and Two Good Ones," *Zygon* 43.2 (2008).

9. This mutual interaction view of the three layers is similar to Larry Laudan's reticulated model of scientific justification. While some take this to be an anti-realist view (since it seems to rely on a coherence theory of justification), the model can be understood realistically if we grant that change in the sciences is a messy business. What emerges over time, says the realist, is approximately true. For a critique of Laudan, see J. P. Moreland, *Christianity and the Nature of Science* (Grand Rapids: Baker, 1999) 186–89.

ology.[10] Let's now consider some of the tensions between specific MSPs and theism. "Tension" is loosely construed here; we are not talking about logical entailment. Views held in theology, metaphysics, science, and the philosophy of science rather have "family resemblances" in the sense that some positions tend to fit together more naturally than others. If one is a Christian, then one is probably not going to be a Marxist, even though there have been movements trying to wed the two.

Reductionism

This principle comes in many varieties. One is *ontological reductionism* whereby the entities at one level of reality are thought to be nothing but composites or states of entities at a more fundamental level. Minds and mental states are nothing but brains and brain states; brains and brain states are nothing but neurons, nerve fibers, and their states, and so on all the way down to molecules, atoms, and fundamental particles, whatever they happen to be. Ontological reduction is thus similar to materialism but with the added doctrine that there are no emergent properties. There is an obvious tension here with theism in that a theist has at least one member of his ontology that is not made up of particles. Most Christian theists also believe in immaterial entities other than God, viz. angels and souls, all of which are incompatible with ontological reduction.

Theory reduction is a distinct, epistemological MSP having to do with our ability to form bridges between recognized theories. We should expect, on this view, that as science progresses higher-level theories will be explained in terms of more fundamental theories. Macro events and laws should become explicable in terms of those at a lower level, much the way thermodynamics has been reduced to statistical mechanics—or so the story goes.[11]

Many theists reject theory reductionism because of the implication that ultimate explanations are only found in physics. If theology is a mat-

10. A naturalistic turn in theology was a factor in the move to uniformitarianism mentioned above. Lyell explicitly lumped in ad hoc appeals to floods, earthquakes, and the like with the theology of demons as an explanation of moral failures. See Owen Anderson, "Charles Lyell, Uniformitarianism, and Interpretive Principles" *Zygon* 42.2 (June 2007) 452–53.

11. The truth is a bit more complex. While there are several ways known to philosophers of science whereby one theory can be reduced to another, there is no sense in which thermodynamics has been fully reduced to statistical mechanics.

ter of knowledge rather than mere value, then that knowledge cannot be reduced to scientific theorizing. Some readers may be surprised to find that most *secular* philosophers today also reject theory reductionism. While they believe that nothing exists beyond the natural order, they do not expect that our theories will one day line up in a neat, reductive hierarchy. These so-called *nonreductive physicalists* believe that we will always need independent theories in biology, psychology, etc. The world is too complex to navigate otherwise.

Methodological Naturalism

MN arose in the seventeenth century as a doctrine akin to separation of church and state. Those in the humanities did not want scientists getting involved in matters outside of their expertise and natural philosophers did not want clergy and kings looking over their shoulders. In 1660, Charles II set the parameters for the Royal Society of London to be, in the words of Robert Hooke, "to improve the knowledge of natural things, and all useful Arts, Manufactures, Mechanics, Practices, Engynes and Inventions by Experiments (not meddling with Divinity, Metaphysics, Moralls, Politicks, Grammar, Rhetoric, or Logick)."[12]

While theists have mixed opinions about MN, many accept it for similar reasons. There are areas of knowledge beyond science and scientists are ill equipped to deal with them. Metaphysics, theology, and ethics are outside of their professional competency. Theistic scientists should therefore use MN even though they are not metaphysical naturalists.

This is an attractive view, one held by several contributors to this volume, and I may well be persuaded someday that it is correct. At present, there are three countervailing arguments for why theists should be wary of MN.

*1. MN has **metaphysical** ramifications that when coupled with scientific realism, theists cannot hold.* Most theists are scientific realists of some variety or other. But notice, if one takes scientific theories to be at least approximately true (realism), and if MN is required to form those theories, then true scientific theories will of course be naturalistic. What if the actual explanation for some phenomenon is supernatural? No matter. Under MN, the best naturalistic explanation *is* the best scientific explanation, and via

12. Robert Proctor, *Value-Free Science?* (Cambridge: Harvard University Press, 1991) 33.

realism, we take that explanation as true. Given that there is little if anything that science does not purport to explain, MN plus realism implies that nearly every phenomenon has a true, naturalistic explanation, at least in principle. As science continues to claim more ground, from evolutionary accounts of ethics to psychological explanations for religious belief, we end up with something very close to *metaphysical* naturalism.[13] This is precisely why atheists point to the success of science as a key reason for accepting naturalism across the board.

2. MN limits the explanatory resources of science. Given the limitations placed by MN, science is sometimes pushed into odd corners. Consider the discovery of finely-tuned cosmological constants, including each of the coupling parameters for the four fundamental forces. Most agree that this discovery requires an explanation. Under MN, when physicist Lee Smolin explains fine-tuning by positing a vast multiverse of possible universes each with different values for these constants, he's doing science. When astronomer Owen Gingerich explains the very same observations by means of design, he's doing religion. This is at best an artificial demarcation. As the SETI project and archeology show, design is an explanatory concept already used in science. Nonetheless, the only scientifically acceptable explanation of fine-tuning at present is an undetectable multiverse. Cosmologists must therefore pursue this hypothesis to win grants, publish papers, and get tenure, *even if supernatural design happens to be the right answer.* As this example shows, MN is actually in conflict with realism. In order to hold scientific realism, one must believe that theories are generally reliable indicators of truth. But if there is a choice between naturalism and truth, MN forces science to choose the former. Once science is limited to certain kinds of entities, it can no longer follow the data wherever it leads. It is forced instead to beat the data until it offers a naturalistic confession.

Another problem for MN is that no one knows what sort of explanatory resources science will need in the future. One can bet that we will never need to use design, but that's a prediction, not a discovery or an inference from established truths. Many of the expectations of late-19th

13. Del Ratzsch presents a similar argument in "Design Theory and its Critics: Monologues Passing in the Night," *Ars Disputandi* 2 (2002) section 3. If one adds a closure principle such that science is able to reach all truth, then MN, realism, and closure logically *entail* metaphysical naturalism.

century physicists were dashed by general relativity, quantum mechanics, and chaos theory. Instead of limiting our explanatory resources, we should adopt the attitude of naturalist extraordinaire W. V. O. Quine. "If I saw indirect explanatory benefit in positing sensibilia, possibilia, spirits, [or] a Creator, I would joyfully accord them scientific status too, on a par with such avowedly scientific posits as quarks and black holes."[14]

3. *MN is superfluous.* Contrary to the conventional wisdom, MN has not rescued science from supernatural design.[15] MN is, in fact, almost always a placeholder in these debates for some other shaping principle. Historical confrontations between naturalistic and design hypotheses were usually settled by appeal to simplicity in the form of Ockham's razor.[16] To cite one (overly used) example, when Laplace presented Napoleon with a copy of his *Méchanique Céleste*, the emperor wished to know why it did not contain any reference to God. Laplace replied, "I have no need of that hypothesis."[17] Nor did he need to invoke MN in order to make his case. Today, many critics of ID begin with MN but then seamlessly switch to complaints about predictability and fruitfulness. The latter two *are* well-established MSPs that can be defended in their own right, but neither is equivalent to MN. In short, MN could be dropped without loss since the work it supposedly does is carried out by other MSPs.

For various reasons then, theists should follow Quine when it comes to MN. If the best explanation for some phenomenon is design, even supernatural design, that would still count as a scientific explanation.

---

14. W. V. O. Quine, "*Naturalism; Or, Living Within One's Means*," *Dialectica* 49 (1995) 252.

15. Eighteenth–nineteenth century debates over flood geology might be an exception. There were certainly theological tensions between uniformitarians and catastrophists.

16. Ratzsch shows how after Darwin the notion of design was pushed back into the more abstract realm of laws and initial conditions. It seemed to all sides that design was no longer needed to explain the operation and function of organisms. Once this move was complete, naturalistically minded scientists and philosophers were free to dismiss design as an unnecessary appendage. The laws themselves were taken to be a sufficient foundation for scientific explanations. See Delvin Ratzsch, "Intelligent Design: What Does the History of Science Really Tell Us?" in *Scientific Explanation and Religious Belief: Science and Religion in Philosophical and Public Discourse*, eds. Michael Parker and Thomas Schmidt (Tübingen: Mohr/Siebeck, 2005).

17. William Herschel recorded this exchange in his diary in 1802. See J. L. E. Dreyer, ed., *The Scientific Papers of Sir William Herschel V1 (1912)* (Whitefish, MT: Kessinger, 2007).

Popular and legal opinion is unfortunately blowing in the opposite direction. Robert Pennock, an expert witness for the plaintiff in the Dover case, not only argued in favor of MN but also claimed that it is simply another name for the scientific method.[18] While this would have been an amusing gaffe in an undergraduate paper, it is deplorable coming from a professor of philosophy. One wonders, if Darwin did not need MN in order to defend against supernaturalism, why does Pennock?

MSPS AND OPEN THEISM

As we have seen, there are tensions between theism and MSPs such as metaphysical naturalism, MN, and reductionism. Let's finally turn to open theism. Are there any special conflicts with this view? The answer is 'yes,' but the list is surprisingly short for reasons to be discussed below.

As we saw earlier, Einstein was a champion of universal, law-governed causation in nature. Since quantum mechanics allows for purely stochastic events, it violates universal causation. Einstein therefore took an *anti*-realist approach toward it. Quantum mechanics works as far as it goes, he thought, but it is not a true and complete theory. Open theists will have a similar attitude about certain theories, but for rather different reasons. Unlike Einstein, open theists reject universal, deterministic causation. They will therefore lean towards anti-realism when it comes to theories that seem to entail that the future is fixed.

The reason for this is that open theists are strong *libertarians* when it comes to freewill: in order for me to be free at this moment, I must have it within my power to make choice A rather than choice B. The future is open, not fixed. Many theists, especially those with an Augustinian/Calvinist background, have a *compatibilist* view of freewill. They believe that the future *is* fixed, God has exhaustive foreknowledge of that future, and yet humans have freewill of some kind or other. Compatibilists can take deterministic theories realistically while open theists cannot.

Prime examples are the theories of special and general relativity. Both treat space and time not as separate physical entities but rather as an integrated four-dimensional space-time or "block universe." Points in the block universe represent place-times from the Big Bang forward. From a purely physical point of view, what we think of as the past and the future are equally real. There is no privileged, moving slice within

18. Kitzmiller v. Dover, 400 F. Supp. 2d 707 (M.D. Pa., 2005) 83.

the block universe that is "the present." This conflicts both with our commonsense view of the passage of time and with libertarian freewill. If all of the points in the block universe have determinate properties, then nothing one does now can change the physical facts elsewhere in the block, including what we think of as the future.[19] Einstein himself understood all this quite well.

There are several anti-realist stances an open theist might take towards relativity. One might be an instrumentalist about all space-time theories. On this view, the equations in both special and general relativity work, but their usefulness is not dependant on their being true. While this might seem initially implausible, consider that many of the theories in the history of science once enjoyed some measure of success even though they have been superseded. (Ptolemaic models of the solar system not only worked well for centuries but also were *more* accurate than the ones first posed by Copernicus.)

There are also more selective forms of anti-realism available to the open theist. One follows from the maxim that entities in physics ought not be automatically hypostatized. Although ray optics entails that certain convergences of light rays (caustics) are infinitely intense, applied scientists dismiss this result as a nonphysical artifact. Ray optics is still extremely useful, but no one takes it in a fully realistic way.[20] Similarly, one might hold that the field equations of general relativity are approximately true, but deny that future space-time points have ontological weight.

19. As Robin Collins has indicated (private correspondence), recent work by philosophers of physics has questioned whether standard general relativity entails a block universe. Indeterminism can reemerge because of the "gauge freedom" of the theory. This is a highly technical debate, but it is clearly the next battleground in the interpretation of relativity. For more, see the exchange by John Earman and Tim Maudlin in the *Philosophers' Imprint* 2.4 (August 2002). Online: www.philosophersimprint.org/002004/.

20. A closely related option is to take an anti-realist view of spacetime as an object in itself. Substantivalists take spacetime to have an independent existence, a thing in which physical objects like stars are located. Several philosophers of physics have argued that spacetime should be understood in a relational rather than substantival way (see David Woodruff's piece in this volume). On this view, spacetime is not a substance but rather a set of relations between possible physical objects. (Cf. brotherhood is not a thing, but rather a relation between certain males in a family.) The relationalist believes in physical objects, but not in a reified block universe. Leibniz argued much the same way against Newton's substantival view of absolute space. For more on this and its relation to the famous hole argument, see Paul Teller, "Substance, Relations, and Arguments About the Nature of Spacetime," *The Philosophical Review* 100 (July, 1991) and John Earman, *World Enough and Spacetime* (Cambridge: MIT Press, 1989).

In other words, there is no four-dimensional space-time manifold.[21] Instead of taking the block universe as a bit of metaphysics entailed by Einstein's field equations, it is merely a convenient device for generating predictions.[22]

One might also be a narrow anti-realist about relativity in the same way Einstein was vis-à-vis quantum mechanics: it's incomplete.[23] On this approach, the open theist is either betting that (i) a successor theory to general relativity will reintroduce an objective flow of time, or (ii) additional physical structure will be discovered that will allow for a non-ad hoc way of foliating (slicing) the space. On the first option, general relativity is understood as a stepping-stone to a more realistic theory without a block universe, something like the way the Rutherford model of the atom was a step toward modern atomic theory. Since quantum mechanics and general relativity are formally inconsistent, a successor theory is certainly forthcoming. On the second option, the block universe it sliced into 3-dimensional (space like) hypersurfaces where each slice is ordered along a temporal axis. This can be done in many different ways. The problem is in finding a sound physical reason for preferring one foliating scheme to another. At present, general relativity lacks any such foliation and does require this additional structure.

Open theists will also tend to be anti-realists about any theory that entails determinism in its many forms since this conflicts with libertarian freewill. Strong reductionist programs in neuroscience imply psychological determinism: our mental states, including the will, are fixed by or identical to brain states. Bohmian mechanics, as we saw earlier, is a deterministic version of quantum physics. Hence open theists side with Bohr rather than Einstein. God may not play dice, but he has ordered the cosmos in such a way that persons can act as free agents.

21. Technically, this requires the denial that spacetime is essentially a four-dimensional, semi-Reimannian manifold. While splitting spacetime into space-plus-time is unproblematic in special relativity, it is a more difficult task in general relativity. See J. Brian Pitts, "Some Thoughts on Relativity and the Flow of Time: Einstein's Equations Given Absolute Simultaneity" (2004). Online: http://philsci-archive.pitt.edu/archive/00002760/.

22. Nobel laureate Steven Weinberg has argued that if anything, naive realism about spacetime has hindered the progress of physics. See his *Gravitation and Cosmology: Principles and Explications of the General Theory of Relativity* (New York: Wiley, 1972) vii–viii.

23. Philosopher Arthur Prior held such a view of special relativity. See his "The Notion of the Present," *Studium Generale* **23** (1970) 245–48.

We have found only two MSPs that conflict with open theism: universal, deterministic causation and global scientific realism. Why is this list so short? There are three reasons. One is that there just aren't many relevant differences between open and classical theism when it comes to science. The two sides agree on most matters and so there isn't much disagreement when it comes to shaping principles. The second is that the logical connections from theology down through the three layers of science are weak. Consider an analogy from politics. Being a Christian influences one's political views, but not in a straightforward way. We all agree that loving our neighbor is a Christian principle. Does that mean government-run health care and more support for the poor? Yes, unless that support creates a ward-of-the-state mentality that undermines the escape from poverty, in which case, no. Does Christian love mean stepping in militarily to protect the oppressed? Or does it mean passive resistance and aid to the victims? There are Christians on both sides. This same kind of underdetermination is present in theology and science. Should open theists support creationism, intelligent design, or theistic evolution? As far as I can tell, open theism is compatible with each. Here and elsewhere, which view one prefers depends on other matters.

Third and most important, open theists are split over the nature of divine action. On one side are those who accept a large degree of divine intervention in the natural order. On this view, miracles and answered prayer are often understood as God's direct action within the cosmos. The other side has principled arguments for noninterventionism, the view that God seldom interferes with his own natural laws. This is an old debate reaching back through Leibniz and Newton into the medieval distinction between primary and secondary causation.[24] Whether a given MSP is in tension with open theism often depends on which side of this divide one falls.

To illustrate, let's again consider MN. Many open theists accept MN except when it is used as leverage for metaphysical naturalism. They agree that science can and should only refer to secondary causes. Since, according to noninterventionists, God seldom intervenes in nature, science doesn't miss much by limiting itself to naturalistic explanations. The alternative view is that the direct action by God in the natural order is a

24. Thomas Aquinas himself argued that God prefers to work through providence and natural law rather than miraculous intervention. See *Summa Theologica* I, q.22, a.3; q.103, a.6; *Summa Contra Gentiles* III, 76, 77, 83, 94.

contingent, empirical matter. God has intervened in the past, especially in the apostolic age, and continues to do so now. "Elijah was a man with a nature like ours, and he prayed fervently that it might not rain, and for three years and six months it did not rain on the earth. Then he prayed again, and heaven gave rain, and the earth bore its fruit" (James 5:17–18, ESV). *Prima facie*, Elijah's prayer was answered in such a way that what would have occurred by way of normal meteorology did not, and this change was due to God's activity. Putting my cards on the table, I have no theological qualms about this type of divine action. God directly acts within the realm of what we normally think of as science. Whether there is any evidence of this direct action should be open to empirical investigation.

Whatever else one might say about science and shaping principles will likewise depend more on this divide within open theism than open theism itself. How excited should one be about chaos and quantum mechanics? For noninterventionists, the ontologically random events in quantum mechanics provide a place where God might work without overriding the laws of nature since the outcomes are not law-governed in a deterministic way.[25] Finding a scientifically acceptable causal joint within which God might act is an important advance in the noninterventionist program. For others, this pursuit is not very interesting. If God isn't limited to working within indeterministic gaps, then the search for *the* causal joint of divine action seems misguided from the start. The same is true when it comes to the question of ontologically emergent properties in chemistry, biology, and elsewhere. Noninterventionists have a special interest in new emergence programs because they provide yet another means for God to influence the world indirectly. The idea is that has God planted the seeds of emergent phenomena within creation itself. There is no need for God to manage further the process whereby nature produces complex organic structures or even conscious human beings. If divine intervention isn't an issue, on the other hand, then one doesn't have a rooting interest one way or the other when it comes to emergence. Perhaps God has used emergent

25. This proposal gets more attention than it merits. Let's say that God had decreed the mass extinction of dinosaurs by way of the asteroid that crashed into the Yucatan peninsula. Assuming that a sufficiently large asteroid were heading towards the earth to begin with, it would have taken 100 million years of quantum tweaking to get the desired impact (David Jones, "Daedalus: God Plays Dice," *Nature* 385 [1997] 122). Given the time scale required in order to bring about some event, there simply isn't much that God can do through the collapse of the wavefunction. As I have argued elsewhere, chaos theory isn't much help ("God, Chaos, and the Quantum Dice," *Zygon* 35.3 (2000) 545–59).

properties, perhaps not. Open theism itself is neutral on this issue. The broader point, again, has to do with why openness has relatively little to say about MSPs. In order for there to be support or tension with a given shaping principle, one needs a fuller set of metaphysical commitments than those that define open theism.

CONCLUSION

As we have seen, open theists are split over many of the same issues that divide Christian academics in general. There are relatively few distinctive doctrines held by the entire group. Consequently, the relation between open theology and science, including MSPs, depends more on these intramural differences than openness itself. To make any real progress, the two sides will have to be less ecumenical. Noninterventionists should pursue their research and see where it leads. They need not speak for all open theists nor have to defend their distinctive views at every turn. The same goes for those with contrary beliefs about metaphysics and divine action. Open theism is a relatively young research program. Each branch should have room to develop. A time for pruning will come, no doubt, but that time is not now.

As we saw in Section 2, MSPs change over time due to a wide variety of influences. Many of these are within the pyramid structure itself, but some are outside of it. Theology is one such influence. If religion is merely the realm of value, faith, and purpose, in contrast to the concrete knowledge of science, then this influence should be resisted. Faith can only interfere with reason. If, however, theology is also knowledge seeking, then theists need not abandon their views if they happen to be in tension with contemporary science. If one has a justified belief in an open rather than determined future, then one should hold on and see if physics will one day catch up. In any case, the science-theology "dialogue" should be a two-way street, rather than, as is tacitly demanded, the dictation of scientific authority to the softer discourse of faith.

3

Religious Belief Formation

A Kantian Perspective Informed by Science

DAVID BASINGER

N O ONE DENIES THAT belief, in general, is influenced by a number of factors outside of our control. But what exactly are these factors, and to what extent do they influence religious belief, especially our belief options and our ability to choose among them? I'll first set forth a number of working assumptions about religious belief formation and retention, assumptions drawn from my reading of the relevant scientific data and my Kantian understanding of reality. Then treating these assumptions collectively as a Kantian hypothesis on the nature of religious belief formation and retention to be confirmed or disconfirmed, I'll explore the explanatory and predictive power of this way of understanding why we affirm the religious beliefs we do. Finally, I'll discuss some significant practical implications that I believe follow if this Kantian hypothesis is assumed true.

INITIAL ASSUMPTIONS

I'm going to assume that individuals possess libertarian freedom. All determinists agree that given the antecedent conditions that precede a choice, no other decision is possible—that the person making the decision cannot choose or act otherwise. And while some determinists have held this to mean that human behavior cannot be considered truly free, most are compatibilists who hold that, even if a person's choices (and thus actions) are determined, this person can be said to have chosen and acted freely, and thus be held morally responsible, under certain conditions— for example, if the immediate cause of the action is a desire, wish, or intention internal to the person and if the person has not been compelled by some external source to make this choice against her will.[1] Proponents of libertarian freedom disagree. They maintain that, given the antecedent conditions that precede any voluntary (truly free) decision, more than one decision must be possible—that the person making the decision must be in a position at that point to choose and act differently.[2]

Proponents of libertarian freedom don't always agree among themselves on the conditions under which it can be said that humans are capable of exercising freedom. They don't always agree, for instance, on the mental capacity, freedom from chemical influence, or freedom from external threat required for meaningful free choice. However, I'm simply going to assume that there are many situations in which individuals do freely choose, in the libertarian sense, to affirm, retain, and/or modify religious beliefs.

I'm also going to assume, though, that religious belief formation and retention is significantly influenced by factors other than libertarian free choice. Three of these factors are well-known and rather noncontroversial, although the extent to which they contribute to belief formation and retention remains the subject of debate.

First, few deny that genetic factors shape both how we form our religious beliefs and how open we are to belief modification. It will surprise no one that studies confirm, for example, that the extent to which a person is inquisitive, accepting of authority, and/or prone to dogmatism is in part based on genetic factors and that these traits significantly influence religious belief formation and retention.[3]

---

1. See John Fienberg, *The Many Faces of Evil* (Grand Rapids: Zondervan, 1994) ch. 6 and Martin Davies, "Determinism and Evil," *Australasian Journal of Philosophy* 58 (1980) 18–27.

2. Randolph Clarke, "Incompatibilist (Nondeterministic) Theories of Free Will," *Stanford Encyclopedia of Philosophy*, http://plato.stanford.edu/entries/incompatibilism-theories/ (accessed February 18, 2008).

3. Martin E. Davies, "Dogmatism and Belief Formation: Output Interference in the Processing of Supporting and Contradictory Cognitions," *Journal of Personality & Social Psychology* 75.2 (1998) 18–19.

It is also widely accepted that subconscious cultural condition-ing shapes our basic religious beliefs. I'm from a Mennonite culture. The Mennonite aversion to violent behavior is not primarily genetic, as is evidenced by the fact that the biological children of Mennonites not raised in a Mennonite culture are less pacificistic than those raised in a Mennonite culture, while the biological children of non-Mennonites raised in a Mennonite culture are just as pacificistic as those who were "born Mennonite." Nor does this pacifistic tendency appear to be solely or primarily the result of explicit personal indoctrination. It seems rather to be primarily the result of the absorption of the pacifistic view of the world that becomes subconsciously ingrained (soft-wired) into the Mennonite child after birth.[4] And the same is true for religious belief formation in general. Our religious perspectives on many issues, from our perspectives on the nature of God to our perspectives on race, sexual orientation, or the role of government in people's lives, have been subconsciously shaped in part by the worldviews (cultural paradigms) to which we have been exposed.

Finally, everyone agrees that what we are explicitly taught early in life by significant others—by parents, pastors, school teachers, and/or friends—influences religious belief formation and retention throughout our lives. Many of my students maintain that their religious beliefs are based primarily on their personal study of the Bible, and in a sense that may be true. However, class discussion reveals quickly that their under-standing of what the Bible says on such basic issues as God's power or knowledge, the destiny of those who have never heard, or the proper Christian attitude toward wealth has been shaped profoundly by the ex-plicit teaching of a parent, pastor, or televangelist. And so it is for most of us with respect to most of our religious beliefs.

There is, though, a fourth factor in the formation and retention of religious belief that is gaining increasing consideration, and that factor is the role of brain function. One of the significant questions here is pri-marily scientific: How does the way the brain works—that is, how does the normal functioning of the brain, the normal way the brain processes information—influence belief (and thus religious belief) formation and retention? This is still a relatively new field of study, but neurophysiolo-

---

4. I have no objective support for this contention. However, my personal experience with Mennonite culture over the past fifty years leads me to believe firmly that pacifistic belief is primarily a function of early immersion in a pacifistic cultural context.

gists are coming increasingly to agree on a number of findings. While these are not totally noncontroversial views, I'm going to assume for our current purpose that the following claims about the belief-shaping functions of the brain are likely true.

1. The normal functioning of our brain is not to proportion belief to the totality of the evidence but rather to make judgments in specific situations apart from all of relevant data of which we are aware.[5] Specifically, "our thoughts tend to be directed at finding the explanation that best makes sense of the specific situation before us, rather than treating it as an observation needing to be integrated with all other relevant evidence before a conclusion can be reached."[6] In fact, several studies have found no relationship or even a negative relationship between a person's confidence in her beliefs and the extent to which these beliefs have been subjected to comprehensive, objective scrutiny.[7]

2. Our brains subconsciously use currently held beliefs to filter the deluge of information we receive and guide our responses. Or, to state this important point more generally, it appears that we are wired in such a way that our preconceptions or expectations significantly affect how we interpret and respond to new claims.[8] In fact, this effect is so dramatic that new information or counter-arguments seem to have little or no effect in many cases. And this may in part explain why it is so easy for people, even educated people aware of diverse perspectives, to "maintain their core beliefs over the course of their lifetime."[9]

3. Our emotive attachment to beliefs strongly influences belief retention. Specifically, current studies seem to indicate that the more strongly we "feel" that our beliefs are correct, the less predisposed we are to examine the evidential basis for these beliefs and the less

---

5. Ronald L. Goldman, "Is There a Cognitive Basis for Religious Belief," *Journal of Psychology and Judaism* 24.3 (2000) 234–41.

6. Ibid., 240.

7. Ibid., 238.

8. Ibid., 236–37.

9. Ibid., 237.

likely we are to modify these beliefs, even when we acknowledge counterevidence.[10]

4.   While the normal functioning of the brain strongly favors belief retention, conscious reflection on beliefs can result in belief modification. Specifically, it has been demonstrated that when individuals are made consciously aware of inconsistencies among their religious beliefs and/or counterevidence to these beliefs in a context where there is strong reinforcement of new or modified beliefs, we can "get a shift in emphasis from one [belief] to the other."[11]

The other, more theoretical question related at least tangentially to brain function is the extent to which our religious belief-forming faculties (our relevant brain activity plus whatever else is involved[12]) are successfully truth-seeking. One currently popular perspective on this question has been championed by Alvin Plantinga. As he sees it, because God desires us to hold true beliefs about such things as God's nature and our duties to God, it's reasonable for Christians to believe God has created us with cognitive faculties that, when functioning properly in a cognitive environment congenial to those faculties, will produce true (warranted) belief.[13] And he believes that our belief-forming faculties do at times func-

10. Ibid., 237–39, 41.

11. Kathleen Taylor, quoted in Alok Jha, *The Guardian*. Online: http://www.guardian .co.uk/science/2005/jun/30/psychology.neuroscience.

12. It needs to be acknowledged here that I may be using a somewhat different understanding of "brain function" in relation to this theoretical question. I have up to this point been discussing the ways the electro-chemical make-up and function of the brain (the hard and/or soft wiring of the brain) influence religious belief. If the use of "religious belief-forming faculty" in this context is simply a descriptor for the way all brains have been programmed (hard-wired) by God to function in belief formation apart from any other sort of additional belief forming influence, then I'm still discussing "brain function" in the same (or a similar) sense as before. However, it is possible that "religious belief-forming faculty" is being used in this context as a descriptor for the normal electro-chemical functioning of the brain plus other belief-forming influences of some other sort—e.g., some form of divine and/or other non-material influence. Either way, it remains the case that religious beliefs are formed in us by a process that significantly involves the functioning of the brain.

13. See, for example, Michael Czapkay Sudduth, "Can Religious Unbelief be Proper Function Rational?" *Faith and Philosophy* 16.3 (July 1999) 298. As most interpret Plantinga, to say that these faculties are "successfully aimed at truth" is to say at least that, under the stipulated conditions, the process is reliable in the sense that there is a high (statistical or objective) probability that the process yields true beliefs most of the time.

tion in environments we can assume are congenial to proper functioning, and thus that we can justifiably maintain in such cases the formed beliefs are true.

I disagree in one significant sense. I don't deny that we possess religious belief-forming faculties. I am also willing to grant that these belief-forming faculties were intended by God to be truth seeking. And I don't deny that these faculties may in fact produce in us religious beliefs that are true. However, given the pervasive, profound diversity in "formed" religious belief among individuals whom I view as equally knowledgeable and sincere (whom I view to be in very similar cognitive environments), I question our ability to determine when our belief-forming faculties are actually functioning in cognitive environments that are congenital to the production of true beliefs and thus question whether we are ever in a position to maintain with any assurance that a religious belief is true (warranted) primarily because we have found this belief formed within us. This, of course, is in no sense a refutation of Plantinga's position. And my skepticism about our ability to determine when our belief-forming faculties are functioning properly does not commit me to the claim that we cannot justifiably maintain that our religious beliefs are true. It is only to say that for whatever reasons we might maintain that our religious beliefs are justified, I don't personally believe that the assumption that these beliefs were formed in a congenial truth-producing environment can reasonable be included among them.

KANTIAN HYPOTHESIS

In addition to these factual (empirical) assumptions about religious belief formation and retention, I also affirm a Kantian metaphysical assumption about the nature of reality, including religious reality. It is my general Kantian belief that while there is an external reality, our understanding of this reality will always be shaped significantly by factors we don't control and can't totally avoid and that these factors always keep us to some extent from seeing reality as it really is.[14] Applied to religious belief forma-

See, for example, Harriet Harris, "Does Analytic Philosophy Clip our Wings" in *Faith and Philosophical Analysis: The Impact of Analytic Philosophy on the Philosophy of Religion*, eds. Harriet Harris and Christopher Insole (Aldershot, UK: Ashgate, 2005) 108.

14. The extent to which I actually believe we should seriously question our understanding of reality in everyday life is contextual and evidence-based. Since the auditory and visual belief-forming faculties of independent listeners and viewers normally pro-

tion and retention, my Kantian assumption is that while there is a truth to the religious issues about which we hold beliefs—for example, our beliefs about God's attributes, how God would have us live, or who can spend eternity in God's presence—and these beliefs can often be held justifiably, we are not, in principle, in a position to demonstrate in an objective, non-question-begging manner that our religious perspectives more accurately describe the relevant reality than those competing religious perspectives that are self-consistent and comprehensive.[15]

And when this Kantian assumption is conjoined with my factual assumptions about belief formation, we find ourselves, I believe, with a helpful basis for understanding religious belief formation and retention. Or, to restate this in the form of a hypothesis that I will argue has significant explanatory and predictive power, it is my contention that the most accurate and useful way to understand religious belief formation/retention is to assume that:

1.   Since we are never in a position to determine with any reasonable assurance that our religious belief-forming faculties are or are not functioning properly, and we can only assume that formed beliefs

---

duce similar sounds and sights, I believe that we can justifiably assume for the purposes of everyday living that these formed beliefs mirror reality as it really is (when experienced by humans). However, since the moral and religious belief-forming faculties of those considering the same data often produce quite divergent moral and religious beliefs, I don't think we are in a position to assume for the purposes of everyday living that these faculties give us clear access to moral and religious reality as it really is.

15. Two clarifications are needed here. First, for a proponent of a perspective on a religious issue to acknowledge that her epistemic competitors are equally justified, in the sense of justification I'm using, does not require that she also acknowledge personally that their reasons for holding their perspectives are as strong and convincing as her own. To acknowledge that her competitors are justified is simply to acknowledge that she cannot demonstrate in an objective, nonquestion-begging way that their perspectives are internally inconsistent or that they have failed to consider all the relevant evidence to which they had access. And she can grant this and still justifiably hold personally that her own perspective should be considered more convincing and still justifiably attempt to convince others to "convert" to her perspective for these reasons. For a more detailed discussion of this point, see David Basinger, *Religious Diversity: A Philosophical Assessment* (Aldershot, UK: Ashgate, 2002) ch. 3.

Furthermore, to say that the perspectives of epistemic competitors are, in principle, equally justified is to say only that there are possible variations of these perspectives that can meet the standards of consistency and comprehensiveness. It is not to say that all actual variations of this perspective held by all competitors do in fact meet these criteria and are thus in fact justified.

are true when we can have this assurance, we cannot rely on such faculties as a source for true religious belief.

2. Both the religious belief options of which we are aware and our choice of options are significantly shaped by our genetic predispositions, our subconscious cultural conditioning, the beliefs we acquired early in life from authority figures, and the way our brains normally process such data.

3. While conscious recognition of these shaping factors can minimize their influence and thus lead to belief modification, we are not, in principle, in a position to demonstrate objectively that our religious perspectives are superior to competing perspectives that are self-consistent and equally comprehensive.

CONFIRMING EXAMPLES

Few religious believers deny that the majority of past adherents to most current religious traditions often affirmed beliefs that are not longer held (or are even explicitly denied) by the majority of adherents to these same religious traditions today. The beliefs in question differ from tradition to tradition. For instance, within many conservative Christian traditions, while the view of Scriptural authority and the hermeneutical principles used for Scriptural interpretation have not changed, beliefs about such things as drinking and dancing and card playing have changed significantly over time. But while few religious believers deny that modifications of this sort occur, few normally find this troubling as most simply see such modification as the understandable adaptation of general religious truth to changing cultural settings.

However, other examples of belief modification are much more significant and troubling. In 1864, John Henry Hopkins spoke for many, many conservative, Bible-believing Christians in America (especially in the South) when he wrote that:

> The Bible's defense of slavery is very plain. St. Paul was inspired, and knew the will of the Lord Jesus Christ, and was only intent on obeying it. And who are we, that in our modern wisdom presume to set aside the Word of God . . . and invent for ourselves a "higher law: than those of Holy Scriptures which are given to us as 'a light

to our feet and a lamp to our paths,' in the darkness of a sinful and
a polluted world."[16]

Yet it seems perfectly clear today to the vast majority of American
Christians who affirm the same high view of Scripture as did Hopkins
that we cannot find in the Word of God any defense for the type of slavery
to which Hopkins is referring.

Or consider the moral intuitions at play in the biblical account of the
killing of Midianite women and children found in Numbers 31. Moses
has sent 12,000 Israelite soldiers to "exact vengeance on the Midianites."
When he discovers that they have killed only the Midianite men and
brought back approximately 100,000 women and children, he commands
them to "kill all the boys, and kill every woman who has slept with a man,
but save for yourselves every girl who has not slept with a man." The story
then ends with the officers returning with an offering to God in thanks for
the fact that they have not lost a single man in this successful effort.

While it appears that these soldiers—who had not only killed about
30,000 men but then chased down and killed about 65,000 woman and
children before taking home with them their share of the 32,000 virgin
girls—did not suffer pangs of moral conscience for their actions, almost
none of my conservative Christian students can understand how anyone,
especially anyone living in relationship with, and attempting to follow the
teachings of, the true God could do such things with gratitude to God for
the outcome. And analogous "moral tensions" could be noted with respect
to the behavior of seeming sincere Christians during the Crusades and
Inquisitions.

One common response to such cases is to say that God has always
considered the behavior/attitudes in question wrong and, therefore, that
those who engaged in such behaviors or held moral attitudes that the vast
majority of Christians now rightly feel are wrong (if not reprehensible)
were in some significant sense at fault for not doing what they should/
could have done to discern how God would in fact have had them act
and feel. It is sometimes argued, for instance, that in contrast to those
European and American Christians who rightly believed slavery to be
wrong in the early 1800s, those like Hopkins who believed slavery to be

---

16. John Henry Hopkins, *A Scriptural, Ecclesiastical, and Historical View of Slavery,
from the Days of the Patriarch Abraham, to the Nineteenth Century* (New York: Pooley,
1864) 16–17.

biblical were guilty of not discerning the correct teaching of Scripture on this issue. However, it seems to me that the Kantian hypothesis in question offers us a much more plausible explanation. As I see it, it's not that the belief-forming faculties of those in the past who believed slavery to be biblical were not functioning in a truth-producing environment while the faculties of those who opposed slavery were functioning in such an environment or that these individuals were less sincerely attempting to live as God would have them live or that they were less open to the Spirit of God. It is, rather, that the dominant worldview of the culture in which they lived set the dispositional and cognitive parameters within which their decisions were made, even when they were doing all in their power to feel, believe, and act in ways that would please God.

Or how ought we respond to the inter-religious and intra-religious diversity of thought surrounding almost every religious issue? That is, how ought we respond to the fact that seemingly sincere, equally knowledgeable proponents of various religions, as well as adherents to the same religion, differ significantly, and often heatedly on everything from the nature of God to the extent to which we can relate to God both now and eternally to the way God would have us treat ourselves and others?

A Plantingian externalist perspective gives us, in principle, one way to view such diversity: those, if any, whose belief-forming faculties are functioning properly in the appropriate context are affirming the correct perspective while those holding differing perspectives are either not fully knowledgeable, not fully sincere, not functioning in a context where the relevant faculties can produce truth, or have faculties that are in some way malfunctioning.

However, it seems to me much more plausible to assume, in keeping with my Kantian hypothesis, that the incompatible perspectives in question are, for all parties, the product of belief-forming faculties functioning within parameters shaped by the relevant individual genetic traits and the culturally instilled cognitive and dispositional states. And these shaping influences, I believe, affect not only the conclusions reached by those on all sides but extend even to what is considered relevant evidence and how it is to be weighed. Furthermore, it seems to me most plausible to assume that the reason most significant religious epistemic conflicts remain unresolved is not because those affirming one perspective have yet to demonstrate objectively that this perspective is superior and/or because one or more of the competitors are not willing or able to acknowledge the truth. The epistemic conflicts in question remain unresolved because the proponents of none of the divergent perspectives are in a position to demonstrate in an objective, non-question-begging manner that their perspective is superior. The best that the proponents of any perspective can do, given the Kantian hypothesis in question, is to justifiably believe (for various reasons) that this perspective is superior.[17]

UNWARRANTED IMPLICATION

What follows if I am right? To accept my Kantian hypothesis clearly does not entail that conscious belief assessment is irrelevant to belief modification. However, it might be argued that if our belief options are prescribed to the extent I claim, there is actually little reason, or at least diminished reason, for an individual to assess her own beliefs or encourage others to reflect on theirs. I think neither is a valid inference.

As I have noted in previous discussions of divergent perspectives, we all hold basic beliefs about ourselves and the world around us; that is not a choice.[18] Moreover, many of these basic beliefs have very significant practical consequences for us and others. Our basic beliefs on the controversial question of how free and morally responsible persons are for their behavior is often the basis for how we as individuals or as a society respond to such behavior. Our basic beliefs on controversial questions related to gender and ethnicity profoundly affect both how we treat others personally and the types of relevant legislation we do or do not support. Our socio-political beliefs can significantly and directly affect hunger and disease in other parts of the world.

And the same holds in the religious realm. Our basic religious beliefs have tremendous impact on how we think about ourselves (for example, how much self-worth we possess or what we see as our purpose for living), how we explain what happens in our lives (for example, the extent to which we believe that God controls our destiny), and how we treat others (for example, how we respond to those who don't share our religious perspectives).

Moreover, we are all aware of the fact that what seems certain (obviously true) can and does change over time. After we get past abandoned belief in Santa Claus or the Tooth Fairy and center on religious beliefs,

17. See again the clarifications in note 15 and Basinger, *Religious Diversity,* ch. 3.
18. Ibid., 18–26.

most individuals can identify what were once held to be fundamental, obvious, non-negotiable religious beliefs that have subsequently either been abandoned or modified. For instance, many Christians have modified over time not only their beliefs on such significant theological issues as the nature of God's power and knowledge, the epistemic status of the Bible, and the eternal destiny of those who have never heard the gospel; they've also modified their beliefs n significant socio-political issues related to gender, ethnicity, and appropriate sexual behavior. And a significant factor in such belief modification, as I have argued before, is almost always serious reflection on such beliefs.

How, though, can such reflection contribute significantly to belief modification, given my contention that our belief options are so strongly shaped and constrained by genetics, culture, and personal interactions? As noted earlier, studies have shown that making individuals consciously aware of inconsistencies in their current religious beliefs and/or of counterevidence to these beliefs can contribute to belief modification, and this is exactly what serious reflection is likely to produce. That is, our belief options are not limited only by our genetics and culturally influenced dispositions and beliefs. They are also limited by our lack of conscious understanding of divergent perspectives and the reasons others hold such perspectives.

Of course, our understanding of any alternative perspective will, itself, always be shaped and limited to some extent by our genetics, culture, and personal interaction with others. And our natural neurological and/or psychological tendency not only to hold but also defend our currently held beliefs in the face of alternative perspectives means that we will seldom experience a sudden significant change in a firmly held belief, especially if this belief has emotive support. Any significant modification to such belief will probably, rather, be the result of a process in which we come first to acknowledge an alternate/modified belief as possible but still clearly wrong, then plausible but still probably wrong, then a reasonable option not personally affirmed, and then finally as the new or modified belief option we do now affirm. But it is compatible with both the relevant scientific evidence and our experience with belief modification to maintain that the shaping influence of genetics, culture, personal interaction with others, and natural brain function can be diminished, even significantly in some cases, by conscious reflection on both our beliefs and alternative perspectives. So I stand by my claim that belief assessment can be of significant value for us personally and thus ought to be encouraged, even given my Kantian hypothesis.

For analogous reasons, I believe that sharing our perspectives with those who hold divergent perspectives can have significant impact on their beliefs and thus ought also to be encouraged. Given my Kantian hypothesis, we aren't in a position to demonstrate objectively to others that the religious beliefs they hold are, in principle, false. And it's true that their ability to listen and understand anything we say will be shaped significantly by their genetic traits, culturally induced dispositional states, and brain function. But helping our epistemic competitors understand that their perspectives have been shaped by such influences, helping them understand that assessing their beliefs is possible and has important practical implications, challenging the consistency and comprehensiveness of their current beliefs, and then finally sharing with them divergent belief perspectives can in some cases set the stage for belief modification.

Likewise, we ought not assume that we are never in a position to influence meaningfully the dominant religious perspective of any given group of individuals. It's true that any attempt on our part to influence such a perspective will occur in a context containing many significant factors over which we have little direct control: the type and amount of access we have to the members of the group we wish to influence, the extent to which those in this group understand what is being said without feeling overly threatened, the extent to which the alternate perspective being proposed already seems possible or plausible to many in this group, the manner in which the guardians of the status quo respond, etc. However, attempts to introduce a divergent perspective can lead to widely accepted, meaningful modification of the dominant view, even acknowledging these constraining factors.

The initial impact and increasing acceptance of open theism in conservative Christian circles is to me a good example. Those of us who helped initiate the open theism movement had little control over the theological climate that proved receptive to the concept of a relational God with self-limiting power who does not have exhaustive knowledge of future free choices. And we had little control over the fact that the number and types of negative responses by evangelical associations and specific denominations would flame interest among conservative Christians. However, there were conscious decisions that did directly affect the impact of open theism. For instance, if we had decided to have the *Openness of God* published by a university press, rather than by InterVarsity Press, it would not have been read by as many of those for whom it was intended, reviewed in as many publications read by those for whom it was intended, or discussed by as many denominations containing those for whom it was intended. If we had not decided to write this book in a style accessible to laypeople, it would not have been so influential. If some of the proponents of open theism had not introduced this concept to Christian analytic philosophers of religion through books and articles, it would not have the prominence in that arena it has today.

In short, while it clearly is true that the impact of open theism is due in no small measure to factors over which the initial proponents had little control in a context which could easily have contained different factors that would have generated a quite different outcome, it is also clearly true, I believe, that the decision to share this divergent perspective in certain ways was also significant. So I stand by the general point here exemplified: we have good reason to encourage dialogue with others, even if my Kantian hypothesis is true.

WARRANTED IMPLICATIONS

There are, it seems to me, some interesting practical implications of my Kantian hypothesis that do hold. I will mention three, all of which are quite controversial.

First, accepting this Kantian understanding of religious belief formation should, I believe, have significant impact on how controversial religious issues are approached in the college classroom.

Not surprisingly, most of us who teach college students usually believe that our own personal perspectives on such issues—for instance, our personal beliefs concerning God's attributes or how God would have us live—are informed and correct. But how should these issues be presented to students, given that we almost always have a significantly greater understanding of the differing perspectives on these issues than our students and ultimately have control over how these issues will be considered—for example, control over the extent to which, and in what manner, the differing perspectives will be discussed?

Given my Kantian hypothesis, while we as instructors may well hold justified beliefs on the issues we discuss, proponents of differing perspectives can, in principle, be justified in their beliefs also.[19] I don't think this

19. See again the discussion of "in principle justification" in note 14.

means that we cannot state our own perspective (although I, myself, seldom do), that we cannot share the reasons why we think this perspective is superior, or that we cannot hope that our students agree. But, given the epistemic humility inherent in my Kantian hypothesis, we ought not at the very least approach these issues utilizing the "debate model" practiced so effectively by advertisers, politicians, and some religious leaders: purposely present only the strongest points of our position (hiding its vulnerability) while presenting only the most vulnerable reading of competing perspectives (hiding their strongest points) in an attempt to convince the students that our perspective is the correct one. We as instructors need at the very least to help our students understand as fully as possible the various perspectives on these issues and acknowledge that none of the self-consistent, comprehensive perspectives on such issues can be demonstrated in a totally objective, non-question-begging manner to be superior to the others.

Second, it is my (admittedly controversial) contention, argued in detail elsewhere, that encouraging belief assessment in a Kantian epistemic environment has the potential to minimize religious intolerance.[20] I acknowledge that religious intolerance is very difficult to define. I don't personally believe, for instance, that critiquing the religious beliefs of others or attempting to convince them to modify these beliefs should normally be considered intolerant behavior. Nor do I feel that purposely attempting to prohibit or restrict the actions of those with divergent religious perspectives should always be considered intolerant in the negative sense of this term. I don't feel, for example, that attempting to restrict the practice of female genital mutilation practiced by some is intolerant, or at least inappropriately intolerant. But there is, I feel, general agreement that attempts by some to prohibit or restrict religious behavior are intolerant in the negative sense normally intended. Most will agree, for instance, that it is inappropriately intolerant to kill those who convert to a different religion or keep those of a different religion from owning property or participating in the political process.

Moreover, I acknowledge that not everyone agrees that encouraging belief assessment will increase religious tolerance. As some see it, for instance, to the extent to which belief assessment weakens commitment to

20. David Basinger, "How Religious Diversity Can and Does Foster Religious Tolerance," in *Religious Tolerance through Humility: Thinking with Philip Quinn*, eds., James Kraft and David Basinger (Aldershot, UK: Ashgate, 2008) 29–42.

a religion in general, commitment to the tolerance-producing aspects of this religion will be weakened and thus intolerant behavior toward those of other religions who hold differing perspectives on given issues may actually increase.[21] However, it seems to me that serious belief assessment will in many cases require a proponent of a given perspective on a religious issue to acknowledge that many of those with whom she differs are at the very least equally knowledgeable and sincere. And the epistemic respect thus engendered will, or at least can, I maintain, lessen the natural tendency of the proponent of a strongly held religious belief to engage in intolerant religious behavior—that is, can lessen the tendency to attempt to prohibit others from acting in accordance with their religious beliefs.

Third, let me note what I view as the most epistemically humbling implication of my Kantian hypothesis. As stated earlier, all of us readily admit that thoughtful, sincere religious believers in the past have affirmed, even passionately, religious perspectives we now consider clearly wrong—for example, beliefs about how the universe came to be, the inherent nature of women, how we can justifiably treat other humans, etc. Moreover, most of us will readily admit that some of the religious beliefs we hold today might be questioned by some (many) in the future. However, to the extent that we believe we have religious belief-forming faculties that can be considered successfully truth-seeking under identifiable conditions and that vigorous intellectual analysis coupled with openness to the spirit of God are often, or at least at times, sufficient conditions for the proper functioning of these belief-forming faculties, we are likely to believe that we are getting closer and closer to an understanding of religious reality as it really is.

What, though, if we deny, as I do, the belief that our religious belief-forming faculties can plausibly be assumed to be successfully truth-seeking for us and seriously question, as I do, the extent to which we are in position to know with increasing certainty religious reality as it really is?[22] What if we accept instead that the religious beliefs we hold today are

21. See essays by William Lane Craig, William Hasker, Robert McKim, and Keith Yandell in *Religious Tolerance through Humility*.

22. It is here that I'm most uneasy with the implications of my own assumptions. I personally believe we are in some ways coming to better understand religious reality as it really is. For example, I personally believe that neither slavery nor the subjugation of women was ever a divine ideal and thus that my perspective on these issues is closer to the actual "religious truth" than divergent perspectives affirmed by many in the past. Moreover, I believe I'm justified in affirming my perspective and continuing to act in

no less restricted and shaped both by individual genetic and dispositional factors and a broader, constantly evolving cultural gestalt than was the case in the past and will be the case in the future? We are then left with the very high probability that some of our most basic, fundamental religious beliefs—including some of those that seem to us today so obviously true—may well not appear at all obvious, or even true, to sincere religious believers in our traditions in the future. Which beliefs these will be I do not know; that there will be such beliefs I do not doubt.

It does not follow from this, let me restate in closing, that we ought not continue to engage in serious belief assessment since we cannot help but hold and act upon significant beliefs that have practical consequences, and belief assessment can clarify our beliefs, focus our belief options, and lead to belief modification. However, it has meant for me personally, to use Philip Quinn's phase, "a thicker phenomenology and a thinner theology."[23] That is, while I do not doubt there is objective religious truth (and that I hold justifiable beliefs about this reality), my Kantian perspective (informed and bolstered by my understanding of the latest science) has led me increasingly to believe that the way I conceptualize such truth is simply one way in which this truth can be understood, a way that is in great part the product of the shaping factors noted previously. However, I also believe that the Spirit of God can work within this context to help each of us better understand that which we are capable of understanding and better act in ways we are capable of acting. And while this may be too "open" for many, it is sufficient for me.

accordance with it. But, given the tremendous shaping power of the sorts of factors that influence religious belief and my Kantian assumption that we are never in a position to see religious reality as it really is, I don't see that I'm in a position to claim that my current perspective on even such things as race and gender can in some objective, nonquestion-begging manner be demonstrated to mirror this relevant religious reality. And I cannot rule out the possibility that 300 years from now, Christians will, as a whole, hold divergent perspectives on such things race or gender, or that (in what is most troubling to me) they will necessarily have deviated further from religious reality as it really is in doing so.

23. See Philip L. Quinn, "Toward Thinner Theologies: Hick and Alston on Religious Diversity," in *The Philosophical Challenge of Religious Diversity*, eds. Philip L. Quinn and Kevin Meeker (New York: Oxford University Press, 2000) 235–43.

PART THREE

Open Theism, Time, and Relativity

4

The Fivefold Openness of the Future

ALAN R. RHODA

O PEN THEISTS ARE THEISTS of a "broadly classical" sort.[1] But why the
qualifier? What puts the "open" in open theism? The answer to that
question has two sides. One concerns the openness *of the future*, meaning,
roughly, that the shape of things to come is not fully given in advance.
Instead, things are progressively "taking shape" as events unfold, as choices are made, as contingencies become resolved one way or the other. The
other side has to do with the openness *of God*,[2] who, according to open
theists, freely enters into dynamic, ongoing, two-way relations with his
creation. As open theists see matters, these two sides to the openness question are intimately related. Having a world with an open future requires a
degree of openness in God. As an essentially perfect knower responsible
for creating and sustaining an open-ended world, God's knowledge and
experience of the world must change to accurately reflect changes in the
world. Conversely, God's openness to creation, particularly his openness
to developing loving relationships with his creatures, requires an open

---

1. I define "broadly classical theism" as the view that there is a unique personal being
(God) who exists necessarily, who possesses a maximal set of compossible great-making
properties, including omnipotence, omniscience, and perfect goodness, and who created
the world *ex nihilo* and can unilaterally intervene in it as he pleases.

2. This concern is reflected in the title of the book most responsible for bringing open
theism to widespread attention, viz., Clark Pinnock et al., *The Openness of God* (Downers
Grove, IL: InterVarsity, 1994).

future in which their free contributions help to determine the shape of things to come.

The foregoing sketch of open theism is, admittedly, quite rough. No doubt there are many non-open theists who, with suitable qualifications, could endorse most or all of it. To refine the sketch, and to make more precise the issues that divide open and non-open theists, I think it is most helpful to focus on the openness of the future. There are several different senses in which the future may be thought of as "open" that need to be carefully distinguished. In this paper I identify five such senses: *causal, ontic, alethic, epistemic,* and *providential*.[3] After defining these, I argue that they are connected in important ways. Working from premises that many, if not most, *non-open* theists accept, I argue for a series of symmetry principles, according to which two or more of the five senses of openness stand or fall together. Using those principles, I give reasons for thinking that *if* the future is causally open, then it is open in *all five* senses. I close by highlighting some ramifications of my argument for both open and non-open theists. In particular, if causal openness entails openness in the other respects, then open theism is the only viable form of free will theism (i.e., theism plus creaturely libertarian freedom). In addition, one major version of open theism[4] is untenable.

FIVE SENSES OF OPENNESS DEFINED

I begin by clarifying some of the terms that I'm going to use in my definitions and arguments. First, by a "state of affairs" I mean *a concurrent arrangement of concrete particulars*. Concurrency is essential for me because I need to be able to speak about states of affairs obtaining *at a time*. With respect to concrete particulars, I mean to stay as neutral as possible on their metaphysical constitution. I don't care whether they are understood as enduring substances, bundles of tropes, Whiteheadian actual entities, or something else entirely. All that is essential for my purposes is that states of affairs be able to serve as truthmakers, be able to obtain at a time, and be able to possess causal powers and/or stand in causal relations.

---

3. Terminological note for non-philosophers: "ontic" means *concerning what exists*; "alethic," *concerning truth*; and "epistemic," *concerning knowledge*.

4. For a description of three important versions of open theism, see Alan R. Rhoda, "Generic Open Theism and Some Varieties Thereof," *Religious Studies* 44 (2008) 225–34.

Second, by a "proposition," I mean an abstract or conceptual representation of a state of affairs. A proposition is *true* if and only if a state of affairs corresponding to the represented state of affairs obtains. Thus, the proposition expressed by the sentence token "My daughter Janelle is hungry" represents Janelle, my daughter, as being hungry and it is true if and only if a state of affairs that includes her being hungry obtains.

Third, I speak of states of affairs obtaining "at a time," as well as of propositions being true "at a time." This needs some defense and clarification. As for defense, some contemporary philosophers reject the notion of a proposition's being true at a time, claiming to find the idea unintelligible.[5] Such worries are misplaced, in my opinion. The standard examples used to question the notion of truth at a time come from mathematics, where the worry, for example, is that to say that 2 + 2 = 4 is true *now* falsely implies that it might have *failed* to be true at some other time. But there is no such implication. That 2 + 2 = 4 is true *now* is fully compatible with its being a necessary truth. Intuitions to the contrary may stem from a conflation of logical implication with conversational implicature.[6] Furthermore, refusal to admit the notion of truth at a time becomes decidedly awkward when we face questions like "Will it be the case *tomorrow* that 2 + 2 = 4?" The question is not incoherent—imagine, if you wish, that it is asked by a child who hasn't yet *realized* that 2 + 2 = 4 is a necessary truth. The obvious answer to the question is "of course." But how can one sensibly affirm that it will be *the case* tomorrow that 2 + 2 = 4 while denying that it will be *true* tomorrow that 2 + 2 = 4? Finally, the notion of truth at a time is harmless so long as we can relate truth at a time to truth *simpliciter*, and that's not a problem.[7]

5. See, for example, Peter van Inwagen, *An Essay on Free Will* (Oxford: Clarendon, 1983) 34–43.

6. See Paul Grice, "Logic and Conversation," in idem, *Studies in the Way of Words* (Cambridge: Harvard University Press, 1989). To say "2 + 2 = 4 is true *now*" does misleadingly suggest that it might have failed to be true at some other time, but this suggestion is merely 'implicated' by the use of the sentence in a conversational context. It is not logically implied by the sentence.

7. Philosophers, of course, may disagree about the proper way to understand that relation. For example, if presentism is right, then only what is true *now* is true *simpliciter*. Alternatively, if truth is omnitemporal, then whatever is true *at any time* is true *at all times*, and so truth at a time reduces to truth *simpliciter*. Finally, if truth is timeless, then a tensed proposition is true at a time just in case a proposition expressing its tenseless truth conditions is true *simpliciter*.

Turning to the issue of clarification, it is important to understand the word "time" in "truth at a time" and "obtains at a time" in an *absolute* sense, not in the *relativistic* sense introduced by Einstein's special theory of relativity (STR). STR defines "simultaneity" in terms of the experimental possibility of synchronizing clocks by light signals. Due to the finite speed of light, what events count as "simultaneous" thus varies from one reference frame to another. It is sometimes claimed, therefore, that STR shows there to be no such thing as absolute time.[8] But, as has been extensively documented,[9] Einstein's definitions of "simultaneity" and of "time" are fundamentally epistemological. He held for broadly verificationist reasons that if we can't experimentally identify absolute simultaneity relations then such relations are physically dispensable.[10] That inference may work fine in the practice of physics, but it won't work for philosophical theology, where the idea of a sempiternal God who experiences succession must be taken seriously.[11] We could suppose on such an account that God is *immediately* acquainted with a fundamentally dynamic reality. Given that God's acquaintance with reality is immediate, the finite speed of light, which creates relativistic issues for us, cannot be an issue for God. Thus, if divine timelessness is false and if God experiences succession, then from God's perspective there is a succession of moments in absolute time.

Fourth, by a "world state" I mean an all-inclusive concurrent state of affairs, the totality of what obtains *at a given time* from an absolute or "God's eye" perspective. A world state is not a possible world, as most philosophers understand the latter. Possible worlds are proposition-like abstract entities. World states, and states of affairs generally, are concrete. History, I take it, has been a continuous succession of world states begin-

8. The classic expression of this argument is Hilary Putnam, "Time and Physical Geometry," in idem, *Philosophical Papers*, vol. 1. (Cambridge: Cambridge University Press, 1975). For an extended response, see William Lane Craig, *Time and the Metaphysics of Relativity* (Dordrecht: Kluwer Academic, 2001).

9. See William Lane Craig, *The Tenseless Theory of Time: A Critical Examination* (Dordrecht: Kluwer Academic, 2000) and Craig, *Time and the Metaphysics of Relativity*.

10. Verificationism is widely regarded as self-refuting. Regardless, it should be clear that the inference from the epistemological claim that we cannot experimentally identify absolute simultaneity relations to the metaphysical claim that there are no absolute simultaneity relations is a *non sequitur*.

11. Recent defenses of divine sempiternality include William Lane Craig, *Time and Eternity: Exploring God's Relationship to Time* (Wheaton, IL: Crossway, 2001), and Garrett J. DeWeese, *God and the Nature of Time* (Hampshire, England: Ashgate, 2004).

ning, if there was a beginning, with an initial world state consisting of God and God alone *sans* creation.

Finally, in some of my definitions I'm going to employ locutions like "for some state of affairs X and some future time *t**" in which I quantify over possible states of affairs and (possible) future times. This is for ease of discourse, and is not meant to imply commitment to the existence of possibilia and futuralia. Those who wish may paraphrase such locutions into talk of propositions representing matters *as if* a state of affairs obtained at a future time.

The foregoing clarifications in place, I now define five different senses in which the future may be conceived of as "open." First, the future may be *causally* open:

> The future is *causally open* relative to time *t* if and only if there is more than one causally possible future relative to *t*.

By a "causally possible future," I mean a complete, non-branching, logically possible extension of the actual past, compatible with holding fixed the laws of nature and supernature.[12] If the future is causally open, then there are multiple such futures, which implies that indeterminism is true, that determinism is false, and that there are "future contingents," i.e., states of affairs that obtain on some causally possible futures and not on others. In other words, there is some state of affairs X and some future time *t** such that neither X's obtaining at *t** nor X's non-obtaining at *t** is guaranteed to happen. If we construe "might" as connoting causal possibility, then we can say that the future is causally open at *t* with respect to X's obtaining at *t** if and only if both <X might obtain at *t**>[13] and <X might not obtain at *t**> are true at *t*.

Second, the future may be *ontically* open:

> The future is *ontically open* relative to time *t* if and only if the world state at *t* does not stand in an *earlier than* relation to a unique and complete series of subsequent world states.

---

12. I include "laws of supernature" in order to allow for the existence of non-physical beings (God, angels, Cartesian souls, etc.) capable of influencing the course of events. Such beings, if they exist, presumably have natures or essences that constrain or limit what they can do, much as the laws of nature constrain what physical beings can do.

13. Angle brackets denote propositions as distinct from the sentences they enclose. Thus, <*p*> refers to the proposition named by the sentence "*p*".

This definition is meant to imply a dynamic, non-eternalist theory of time—one which either denies the existence of future world states altogether or which admits their existence but denies that they constitute a *unique and complete* series. One view that denies the existence of future world states is "presentism." According to presentism, there is only one world state, the present one. Past world states no longer exist. Future ones do not yet exist. The present world state, in virtue of its intrinsic features, is evolving into a new world state that will replace it. Another view that eschews future world states is the "growing block" view. According to this position, the present world state is the leading edge of a series of world states stretching back into the past. All past and present world states exist. They are not replaced, as on the presentist view, but are succeeded as new world states come into being. Another model that entails ontic openness is the branch attrition model[14] according to which all of many causally possible futures exist, such that there is no *unique* series of future world states. As for completeness, no one to my knowledge has seriously proposed that some but not all future world states exist. It's hard to see what could motivate such a view. Not only would it face all of the standard objections to dynamic theories of time without any of the standard advantages,[15] but it would create new problems to boot: Why do only some future states of affairs exist? Why these and not others? I propose, accordingly, a *no partial futures* (NPF) thesis: It is not possibly the case that some but not all future world states exist.

Third, the future may be *alethically* open:

> The future is *alethically open* at time t if and only if for some state of affairs X and some future time t^* (i) neither <X will obtain at t^*> nor <X will not obtain at t^*> is true at t and (ii) neither of their tense-neutral counterparts, <X does obtain at t^*> and <X does not obtain at t^*>, is true *simpliciter*.

Simply put, the future is alethically open just in case there is no "complete true story" depicting a unique series of events as *the* actual future. There

---

14. Storrs McCall, *A Model of the Universe: Space-Time, Probability, and Decision* (Oxford: Oxford University Press, 1994).

15. Standard objections to dynamic models include those stemming from McTaggart's paradox and from the special theory of relativity. Standard arguments for dynamic models appeal to their better fit with our psychological experience of time and with a realist understanding of causality. For a helpful discussion of these and related issues issues, I recommend DeWeese, *God and the Nature of Time*, ch. 2.

are at least two ways in which alethic openness can be satisfied. The first approach denies bivalence, the principle that every proposition is either true or, if not true, then false. Thus, it has been suggested by some that, if X's obtaining at t^* is a future contingent, then <X will obtain at t^*> and <X will not obtain at t^*> (and their tense-neutral counterparts) either have a third indeterminate truth value or have no truth value at all.[16] The second approach retains bivalence by holding that <X will obtain at t^*> and <X will not obtain at t^*> (and their tense-neutral counterparts) are contraries, not contradictories. On this account, <X will obtain at t^*> and <X will not obtain at t^*> are both false at t just in case <X might obtain at t^*> and <X might not obtain at t^*> are both true at t.[17] Likewise, <X does obtain at t^*> and <X does not obtain at t^*> are both false *simpliciter* at times prior to t^*.[18] While I favor the second approach,[19] I won't presuppose it in what follows.

Fourth, the future may be *epistemically* open:

> The future is *epistemically open* at time t if and only if for some state of affairs X and some future time t^* neither <X will obtain at t^*> nor <X will not obtain at t^*> (nor their tense-neutral counterparts) is infallibly known either (i) at t or (ii) timelessly.

What this says, essentially, is that the future is epistemically open just in case it is alethically open *as far as anyone infallibly knows*. The adverb "infallibly," and clause (ii) at the end, are there to avoid trivialization. It is, after all, boringly obvious that the future is epistemically open to fallible beings like ourselves. Epistemic openness only becomes an interesting and controversial thesis when it concerns an essentially perfect and infallible knower, like God. If there is no God, epistemic openness is trivially true. As for (ii), a timeless God has no temporal properties and stands

---

16. See, for example, Jan Łukasiewicz, "Many-Valued Systems of Propositional Logic," in *Polish Logic*, Storrs McCall, ed. (Oxford: Oxford University Press, 1967).

17. Here and throughout, "might" is to be understood as connoting causal possibility, not epistemic possibility.

18. One way to argue for this is by appealing to reference failure. Arguably, both <The present king of France is bald> and <The present king of France is not bald> are false *simpliciter* because there is no present king of France. Similarly, arguably, both <X does obtain at t^*> and <X does not obtain at t^*> are false *simpliciter* if there is no time t^*, as would be the case on either the presentist or growing block model of an ontically open future.

19. I defend it in Alan R. Rhoda, Gregory A. Boyd, and Thomas G. Belt, "Open Theism, Omniscience, and the Nature of the Future," *Faith and Philosophy* 23 (2006) 432–59.

in no temporal relations and so cannot know anything *at a time*. Since I'm sure that advocates of divine timelessness don't want to be committed to epistemic openness simply on that account, (ii) adds a necessary restriction.

Fifth and finally, the future may be *providentially* open:

> The future is *providentially open* as of time *t* if and only if for some state of affairs X and some future time *t** neither X's obtaining at *t** nor X's non-obtaining at *t** has been efficaciously ordained either (i) as of *t* or (ii) timelessly.

For an agent S to *efficaciously ordain* X is for S deliberately to act in a way that guarantees the eventual occurrence of X and for S to know with certainty that in so acting he is guaranteeing the eventual occurrence of X. In Plantinga's terms, S efficaciously ordains a state of affairs if and only if S either "strongly" or "weakly" *actualizes* it.[20] If S strongly actualizes X then S's actions are intrinsically efficacious (i.e., causally sufficient) for bringing about X. If S weakly actualizes X then S's actions satisfy the antecedent of a true counterfactual of freedom having <X obtains> as a consequent. In this latter case, S's actions are extrinsically efficacious (and not causally sufficient) for bringing about X. Presumably, the only agent possibly in a position to render the future providentially settled is God.[21] Hence, we may say that the future is providentially settled if and only if God exercises "meticulous providence," that is, if and only if God efficaciously ordains "whatsoever comes to pass."[22] If, on the contrary, God exercises non-meticulous or "general" providence, then the future is providentially open.[23]

---

20. Alvin Plantinga, *The Nature of Necessity* (Oxford: Clarendon, 1974) 173.

21. If there is no God, of course, then providential openness is trivially true.

22. Westminster Confession of Faith 3.1. A more elaborate statement of meticulous providence is given by Alfred J. Freddoso, "Introduction" to Luis de Molina, *On Divine Foreknowledge: Part IV of the Concordia*, Alfred J. Freddoso, trans. (Ithaca, NY: Cornell University Press, 1988) 3: "God, the divine artisan, freely and knowingly plans, orders, and provides for all the effects that constitute His artifact, the created universe with its entire history, and executes His chosen plan by playing a causal role sufficient to ensure its exact realization. Since God is the perfect artisan, not even the most trivial details escape His providential decrees."

23. For one account of how this could be, see Peter van Inwagen, "The Place of Chance in a World Sustained by God," in *Divine & Human Action: Essays in the Metaphysics of Theism*, Thomas V. Morris, ed. (Ithaca, NY: Cornell University Press, 1988). Van Inwagen proposes that God may ordain "either *a* or *b*" without specifically ordaining *a* and without specifically ordaining *b*.

Of these five senses of openness, causal openness is widely, though not universally, accepted, whereas the other four—ontic, alethic, epistemic, and providential—are all highly controversial. Causal openness is rejected by causal determinists but affirmed by proponents of the "libertarian" conception of free will, and also by those who think that quantum mechanics reveals the existence of causal indeterminacy in nature.[24] Ontic openness is rejected by philosophers who hold to a static block theory of time, as well as by those who hold to certain versions of the dynamic theory of time, such as the so-called "moving spotlight" view. It is accepted, however, by both presentists and growing blockers.[25] As for alethic openness, many philosophers reject it. Most, however, seem to take its falsity for granted, assuming with little to no argument that there is such a thing as a unique and complete series of events that either is or will be *the* future.[26] Finally, epistemic and providential openness are hotly contested issues among theists. A growing minority (open theists) say that the future is open in both respects, but many others (theological determinists, Molinists, etc.) hold that the future is settled in at least the epistemic, if not the providential, sense.

As we can see, there are several distinct yet interrelated debates concerning the openness of the future. I believe that we can make significant headway on many of these debates, in particular the open theism debate, by identifying interdependencies among the five senses of openness that I have distinguished. To that project I now turn.

IDENTIFYING INTERDEPENDENCIES

In what follows, I shall assume the existence of God.[27] Moreover, I assume that God is an essentially perfect knower, that is, a being who essentially knows all that can be known as well as it can be known. As such, I take it

24. See, for example, Abner Shimony, "The Reality of the Quantum World," *Scientific American* 258 (1988) 46–53.

25. For an introductory overview of major views on the metaphysics of time, I recommend Craig Bourne, *A Future for Presentism* (Oxford: Oxford University Press, 2006) ch. 1.

26. William Lane Craig, for example, takes the alethic settledness of the future as axiomatic. He writes (in *Time and Eternity*, 262) that "the future, *by definition*, is just as unalterable as the past. . . . To change the future would be to bring it about that an event which will occur will not occur, which is self-contradictory" (emphasis added).

27. Readers who are non-theists can substitute a hypothetical ideal knower for God.

that God has maximal knowledge in both the propositional sense of infallibly believing all truths that can be known and in the experiential sense of being fully acquainted with all of reality. In sum, I assume that God is essentially as close to being unqualifiedly omniscient as it is possible for a being to be. Theists on all sides of the open theism debate can, I think, agree on that much.

To simplify matters, I'll use bold letters **A**, **C**, **E**, **O**, and **P** to stand for the alethic, causal, epistemic, ontic, and providential openness of the future, respectively. I'll represent their denials, the theses that the future is *settled* in the corresponding respects, by putting a tilde, ~, in front of the letter. Thus, **A** means that the future is alethically open and ~**A** (read "not-**A**") means that the future is alethically settled. In addition, I use "→" to symbolize entailment,[28] "↔" for two-way entailment, "⊃" for the material conditional, "≡" for material equivalence, "∨" for truth-functional inclusive disjunction ("or"), "∧" for conjunction ("and"), and "□" for broadly logical necessity. I begin with the most obvious derivations.

A→**E**: This is a necessary truth. It follows from the platitude that knowledge entails truth (KET). If neither <X will obtain at t^*> nor <X will not obtain at t^*> is true at t, then God cannot know either of those propositions at t. Similarly, if neither <X does obtain at t^*> nor <X does not obtain at t^*> is true *simpliciter*, then God cannot know those propositions either.

E→**C**: This follows from core theistic commitments. Suppose ~**C**. That is, suppose that the future is causally settled, such that the present world state and causal laws determine a unique series of future world states. In that case, like Laplace's demon, a God fully acquainted with the present world state and the laws could predict with certainty the unique and complete course of future history. It follows that ~**C**→~**E**, which contraposes to **E**→**C**.[29]

---

28. By entailment, I mean strict implication. Thus, p→q is equivalent to $\square(p \supset q)$.

29. One may wonder whether I am entitled to use contraposition as an inference rule since I am not presupposing bivalence and since contraposition is not valid for multivalued logics. Nevertheless, inference rules that are not generally valid may still be valid for a *restricted class* of propositions. While contraposition fails for propositions that lack truth values, or that have indeterminate truth values, it remains valid for propositions that are *essentially bivalent*, as **A**, **C**, **E**, **O**, and **P** most certainly are. Because they specify *necessary and sufficient* conditions, each is either true or, if not true, then false. (I thank Mike Rea for bringing this issue to my attention.)

E→O: This also follows from core theistic commitments. According to theism, everything that exists is either an aspect of God's being or a part of God's creation. As an essentially perfect knower, God has perfect self-knowledge. As omnipresent creator and sustainer of everything else, God is fully acquainted with all of creation. Hence, nothing in all of reality can be hidden from God.[30] Now, either there is a unique and complete series of future world states or there isn't. If there is, then God is fully acquainted with it, in which case the future is not epistemically open. It follows that ~O→~E, which contraposes to E→O.[31]

E→P: It follows from the definition of "efficaciously ordain" that God knows what he has efficaciously ordained. Hence, if the future is providential settled, that is, if all its details have been efficaciously ordained by God, then the future is epistemically settled as well. It follows that ~P→~E, which contraposes to E→P.

The foregoing derivations will be accepted by nearly all theists. From here on, however, things get more controversial, so let's pause to note some consequences.

First, from A→E and E→C it follows that A→C.

Second, from A→E and E→O it follows that A→O.

Third, from A→E and E→P it follows that A→P.

Combining these, we get the result that A→(C ∧ O ∧ E ∧ P). In other words, if the future is alethically open, then it must be open in all of the other four senses. Let's continue.

E→A: This follows if God essentially knows all truths,[32] an assumption that all non-open theists, and many open theists, will grant. Thus, if

30. Cf. Hebrews 4:13, "Nothing in all creation is hidden from God's sight. Everything is uncovered and laid bare before the eyes of him to whom we must give account" (NIV).

31. Joseph Jedwab pointed out to me that a theist could resist this inference by allowing for the possibility of future world states subsequent to *t* that are inaccessible to God at *t*. This would require denying that God's perspective on reality is necessarily identical with the proverbial "God's eye" or absolute perspective on reality.

32. Strictly speaking, E→A follows from the weaker assumption that God essentially knows all truths *about the future*. On a separate note, some philosophers believe that first-person truths, such as the one I know when I know <I am Alan Rhoda>, are essentially unknowable by anyone else. This view is controversial, but if correct, it affects all theists, and not just open theists. For discussion, see Edward R. Wierenga, *The Nature of God: An Inquiry into Divine Attributes* (Ithaca, NY: Cornell University Press, 1989) ch. 2.

the future is alethically settled, then for every possible state of affairs X and every future time t^* there is a true proposition stating whether or not X obtains at t^*. Hence, if God essentially knows all truths, then the future is epistemically settled for God. In short, ~A→~E, from which it follows that E→A. *Some* open theists, however, reject E→A. According to Richard Swinburne and William Hasker, for example, God is not omniscient in the sense that he essentially knows all truths, but rather in the sense that he essentially knows all truths *that can be known*,[33] which is presumed to be a proper subset of all truths. For now, I set this view aside. (I'll argue against it later.) Since non-open theists concede E→A, let's accept it and see what follows.

We have derived E→C, E→O, E→P, and E→A. Combining these gives us the result that E→(C ∧ O ∧ A ∧ P). In other words, if the future is epistemically open, then it must be open in all of the other four senses. In addition, combining E→A and A→E, gives us an important symmetry principle:

A↔E: Necessarily, the future is alethically open (settled) if and only if it is epistemically open (settled).

Moving on, let's consider what, if anything, follows from a providentially open future, **P**, regarding A, C, O, and E. What we can conclude here depends on whether it is impossible for the future to be (alethically, causally, epistemically, ontically) settled unless it is providentially settled. That is, does ~~P entail ~~A, ~~C, ~~E, or ~~O? Apart from theism, I doubt that these entailments have much plausibility. Certainly many non-theists have thought the future could be causally, ontically, or alethically settled without there needing to be an agent who has efficaciously ordained all the details. But given a God who exists necessarily and who is the creator and sustainer of all other (concrete) existents, it makes sense to wonder how the future could be settled in those respects apart from God's exercising meticulous providence. We must, however, distinguish between *the future's* being settled in a given respect and things always *having been* settled in that respect. It would seem that a God exercising general providence could have set up the world so that it starts out as causally open, but

---

33. See Richard Swinburne, *The Coherence of Theism*, rev. ed. (Oxford: Oxford University Press, 1993) 180; William Hasker, *God, Time, and Knowledge* (Ithaca, NY: Cornell University Press, 1989) 187; idem, "The Foreknowledge Conundrum," *International Journal for the Philosophy of Religion* 50 (2001) 110–11.

then eventually *becomes* causally settled. Indeed, open theists are committed to this possibility since God, on their view, has the power to determine all events in history and therefore the power to set whatever limitations on future contingents he wants to. And since they believe that alethic and epistemic openness are consequent upon causal openness, they are also committed to the possibility that the world could start out as alethically or epistemically open but eventually become settled in those respects. So open theists, at least, cannot endorse P→A, P→C, or P→E.[34] Matters are different, however, for many non-open theists. According to theological determinists and Molinists, for example, P is *necessarily false*. As such, it trivially entails A, C, E, and O.

What about P→O? A strong case can be made that theists generally are committed to it. Suppose ~O. That is, suppose that a unique and complete series of future world states exists. Given the theistic doctrine of creation, there can be no non-divine (concrete) beings apart from God's creative and sustaining activity. Hence, it follows that all future world states owe their existence to God's creative and sustaining activity. Given that such activity on God's part is essentially efficacious and that God cannot fail to know exactly what he is doing, ~O entails ~P, which entails P→O. It seems, then, that theists generally, or at least those committed to a traditional doctrine of creation,[35] should affirm P→O.

Now let's shift our focus to ontic and causal openness. We'll start with O→A, O→E, and O→P. All of these, it turns out, are *false* unless C is necessarily true.[36] As noted above, if the future were causally settled, a God fully acquainted with the present world state (and causal laws) could predict with certainty a unique and complete series of future world states. In that case the future would be epistemically settled even if it was ontically open. It follows that (~C ∧ O)→~E. From A→E, it also follows that (~C ∧ O)→~A. Similarly, it follows from the doctrine of creation that if the future were causally settled God would be knowingly and efficaciously

---

34. They might, however, endorse P⊃A, P⊃C, or P⊃E if they believe that God has *de facto* policies in place which preclude the possibility of the world's ever becoming causally, alethically, or epistemically settled.

35. Process theists are a notable exception.

36. O→C is trivially true if C is necessarily true, but almost certainly false otherwise. Most theories of time that affirm an ontically open future, such as presentism and the growing block theory, are compatible with a causally settled future. I will therefore set O→C aside.

responsible for that fact. Hence, $(\sim C \wedge O) \rightarrow \sim P$. Now, most theists have wanted to say that C, if true, is only *contingently* true.[37] Since that seems to me the right thing to say, I will not try to defend either $O \rightarrow A$, $O \rightarrow E$, or $O \rightarrow P$. Instead, I will argue for the weaker $(C \wedge O) \rightarrow A$, $(C \wedge O) \rightarrow E$, and $(C \wedge O) \rightarrow P$.

My argument requires the assumption that (contingent) *truth supervenes on being* (TSB). According to TSB, every (contingent) difference in truth corresponds to a (contingent) difference in being, such that if anything that is true had not been true, then there would have been a corresponding difference in reality.[38] In other words, reality must be sufficiently robust to discriminate propositions that are (contingently) true from those that aren't. I take TSB to be a necessary truth. It is, I submit, indispensable for a realist (as opposed to anti-realist) approach to metaphysics and theology. To deny TSB is to admit that (contingent) truths can "float free" of being. Some may be comfortable with that idea.[39] I am not.

Now, suppose that the future is alethically settled ($\sim A$), such that for all possible states of affairs X and all future times t^*, either $<$X will obtain at $t^*>$ or $<$X will not obtain at $t^*>$ is now true, or alternatively, either $<$X does obtain at $t^*>$ or $<$X does not obtain at $t^*>$ is true *simpliciter*. Form the

---

37. Again, process theists are a notable exception. In distinction from broadly classical forms of theism, they hold that C is necessarily true and $\sim$C necessarily false. Conversely, many theological determinists hold that C is necessarily false and $\sim$C necessarily true. Broadly classical free will theists generally take C to be contingent on the grounds that God could have created a causally settled world, but didn't.

38. Aquinas argues for the stronger principle that *ens et verum convertuntur*, being and truth are convertible (*Summa Theologica* 1a.16.3). This entails TSB and adds to it the claim that every difference in being corresponds to a difference in truth. This addition may be controversial, particularly if one thinks that truth depends on the existence of minds and that the existence of minds is contingent. If that's right, then presumably it is possible for there to be being without truth (for example, before any sentient life has evolved). That objection, however, is not available to theists who believe in the necessary existence of an essentially omniscient Mind (i.e., God).

39. Molinists may object to TSB because it creates problems for them vis-à-vis the well-known "grounding objection," but I think the proper response to that is "so much the worse for Molinism." As Graham Oppy ("Arguments from Moral Evil," *International Journal for Philosophy of Religion* 56 [2004] 69) puts it, "The principle that there are no pairs of possible worlds with minimal supervenience bases that differ *only* with respect to the truth-values of counterfactual claims is . . . a pretty secure piece of metaphysical doctrine" (emphasis his), one that is well-motivated independently of issues in philosophical theology.

conjunction Ω of all such truths. Either a sufficient metaphysical ground obtains for the truth of Ω or it does not. If not, then we have a violation of TSB, for reality fails to discriminate between the truth of Ω and contrasting alternatives. If, however, a sufficient ground obtains for the truth of Ω, then either that ground is constituted by wholly *non-future* states of affairs or it is constituted at least in part by *future* states of affairs. If the former, then the future is causally settled, which violates C. For if any possible state of affairs were still such that it both *might* and *might not* obtain in the future, then wholly non-future grounds would not yet be *sufficient* to ground the truth of Ω, contrary to hypothesis. If, however, a sufficient ground for the truth of Ω exists and is constituted in part by future states of affairs, then it follows from NPF (no partial futures) that a complete series of future states of affairs obtains. Moreover, since this series of future states of affairs must discriminate between Ω and contrasting alternatives, it must be unique. We are therefore led to posit a unique and complete series of future states of affairs, which violates O.[40] So there we have it: Given TSB and NPF, ~A entails either ~C or ~O, which is equivalent to $(C \wedge O) \rightarrow A$.

Combining $(C \wedge O) \rightarrow A$ with $A \rightarrow E$ gives us $(C \wedge O) \rightarrow E$. And combining that with $E \rightarrow P$ gives us $(C \wedge O) \rightarrow P$. From here we can derive several significant results. $(C \wedge O) \rightarrow A$ is equivalent to $\Box((C \wedge O) \supset A)$, which is equivalent to $\Box(C \supset (O \supset A))$, which is equivalent to $C \rightarrow (O \supset A)$. From that and $A \rightarrow O$ we get $C \rightarrow (O \equiv A)$. Parallel derivations yield $C \rightarrow (O \equiv E)$ and $C \rightarrow (O \equiv P)$. We thus arrive at a trio of conditional symmetry principles.

$C \rightarrow (O \equiv A)$: Necessarily, if the future is causally open, then the future is ontically open (settled) if and only if it is also alethically open (settled).

40. A similar argument is developed in Michael C. Rea, "Presentism and Fatalism," *Australasian Journal of Philosophy* 84 (2006) 511–24, and in Alicia Finch and Michael Rea, "Presentism and Ockham's Way Out," *Oxford Studies in Philosophy of Religion* 1 (2008) 1–17. William Lane Craig (*The Tensed Theory of Time: A Critical Appraisal* [Dordrecht: Kluwer Academic, 2000] 213–14) tries to skirt the issue by proposing that a contingently true proposition about the future (e.g., <X will obtain>) is true not in virtue of what *exists* at a future time but rather in virtue of what *will exist* at a future time. But this reduces to the options in the text, for what will exist either consists of wholly *non-future* states of affairs or it includes *future* states of affairs or it consists of no states of affairs at all, in which case TSB is violated. For further discussion, see section four of Rhoda, Boyd, and Belt, "Open Theism, Omniscience, and the Nature of the Future."

C→(O≡E): Necessarily, if the future is causally open, then the future is ontically open (settled) if and only if it is also epistemically open (settled).

C→(O≡P): Necessarily, if the future is causally open, then the future is ontically open (settled) if and only if it is also providentially open (settled).

We can combine these into a single principle:

C→(O≡A≡E≡P): Necessarily, if the future is causally open, then it is either ontically, alethically, epistemically, and providentially open or ontically, alethically, epistemically, and providentially settled.

Because these principles are applicable only on the condition that C is true, they can be ignored by theological determinists. But free will theists ought to admit them unless they bite a bullet and reject either KET, TSB, NPF, the idea that God is essentially fully acquainted with all of reality, or the standard theistic doctrine of creation.[41] Since the first three of those assumptions are highly plausible independently of theism, and the last two are highly plausible given theism, it's pretty tough to avoid the conclusion that C→(O≡A≡E≡P). And if that's right, then one cannot consistently be a free will theist *and* affirm either an ontically or alethically open future without also being an open theist, which I define as broadly classical theism plus C, E, and P.[42] It also means that a successful argument from C to *any* of O, A, E, or P automatically gives us the rest. Accordingly, let's see what we might be able to derive from C.[43]

41. KET grounds the inference from A→E; TSB and NPF ground the derivation of C→(O⊃A); God's being essentially fully acquainted with reality grounds the inference from E→O; and the doctrine of creation grounds the inference from P→O. E→P is true by definition of providential openness. From there we can derive all of the symmetry principles.

42. In Rhoda, "Generic Open Theism" I proposed defining open theism in terms of broadly classical theism, C, and E. I now wish to add P to that set of requirements.

43. In what follows I am not seeking to give airtight arguments to establish that C entails O, A, E, or P. It would take several papers to explore those issues in adequate depth. Instead, I am simply pointing out that there are *prima facie* plausible reasons for thinking that C entails one or more of O, A, E, and P.

THE IMPLICATIONS OF CAUSAL OPENNESS

Let's begin by considering whether C entails A. Suppose that a fair coin has just been flipped and that the world, immediately after the moment of its toss, is perfectly indeterministic (50/50) with respect to whether the coin lands heads or tails. Suppose that a few moments later the coin lands heads. Call the time at which the coin is flipped F. Call the time at which it lands L. Now consider this question: Was it true *at F* that the coin was going to land heads at L? There are two plausible answers.[44] According to the "Ockhamist" proposal, <X will obtain at t^*> is true at all times prior to t^* and just in case X obtains at t^*. With respect to the coin, therefore, it all depends on what happens *at L*. Since the coin did land heads at L, it was true at all previous times (and thus at F) that it was going to land heads at L. According to the contrasting "Peircean" proposal, <X will obtain at t^*> is true *at t* just in case sufficient grounds for its truth obtain *at t*. With respect to the coin, therefore, it all depends on what obtains *at F*. Since *ex hypothesi* sufficient grounds were not in place at F for the coin to land heads at L, it was not true then that it was going to land heads at L.

Clearly, C entails clause (i) of the definition of alethic openness if the Peircean semantics is correct.[45] (Recall that the definition has two clauses: clause (i) concerns truth *at a time*; clause (ii) concerns truth *simpliciter*.) Thus, C entails that for some possible state of affairs X and future time t^*, X's obtaining at t^* is a future contingent. This entails that sufficient grounds are not *now* in place either for X's obtaining at t^* or X's non-obtaining at t^*, from which it follows by the Peircean semantics that neither <X will obtain at t^*> nor <X will not obtain at t^*> is now true.

Moreover, there are reasons for thinking that the Peircean semantics is correct. Here is an argument from elimination:[46]

1. Either the Peircean or the Ockhamist semantics is correct.

2. The Ockhamist semantics is incorrect.

3. The Peircean semantics is correct. (from 1 and 2)

44. The distinction between the following semantic proposals comes from Arthur Prior, "The Formalities of Omniscience," in *Papers on Time and Tense*, Per Hasle *et al.*, eds. (Oxford: Oxford University Press, 2003) 39–58.

45. I assume that whether the Peircean or Ockhamist semantics is correct is not a contingent matter.

46. I develop an independent argument for the Peircean semantics in Alan Rhoda, "The Philosophical Case for Open Theism," *Philosophia* 35 (2007) 301–11.

Premise (1) is very plausible. The Ockhamist and Peircean semantic traditions have each had a long history and many able defenders (though not generally under those labels, of course).[47] Apart from recent attempts to construct a hybrid semantics,[48] there are no other serious proposals. Sure, one *could* pick a time (or a set of times) distinct from either F or L as the relevant moment of evaluation for determining whether <The coin will land heads at L> is true at F, but why? If anyone thinks there is a defensible alternative, the burden of proof is on them to explain why we should take it seriously.

As for premise (2), if the Ockhamist semantics is correct, then the only way the future can be alethically settled is for it to be ontically settled. In short, $\sim$A$\rightarrow\sim$O. This is because, on the Ockhamist semantics, propositions about the future depend for their truth on *future* states of affairs. By NPF, if some future states of affairs obtain, then a complete series of obtains. By TSB, this series must be unique, else it wouldn't suffice to ground the unique "complete true story" of the future required for alethic settledness. Hence, $\sim$A entails $\sim$O given the Ockhamist semantics, TSB, and NPF.[49] $\sim$A$\rightarrow\sim$O, in turn, entails O$\rightarrow$A, which (by A$\rightarrow$E) entails

47. The Peircean semantic tradition goes back at least as far as Aristotle (*De interpretatione* 9), and was the received view in antiquity. Jonathan Barnes, *Truth, etc.* (Oxford: Oxford University Press, 2007) notes of a recognizably Peircean semantic proposal that it was accepted "by Plato, by Aristotle, by Epicurus, by the Stoics; and no doubt by everyone else" (ibid., 72). Modern champions of the Peircean semantics include Arthur Prior ("The Formalities of Omniscience") and Charles Hartshorne ("The Meaning of 'Is Going to Be,'" *Mind* 74 [1965] 46–58). The Ockhamist tradition, in contrast, is more or less the received view among modern philosophers, but was very rare in antiquity. The earliest known proponent seems to have been Carneades (214–129 BC), a Platonist of the skeptical or "new" Academy. See Cicero, *De fato* 32–33, and Barnes, *Truth, etc.* 27–29, 71–72.

48. Sophisticated hybrid positions have been proposed by J. R. Lucas, *The Future: An Essay on God, Temporality, and Truth* (Oxford: Basil Blackwell, 1989); and by John MacFarlane, "Future Contingents and Relative Truth," *The Philosophical Quarterly* 53 (2003) 321–36. One problem with such accounts is that they render the notion of "truth" systematically ambiguous. Thus, Lucas distinguishes between "predictive" and "valedictory" truth. The first behaves in a Peircean manner; the second in an Ockhamist manner. Similarly, MacFarlane relativizes the truth of propositions about the future to the evaluator's temporal standpoint vis-à-vis the putative future event. Prior to the event, truth values are assigned in a Peircean fashion. Afterwards, they are assigned in an Ockhamist fashion. On either proposal, it becomes unclear how to talk about what is true *simpliciter*, and that's what we need to do when dealing with questions concerning *God's* knowledge, which is inherently absolute and non-relative.

49. Again, I assume that whether the Peircean or Ockhamist semantics is correct is not a contingent matter. For a related argument from Ockhamism to $\sim$O, see Finch and

O→E. But the latter is *false* unless C is a necessary truth. After all, given ~C God could know with certainty exactly how the future will turn out even if no future states of affairs obtain. On any version of broadly classical theism, however, C is not a necessary truth, for God could have created a fully deterministic world if he had wanted to. Broadly classical theists, therefore, should conclude that the Ockhamist semantics is false because it entails something false.

However, while the above considerations may suffice to show that C entails clause (i) of the definition of alethic openness, they don't suffice to show that C entails A. That would require also showing that C entails clause (ii) of the definition. Arguably, it doesn't. Given ~O, either <X does obtain at t^*> or <X does not obtain at t^*> would be true *simpliciter* for all states of affairs X and future times t^* *even if C was true*. Hence, C does not entail A (unless there is some way of showing that ~O is necessarily false).

Let's now consider whether C entails E. The obvious strategy for arguing that it does is to show that exhaustive divine foreknowledge (understood so as to imply ~E) is incompatible with future contingency (which implies C). Given an Ockhamist semantics, such a strategy may look unpromising, for Ockhamism entails a distinction between "hard facts" and "soft facts" that seems to resolve the incompatibilist worry. Roughly, a *soft fact* relative to time t is one that is a future contingent relative to the world state at t and thus is true at least partly in virtue of states of affairs that are future relative to t. Conversely, a *hard fact* relative to time t is one that is either not contingent or not even partly about the future relative to the world state at t; hence, sufficient grounds for its truth are given by states of affairs that are past, present, or otherwise non-future relative to t. Given Ockhamism, it follows that past truths about future contingents are soft facts. So if I freely drive to work tomorrow, then it was a soft fact 200 years ago that I will drive to work on that date. Since that soft fact is past I cannot now change it, but this poses no difficulty for my freedom

---

Rea, "Presentism and Ockham's Way Out." I should add that William Hasker and I have vigorously disagreed on this issue in correspondence. A self-professed TSB-affirming presentist and semantic Ockhamist, Bill maintains that propositions like <X will obtain> do not require for their truth the existence of a *future state of affairs* which includes X, but rather the *future existence* of a state of affairs which includes X. I maintain that his position is incompatible with the combination of TSB and presentism. On presentism, future existents have *no metaphysical status*, and so are not available as bases for truths to supervene upon or as relata in a correspondence relation.

because the only reason it was a fact 200 years ago is because I freely drive to work tomorrow. So far so good. The Ockhamist semantics reconciles creaturely freedom with *foretruth*. But arguments for the incompatibility of God's *foreknowledge* or infallible *forebelief* and creaturely freedom are not so easily parried.[50] Several authors, notably Nelson Pike and William Hasker, have argued that *God's past beliefs* qualify as hard facts.[51] If that's right, then C→E *even if* an Ockhamist semantics be granted.[52] From there, along with E→O, E→A, and E→P, we can derive C→(O ∧ A ∧ E ∧ P).

Now let's consider whether C entails O. Unfortunately, I know no simple argument for this result that is likely to meet with wide acceptance.[53] Establishing C→O would require defending a robust causal theory of time according to which time flow consists in the absolute becoming of new world states as a result of prior world states. The details of such an argument are too complex to pursue here.[54] Instead, I'd like to consider the weaker claim that C *materially implies* O, i.e., C⊃O. This result may be obtained via C→E and C→(O≡E), but there is an independent line of reasoning worth exploring. It is an inductive argument, one that appeals to explanatory considerations, in order to show that O is more plausible, given C, than is ~O. Suppose, then, that C is true. To make matters definite, let's consider a setup similar to that in the famous EPR experiment.[55] A source emits at time *t* a pair of electrons, A and B, moving in opposite directions. The electrons are in a state of quantum entanglement, such

50. For discussion of Ockhamist responses to incompatibilist arguments see John Martin Fischer, ed., *God, Foreknowledge, and Freedom* (Stanford, CA: Stanford University Press, 1989).

51. Nelson Pike, "Divine Foreknowledge and Voluntary Action," *Philosophical Review* 74 (1965) 27–46; William Hasker, *God, Time, and Knowledge.*

52. Of course, if the Ockhamist semantics is *false*, as I have argued above, then the incompatibilist's case is strengthened. Appeal to divine timelessness may help to parry the incompatibilist's argument. As Linda Zagzebski has pointed out, however, it's not clear that we could have the power to bring about what God timelessly knows. Cf. Linda T. Zagzebski, "Recent Work on Divine Foreknowledge and Free Will," in *The Oxford Handbook of Free Will*, Robert Kane, ed. (Oxford: Oxford University Press, 2002) 45–64.

53. Obviously, any eternalist who wants to affirm a causally open future will reject the entailment.

54. But see Michael Tooley, *Time, Tense, and Causation* (Oxford: Oxford University Press, 1997) for a sophisticated argument along these lines.

55. For a helpful account of the EPR (Einstein–Podolsky–Rosen) argument, see Arthur Fine, "The Einstein-Podolsky-Rosen Argument in Quantum Theory," *The Stanford Encyclopedia of Philosophy (Summer 2004 Edition)*, Edward N. Zalta, ed. Online: http://plato.stanford.edu/archives/sum2004/entries/qt-epr/.

that a measurement on one of them to determine its spin instantly correlates to an opposite spin on the other electron, regardless of their distance apart. Prior to measurement, the quantum system has two possible outcomes: {(A – spin up, B – spin down), (A – spin down, B – spin up)}, and it cannot be predicted which will obtain. In short, the world state at *t* causally underdetermines which of two possible successor states obtains at *t**. Now, how should we model this situation? There seem to be three possibilities:

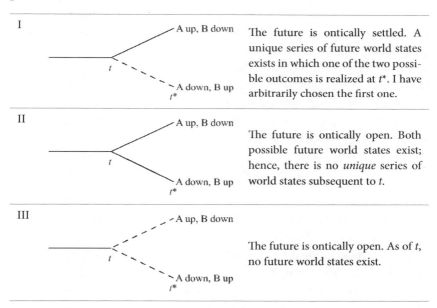

I — The future is ontically settled. A unique series of future world states exists in which one of the two possible outcomes is realized at *t**. I have arbitrarily chosen the first one.

II — The future is ontically open. Both possible future world states exist; hence, there is no *unique* series of world states subsequent to *t*.

III — The future is ontically open. As of *t*, no future world states exist.

All other things being equal, it seems that (III) is the best model. (III) is preferable to (I) because, like (II), it preserves symmetry between the possible outcomes. The empirical data give us no reason for thinking that either possible outcome is privileged in advance as the "actual" outcome. Second, (III) is preferable to (I) and (II) for reasons of parsimony. Positing future world states does no explanatory work because it is only *when the measurement occurs* that the nature of the world state at *t** becomes settled. The direction in which the quantum system collapses is not explained by future world states; rather, it is the collapse of the quantum system that explains which possible future world state becomes actual. At any rate, either (II) or (III) would give us an ontically open future. In the absence of other considerations favoring ~O, therefore, it seems that C gives us good reason for accepting O. Given C⊃O, along with C→(O≡A), A→E, and E→P, we can derive C⊃(O ∧ A ∧ E ∧ P).

Finally, let's consider C→P. This claim could be established by first arguing for C→E and combining that with E→P. But there is an independent line of argument that stands a good chance of being sound. The strategy is simply to refute Molinism. It is widely agreed that Molinism offers the only real hope for reconciling meticulous providence (~P) with future contingency (C).[56] If that's right, and if Molinism fails, then ~P entails ~C, which gives us C→P. Moreover, Molinism is subject to several well-known objections that threaten the very coherence of the position.[57] Length considerations prohibit us from exploring this line of argument. Suffice to say, while Molinism has its share of earnest defenders,[58] they haven't made much headway toward convincing non-Molinists that the objections can be satisfactorily answered. If this strategy works, then we get C→P. From there, along with P→O, C→(O≡A), A→O, and A→E, we can again derive C→(O ∧ A ∧ E ∧ P).

RECAP AND CONCLUSIONS

Let's review the major results. That knowledge entails truth (KET) gave us A→E. From the thesis that God is essentially fully acquainted with all of reality, we got E→C and E→O. From those and A→E we derived A→C and A→O. The definition of providential openness gave us E→P. The thesis that God essentially knows all truths then gave us E→A, which allowed us to derive A↔E. From the theistic doctrine of creation, we derived P→O. From there, with the additional assumptions that truth su-

56. Both Bill Hasker (a prominent anti-Molinist) and Tom Flint (a prominent Molinist) agree that if meticulous providence and future contingency are desired, then Molinism is "the only game in town." See William Hasker, "Response to Thomas Flint," *Philosophical Studies* 60 (1990) 117–26; and Thomas P. Flint, *Divine Providence: The Molinist Account* (Ithaca, NY: Cornell University Press, 1998) ch. 3.

57. Chief among these is probably the "grounding objection," the charge that Molinism violates TSB when it comes to counterfactuals of creaturely freedom (CCFs). Another important charge is vicious explanatory circularity: My free decisions would seem to be explanatorily prior to the truth values of my CCFs, which truth values, in turn, would seem to be explanatorily prior to God's decision to create me, which decision would seem to be explanatorily prior to my free decisions. For detailed discussion of all of the issues surrounding Molinism, see Flint, *Divine Providence*; and William Hasker, David Basinger, and Eef Decker, eds., *Middle Knowledge: Theory and Applications* (Frankfurt: Peter Lang, 2000).

58. Notably, Flint, *Divine Providence*; and Alfred J. Freddoso, "Introduction."

pervenes on being (TSB) and that there can be no partial futures (NPF), we derived (O ∧ C)→A, (O ∧ C)→E, and (O ∧ C)→P, from which (along with previous results) we derived C→(O≡A≡E≡P). Finally, I argued that there is at least a *prima facie* plausible case to be made on behalf of C→E, C⊃O, and C→P. If any *one* of those is correct, then from C→(O≡A≡E≡P) we can derive C→(O ∧ A ∧ E ∧ P), or at least C⊃(O ∧ A ∧ E ∧ P). Either way, it follows that if the future is causally open then it is open in all five respects.

From this we see that there are several routes to open theism, defined as a commitment to broadly classical theism, C, E, and P:

d) If a broadly classical theist accepts C and O, then he is committed to A (by (O ∧ C)→A), and thus to E (by A→E) and P (by E→P).

e) If a broadly classical theist accepts C and C→E, then he is committed to E and thus to P (by E→P).

f) If a broadly classical theist accepts C and C⊃O, then he is committed to E (by (O ∧ C)→E), and thus to P (by E→P).

g) If a broadly classical theist accepts C and C→P, then he is committed to P and thus to E (by P→O and (O ∧ C)→E)).

h) If a broadly classical theist accepts A, then he is committed to E (by A→E), P (by E→P), and C (by A→C).

i) If a broadly classical theist accepts E, then he is committed to P (by E→P) and C (by E→C).

These entailments can, of course, be blocked if one is prepared to jettison theses like KET, TSB, NPF, God's exhaustive acquaintance with reality, God's knowledge of all truths, and the standard theistic doctrine of creation. But the first three of those theses have high intuitive plausibility independently of theism, the next two seem to follow from the idea that God is the greatest possible being, and the last is a core commitment of theism. Non-open theists are thus left with a choice between biting a bullet by denying one or more of those theses and denying C, O, or both. If all six of those theses be granted, the options are few. Theological determinists deny C, but pay a price by setting themselves up for an especially difficult time with the problem of evil.[59] Non-open free will theists, on the

---

59. For discussion of theological determinism in relation to the problem of evil, see William Hasker, *Providence, Evil, and the Openness of God* (London: Routledge, 2004) ch. 7.

other hand, are committed to **C**, so we would expect them to deny **O**, as well as **A**, **E**, and **P**.[60] The tenability of the resulting position {**C**, ~**O**, ~**A**, ~**E**, ~**P**} depends on being able to block all inferences from causal openness to the other four. Interestingly, however, many non-open free will theists affirm *both* **C** and **O**.[61] If my arguments are right, then they *have* to reject either KET, TSB, or NPF. Otherwise, we can use those to derive (**O** ∧ **C**)→**A** and (**O** ∧ **C**)→**E** and generate an inconsistency. For similar reasons, versions of open theism that affirm **C**, **E**, and **P**, but deny either **A** or **O**, are problematic. Hasker, for example, accepts **C**, **O**, **E**, and **P**, but denies **A**. Accordingly, he must deny (**O** ∧ **C**)→**A**, and along with it one or more of KET, TSB, or NPF. In addition, he has to deny that God essentially knows *all* truths (otherwise we could derive **E**→**A** and generate an inconsistency).[62] What Hasker can (and does) say is that God knows all that *can* be known while admitting that there are truths about which future contingents "will" or "will not" obtain that cannot be known. But in the absence of a compelling account of how there can be truths that are in principle unknowable *even for God*, qualifying divine knowledge in this way puts open theists at a polemical disadvantage vis-à-vis their competitors.[63] Moreover, it's not at all clear why the qualification is necessary. Whatever reasons we have for thinking that "will" or "will not" (or "does" and "does not") propositions about future contingents are not knowable are also reasons for thinking that they are *not true*. After all, given **C** and **O**, there is no combination of states of affairs—past, present, or otherwise—upon which such truths could supervene. Recognizing this allows the open theist to restore polemical parity by arguing that it is precisely *because* God believes all and only truths that the future is epistemically open for God. Open theists, then, are much better off if they affirm **A** and **O** in addition to **C**, **E**, and **P**.

In closing, I would like to comment briefly on the significance for theists of the **C**⊃(**O** ∧ **A** ∧ **E** ∧ **P**) thesis. If this is right then the theist's

---

60. Given **C**≡(**O**≡**A**≡**E**≡**P**), **C**, and ~**O**, it follows that ~**A**, ~**E**, and ~**P**.

61. See, for example, Craig, *Time and Eternity*; and DeWeese, *God and the Nature of Time*.

62. Similarly, open theists who deny **O** would have to deny God's exhaustive acquaintance with reality. Otherwise, we could generate an inconsistency from **E**→**O**.

63. Critics of open theism, like Bruce A. Ware, *God's Lesser Glory: The Diminished God of Open Theism* (Wheaton, IL: Crossway, 2000) often charge that the God of open theism is not *really* omniscient and is therefore a "diminished God," or not even a God at all.

options are limited to open theism and theological determinism. The first option commits one to the fivefold openness of the future—causal, ontic, alethic, epistemic, *and* providential—and with it a dynamic world of open-ended possibilities in which the shape of things to come is, in some respects at least, yet to be decided. The story is only partially written and it is one to which we, if we have libertarian freedom, have the privilege of contributing a chapter. The second option, in contrast, commits one to a future that is settled in *at least* causal, alethic, epistemic, and providential respects.[64] It may still be ontically open, but not open-ended. In such a world, the shape of things to come is already fully present in its causes. The story is fully written; there remains only to play it out and to enjoy it along the way—assuming, one hopes, that is part of the script.[65]

64. Given the falsity of Ockhamism and the non-necessity of C, there is no entailment from ~C, ~A, ~E, and ~P to ~O. (And if C were necessary it would be a trivial entailment, since a necessary falsehood entails anything and everything.)

65. My sincere thanks to Bill Hasker, Joseph Jedwab, Mike Rea, Kevin Diller, and members of Notre Dame's Center for Philosophy of Religion discussion group for helpful comments on earlier drafts of this paper.

5

Presentism and the Problem of Special Relativity

David M. Woodruff

". . . one can extract only so much metaphysics from a physical theory as one puts in."

—Lawrence Sklar

INTRODUCTION

RELATIONAL THEOLOGIES, SUCH AS Open Theism, are committed to the belief that a rich and dynamic relationship with creation is a fundamental divine value.[1] We might describe a theology as a relational theology in that it understands the range of God's actions, purposes, and revelation according to the value God places on relationships.[2] A notice-

---

1. There are a number of good introductions to open theism, see for example: Clark H. Pinnock et al., *The Openness of God: A Biblical Challenge to the Traditional Understanding of God* (Downers Grove, IL: InterVarsity, 1994); Gregory A. Boyd, *God of the Possible: A Biblical Introduction to the Open View of God* (Grand Rapids: Baker, 2000); John Sanders, *The God Who Risks: A Theology of Divine Providence*, 2nd ed. (Downers Grove, IL: InterVarsity, 2007); or Clark H. Pinnock, *Most Moved Mover: A Theology of God's Openness, Didsbury Lectures* (Grand Rapids: Baker Academic, 2001). I develop the notion of a divine value and the role this concept plays in theological discussions surrounding open theism in, David M. Woodruff, "Being and Doing in the Concept of God," *Philosophia: Philosophical Quarterly of Israel* 35.3–4 (2007)."Being and Doing in the Concept of God" *Philosophia* 35.3–4 (December, 2007) 313–20.

2. See David M. Woodruff, "Examining Problems and Assumptions: An Update on Criticisms of Open Theism," *Dialog* 47 (2008) 53.

able consequence of this commitment is that Open Theists affirm that the future is open in the sense that in many cases what will occur is not specifically foreordained by God, but is also the result of the free acts of humans. According to most Open Theists this entails God is in time[3] and that God does not have exhaustive definite foreknowledge. These controversial views have attracted a wide variety of criticisms, some seemingly wide of the mark, but some which are quite significant. Of the significant criticisms, one of the most poignant is that Open Theism's conception of reality is inconsistent with the best established claims of physics. I wish to argue that the range of interpretations of the data that 'the best of physics' has to offer leaves open the possibility of accepting the empirical findings of physical sciences without having to accept metaphysical conclusions inconsistent with open theism. Two things are critical to the open theist's view as I have presented it. First, there need to be alternatives, or alternate possible futures; that is Open Theism must reject the idea that there is a single, complete and presently existing future. Second, we need to be able to actualize or be an essential part of the process that actualizes what occurs from the range of possibilities. The problem this paper addresses is that some have criticized open theism claiming these comments are fundamentally at odds with the best physics and in particular these features are seen to be at odds with Minkowski's spacetime and hence the special theory of relativity (STR).[4] Because I am a philosopher, I want examine this as a philosophical theory. I want to develop some purely metaphysical motivations for considering alternatives to the Minkowski interpretation of Special Theory of Relativity. A successful conclusion of the project would neither reject nor radically revise relativity theory. To understand better Open Theism's commitments and the problems they raise with relativity theory, we will start with the nature of presentism, the preferred temporal ontology for those affirming Open Theism.

3. Being "in time" is a metaphor. Perhaps it would be better to speak of God as experiencing temporal succession; however, this is a bit wordy and speaking of God or other things as being "in" time is used widely enough that it is commonly understood.

4. Some examples of this are: Brian Leftow, *Time and Eternity, Cornell Studies in the Philosophy of Religion* (Ithaca: Cornell University Press, 1991) 231–35; Hilary Putnam, *Mathematics, Matter, and Method* (Cambridge: Cambridge University Press, 1975), "Time and Physical Geometry" 198–205; Theodore Sider, *Four-Dimensionalism: An Ontology of Persistence and Time* (Oxford: Clarendon, 2001) 42–52; Wesley Wildman—personal conversations.

PRESENTISM

The Basic Concept of Presentism

To begin to get traction in this discussion we need, at the very least, a reasonably clear idea about what the thesis of presentism is and how it differs from eternalism. The difficulty is stating this in a way that makes clear the differences without committing oneself to an obviously false position. (Just to be fair I take it there are similar difficulties with clarifying the eternalist thesis). One way to help in avoiding such difficulties is to state what the position denies and see if we can work from there to what it affirms. The thesis of presentism denies that past things and future things exist on an ontological par with that which exists in the present. Caesar or Plato would be paradigmatic cases of past things; things which presentism asserts no longer exist.[5] As I write this, my grandchildren or intergalactic human explorers would be, if they ever come to be at all, future things. In showing this, some things are easy enough to order in relationship to each other because of their causal connections. Other things bear the relationship without having much if anything of a causal connection. Hence, one way to get at the thesis of presentism is to say that anything that does exist is part of the present whereas things that no longer exist are past and things that will exist but do not yet exist are future. This will be somewhat incomplete as many of the existing things themselves have states that no longer exist and states that will exist but do not yet exist. To avoid the apparent commitment to states we might say it this way, the things which exist now have certain properties and stand in relation to other things. The properties and relations that they did stand in but no longer hold are past properties and relations. The properties and relations they may come to have but do not yet have are their future properties and relations. Presentism contrasts with eternalism. Eternalism is the thesis that the present is not ontologically unique. The past and future are just as real as the present. Time, like space, has extension and temporal extension is like spatial extension in that all points in the extension are equally real.[6] Presentism denies this point of similarity between time and space.

5. Here I am ignoring the possibility of an afterlife.

6. We might wish to distinguish "full blown eternalism" from what we might call "manifold eternalism." A full-blown eternalist includes the things in the temporal extension. This is four-dimensionalism where in addition to their spatial extension and spatial parts things have temporal extension and temporal parts. "Manifold eternalism" on the other hand is not committed to this view of the nature of things. It posits the extension

Mark Hinchliff points out that depending on our use of "exist," the eternalist is not committed to the view that everything that exists presently exists.[7] He makes this distinction to show what is at issue in presentism and to clarify the substance of the debate between the presentist and eternalist. Hinchliff's point is that presentists and eternalists disagree about the claim that, "only presently existing things exist." He shows that there is a significant metaphysical disagreement when "presently" is an indexical tense operator. The eternalist claims that Socrates exists, but not that his existence is simultaneous with my existence. The eternalist does not say that Socrates exists now, where "now" because of its indexical character refers to the present say at 3 pm on 1 June 2009. Socrates exists at his time and what the eternalist wants to say is that there is no ontologically relevant distinction between that time and my time or between that temporal slice and my temporal slice. The whole of the temporal manifold shares the same existence. No part of that manifold is ontologically privileged. The presentist on the other hand wants to say that there is a relevant ontological distinction to be made between the past or future on the one hand and the present on the other hand. We might then summarize this way: the eternalists think that everything's existence occurs at a time but that there is nothing special with reference to existence between one time and another whereas the presentists think there is something unique about the present such that only presently existing things exist.[8]

---

of the temporal manifold without accepting that things themselves are spread out in that manifold. It thus rejects the notion that things have temporal parts while accepting that past and future times exist. Because the current description makes no reference to things it might easily be taken as "manifold eternalism." In fact, this is only due to my efforts to introduce the concept in a basic and neutral way. While I think we should take seriously the notion of manifold eternalism, it is the less common view and it does not entail the problematic features of relativity that are discussed here. Although I think its solution to the criticism I am addressing is worthy of consideration, it would also be considered to be a "radical" solution to the problem. Here after when I refer to eternalism I will be referring to "full blown" eternalism.

7. Mark Hinchliff, "A Defense of Presentism in a Relativistic Setting," *Philosophy of Science* 67.3 Supplement (2000) S575–S586

8. While I think this distinction is useful I will offer a modification of presentism that I hope to show can be harmonized with STR without radical revisions of either Presentism or STR.

The Intuitive Appeal of Presentism

Perhaps the appeal of presentism is already obvious, but as this will be a relevant issue in how I develop my response to criticisms of presentism I would like to cover briefly some of the appealing features of the theory.[9] Probably the most significant feature of presentism is that it captures our experience of the uniqueness of the present. Our common sense descriptions of our experience of time better fit the presentist's description, than the way directly analogous to space as the eternalists describe. A second appealing feature is that it describes our sense of the existences of substances. We typically understand substances as existing as complete things in the present and as changing their properties over time.[10] Presentism gives the temporal structure for this where eternalism is generally worked out with objects having extension in four dimensions, thus having temporal parts of their temporal extension. The next two features are related to these but are significant enough that they are worth independent discussion. Our experience of change is that it is inexorable and directional. This is often discussed as the flow of time. I think this is an unfortunate metaphor, but it is entrenched enough in our thinking that it is difficult to avoid. We experience the present as something that cannot remain unaltered. And once the present moment is past we cannot restore or revisit it. In addition, presentism captures our sense that we cannot move backward in time and our movement forward is limited and forced.

Finally given the broader context of this paper I wish to point out that presentism fits well with the thesis of Open Theology. As noted above, Open Theology is a form of relational theology, in that it posits that God's rich and dynamic relationship with creation is a divine value. Open Theology connects this value with the structure of creation. On the eternalist view God could stand in relationship to entities that populate the manifold of spacetime as described by eternalists; however, our ordinary intuition is that something of the richness of that relationship is lost and

9. I don't mean to imply here that eternalists cannot account for some of these features, but rather to set the standard here, to establish that these features need to be accounted for by theories that reject presentism.

10. Here I am not trying to imply that this common sense view is unproblematic, but rather that it fits with presentism, it is a common sense view of objects and an analysis of time needs to account for it somehow. Simply ignoring it will not do. See the introduction of David K. Lewis, *Philosophical Papers* (New York: Oxford University Press, 1983) for a discussion of addressing our common sense perspectives in our technical philosophical theories.

in particular it is lost when the dynamic and open character of change is limited by the existence of the complete temporal manifold.[11] How big a problem this is and whether it justifies the claims that Open Theists make is clearly a matter of dispute. Nonetheless, there is an intuitive appeal we sense for the dynamic relationships that presentism makes possible. At any moment I view myself as completely present in that relationship.

Some Problems of Presentism

The above appeal of presentism is not intended to imply that presentism is without problems. One of the most interesting things about science is its ability to shape the way we think about the world. Its empirical character provides us with justification for giving up what otherwise might seem intuitively obvious and embracing ideas that we come to believe are true. The Copernican Revolution is a prime example of this. It just seems clear and obvious from our ordinary perspective that the earth is not moving, let alone hurtling through space. Science has the power to justify the rejection of this belief. Similarly we must ask, does science give us good reason to reject presentism regardless of its otherwise intuitive appeal? We can begin to answer that question by looking at some of the problems with presentism. The first is the connection between presentism and the flow of time. What is time that it can flow? How can we measure the flow of time? What would it be measured against? The notion of the movement of time raises a whole collection of problems. The second set of problems centers around the notion of the present itself. Is the present a literal instant, having no extension, between the past and the future? If it has no extension how can the present account for the things we think about it? If it is extended how can we understand that extension? Is there any empirical evidence for the extension or of the uniqueness of the present? A related problem has to do with our perception of the passage of time. Our immediate impression is that the passage of time is regular; however, upon closer inspection it would appear that much of our experience of the regularity of the passage of time is dependent upon us. In fact we experience compression and extension of "the present," giving us reason to wonder if it is nothing more than a description of our experience. In high stress or threatening situations we can identify the extension of time, that is, our experience of the passage of time seems to slow.

11. See Woodruff, "Being and Doing in the Concept of God," 313–20.

We experience a whole progression of events; say an automobile accident that we would expect to pass by quickly as being extended over a longer period of time and we notice many particular details as the event unfolds. In other circumstances time literally seems to "fly by." We just get started doing something we enjoy and in what seems like a few moments hours have passed by. Simply put our experience of the passage of time may well be telling us about us and not about time. Finally, there is something to the notion of spacetime that our ordinary concept of time does not embrace. Because this seems to be the most valuable contribution that science offers to correct our ordinary conception of time we will look more fully at spacetime as a unified structure.

Relativity theory poses a particularly significant problem for presentism. The general background for this criticism comes in the context of deeper issues about the nature of what constitutes a good philosophical theory. Logical consistency is by most accounts a critical component; however, it clearly will not do as a sufficient criterion of what makes a philosophical theory successful. Another criterion, given in various ways, is factual adequacy. For a theory to be a valuable theory it must fit the facts. If this is right, and I think it is, then our philosophical theories should fit the facts, or we might say it should fit with what we believe are the facts. We ought to rely on science for the facts when it comes to the structure of the universe and of space and time.[12] A philosophical theory that ignores what the best of the physical sciences says about relevant fields is simply inadequate. This may not be as obvious as it sounds. The structure and nature of science as a discipline turns out to cause some difficulty here. No scientific theory is without anomalies; scientific theories often posit theoretical entities and sometimes they rely on philosophical commitments in critical areas. As a result the question of when a philosophical theory should be accountable to a scientific theory and when it should be critical of it cannot be answered in a straightforward principled way.

Even if we cannot elucidate specific principles there are cases where all would agree that a philosophical theory simply cannot ignore the success and wide spread agreement about scientific data and theories.

---

12. It might be noted that we do not rely solely on science in that scientific theories are subject to issues of logical consistency and conceptual problems (problems of a conceptual nature where the conceptual issues are strong enough for us to doubt the explanations given by the scientific theory). For example some interpretations of general relativity are rejected because they violate our concept of causal order.

Presentism faces this situation regarding relativity theory. Sider sums it up this way, "The notion of the *present* time that is so crucial to presentism is meaningless within Minkowski spacetime, in which there is no distinguished partition of spacetime into space and time, and no observer-independent notion of simultaneity."[13] If Sider and others are right in holding that, given Minkowski's interpretation of spacetime, a key concept of presentism is meaningless or that fundamental implications of presentism are contrary to special relativity theory, then it would appear that presentism faces a significant if not conclusive criticism.

To address this criticism we need to be specific about where the alleged inconsistencies are between presentism and relativity theory. A quick review of the issue of simultaneity in the special theory of relativity will enable us to get down to the critical issues. A classic example of this involves two observers one at the side of a train track and the other on a train moving significantly close to light speed.[14] As the two observers pass each other lightening strikes two places, one up the track and one down, equal distance from the observers. A pivotal step in Einstein's theory is that light moves at the same velocity in all inertial frames. The result of the fixity of light speed is that the two observers will observe different things. One will observe the lights as simultaneous and the other will not. If an observer knows the relative speed of the other observer, they will conclude something like the following: "of course I know the lights were simultaneous (or not), but that poor soul will form the false impression that they were not (or were, as the case may be)." There are a number of "paradoxes" found in relativity theory that are relevant. For example, relativity theory presents the differential in age of twins who are a part of radically different inertial frames as a "paradox." My point is not to disagree with relativity theory but to note that it is a paradox given our ordinary expectations. But there is a deep expectation about the nature of time that is not at issue in the "twin paradox." In each inertial frame time operates in the same way, events which have not yet happened, occur, then are past.[15] The "moving" twin does not jump in time; rather by taking ad-

13. Sider, *Four-Dimensionalism : An Ontology of Persistence and Time*, 42.

14. Of course one of the issues will be who is moving? All we can actually say is that they are moving relative to one another.

15. Relativity theory does call some of our ordinary sense of time into question. In particular here what it calls into question is the universality of the rate of this progression. Some physicists will argue that time travel is possible in the sense that we can travel

vantage of time dilation, she experiences a temporal disconnect with the "stationary" twin who remains in the initial inertial frame. The common sense idea here is that space is different from time in that I can leave and return to the same place in space[16] but I cannot leave and return to the same time. So far it may not be obvious that there is anything that poses a particularly significant problem. That we make different observations of the same phenomena from different perspectives is not particularly surprising.[17]

The problem that relativity established was that the two observers would appeal to the same principles to arrive at their different conclusions. However, there would be no agreed upon data that could be used to adjudicate the dispute. The most anyone can justify by empirical data is that whether or not the flashes were simultaneous was relative to the observer. What was needed to decide the issue was some framework of absolute simultaneity[18] that could be used to adjust the observations given their different inertial frames. A consequence of relativity theory is that in principle no such framework of absolute simultaneity could be meaningfully determined. Because simultaneity is necessarily determined from within an inertial frame, any evidence for a claim about what is absolutely simultaneous would be equally well-based with another different claim

---

into the future. I think this is largely misleading, but in one sense technically correct. By being accelerated relative to the earth, to near light speed I can travel and return and meet my great, great, great grandchildren without either living extremely long or having my children marry and have children at an unusually young age. My age relative to the aging experience by those remaining on earth appears to have slowed. Our ordinary expectation, would be that you age at the same rate compared to all other things regardless of how they travel. Here the ordinary belief I wish to call attention to is that we cannot escape the progression from future to present to past. We still age, changes still occur. Relativity does not give us access to an existence free from the orderly progression of time. We are not free to move back and forth in the temporal plane as we can in the spatial frame.

16. Granted this becomes much more difficult when we reject the notion of an absolute space or even merely broaden our perspective to realize that the earth is moving in space. Nonetheless the point is we do not see the same restrictions for movement in space that we do with time.

17. Consider two observers in the same inertial frame, one half way between two lightening strikes and the other split 1/3–2/3's of the way between the two. The two will make different initial observations about the simultaneity of the flashes. However, if they know their distances the two could correct their initial observations. Once they make corrections for distance they will be able to agree on who's observation was correct.

18. See the subsequent discussion of temporal hyperplanes in spacetime.

made from within a different inertial frame. The present then is relative to the observer and not a feature of the nature of time itself.

This situation can be discussed in terms of the geometry of Minkowski spacetime. In Minkowski spacetime the connection between space and time is given a graphic representation where in addition to the three dimensions of space, time forms an additional dimension. Although Einstein worked out his theory without the four-dimensional representation Minkowski offered and the above problem of simultanity can be demonstrated without Minkowski's representation, it is without doubt that Minkowski's spacetime was a valuable addition to Einstein's work. Using Minkowski spacetime we can graphically represent world lines and light cones. In Minkowski spacetime, because we are working with a 4-dimentional space any three-dimensional region that divides the space is called a hyperplane.[19] The question then in Minkowski terms is whether there is a unique, privileged temporal hyperplane that unifies different inertial systems. If we could identify an ontologically privileged temporal hyperplane that was common to two different inertial systems we would, in doing so, give the basis for adjudicating disputes between observers in the different inertial frames. In short the lack of a privileged unifying temporal hyperplane graphically illustrates the point of STR that there is no information independent of a reference frame to act as a privileged frame of reference and hence no basis for absolute simultaneity nor a unique privileged present.

Although Minkowski introduces the concept of spacetime as a unified manifold, [20] the notion can be applied to both Newtonian and Galilean (or neo-Newtonian) frameworks as well. Galileo introduced the idea of relativized inertia or perhaps more correctly the Galilean relativity principle. He showed that if we were to do an experiment in a lab, say dropping a ball or shooting a projectile without some reference point we

19. A hyperplane for a 4d space is a 3d volume of that 4d space, just as a plane is a 2d surface of a 3d volume. The concept of a hyperplane is one that can be generalized to any space regardless of the number of dimensions of that space. The hyperplane completely divides the space and will have one less dimension than the space it divides. It should also be noted that because we represent Minkowski spacetime three dimensionally, we represent the hyperplane as a 2d plane dividing spacetime.

20. The connection between space and time was not original with Minkowski. In fact Minkowski himself credits several individuals as influential in how he developed the concept. Nonetheless, he was the first to actually work it out by bringing together a number of ideas and introducing several unique ideas himself.

would not be able to tell whether the lab was stationary or moving at constant speed. What is of interest for our discussion is that in the neo-Newtonian framework we lack a uniquely privileged distance relation and thus we can offer a transformation from any inertial frame to any other frame (which will maintain all distinctions of relative and accelerated motion). Without a fixed spatial point there is no basis to determine which inertial frame is privileged.[21] Instead we can transform information from any inertial frame into any other inertial frame.[22]

In STR the speed of light is constant. This constancy leads to interesting consequences when we look at the transformation from one inertial frame to another. The conversions were given by Lorentz.[23] As before these transformations enable us to use information from one reference frame along with the relative speed to get information of the other reference frame. The point of interest here is that Lorentz transformations yield the result that when we make the transformation from one inertial frame to another while holding the speed of light as constant there is a spatial contraction and temporal dilation. This can be given a graphical representation on Minkowski's spacetime. Like the Galilean transformation, this transformation can be made in either direction hence it is a relativistic system. The connection between space and time, that is that both spatial and temporal measurements change when moving from one inertial frame to another, was the starting point for Minkowski's four-dimensional geometric representation STR. When this is represented the result is that there is no basis to prefer one inertial frame with its temporal hyperplane over another. For presentism the alleged problem is that according to SRT there is no preferred or absolute temporal hyperplane—no way to break reality up so we can say here is what is simultaneous, in short, there is no unique present. With the geometry provided by

21. For a discussion of this see for example Barry Dainton, *Time and Space* (Montreal; Ithaca, NY: McGill-Queen's University Press, 2001) 184–85; or Craig Bourne, *A Future for Presentism* (Oxford: Clarendon, 2006) 142–46.

22. Transformations are a means of converting the information in one reference frame into information of another reference frame. Here the distance measurements of one reference frame are transformed into the distance measurements of another. In a very simplified instance, by knowing that I am traveling at 60 miles an hour and you are passing me with an overtake speed of 10 miles an hour I can use this information to determine that in your car the country side is passing by at 70 miles an hour.

23. Note that Einstein and Lorentz each came up with the transformation and had different interpretations of them.

Minkowski that was four-dimensional (thus including temporal extension) it is a quick step from its success at representing STR to the conclusion that there is no ontologically relevant sense of 'present' and on to the ontological commitments of eternalism. This raises a clear problem for the openness of the future. I think it is a key point here that the move from STR to four-dimensionalism and eternalism is grounded in the success of Minkowski spacetime.

ONTOLOGICAL CONSIDERATIONS

Minkowski had to work out the nature of the spacetime that was connected to STR. This is not merely adding a temporal dimension to the already accepted three spatial dimensions. To make the intervals match the conclusions of the Lorentz transformation time is treated differently from the spatial dimensions.[24] What Minkowski was able to show with his version of spacetime was a geometry consistent with Einstein's STR. Minkowski himself thought that the success of his geometry established that space and time could no longer be considered in isolation. Since he had no reason to think that prior attempts to represent space were intended as helpful representations and not actually descriptive of space, he would have had no reason to think of his spacetime as limited in its ontological consequences to the status of a pedagogical tool. Furthermore, Minkowski saw his work as deeply connected to the structure of the universe. The one thing that STR held as invariant that was capable of providing a basis for a geometrical representation was the speed of light. Minkowski began there, with the path of light as the basis for his spacetime. Dainton notes, "The idea that luminal trajectories are built into the very fabric of spacetime is a natural response to the abolition of the æther, . . . it seems there is only one candidate for the structure that constrains or determines the paths light rays can take: spacetime itself."[25] Minkowski and most of physics following him took it for granted that the concept of spacetime was not merely a useful aid in explaining STR but it actually describes the spatio and temporal structure of the physical universe as being a unified complete manifold. A four dimensional manifold of this

24. See Fritz Rohrlich, *From Paradox to Reality : Our New Concepts of the Physical World* (Cambridge: Cambridge University Press, 1987) 75–86; Bourne, *A Future for Presentism*, 151–59 or most any text on the nature of STR.

25. Dainton, *Time and Space*, 263–64.

sort is at best problematic for presentism. Sider makes the point this way, "There is a superficial inconsistency right at the surface since Minkowski spacetime includes all of history's events in a single existent manifold. . . . This is not surprising: Scientific spatiotemporal theories are typically formulated under eternalist assumptions since the formulation is much easier and since scientists do not typically share philosophers' scruples about the ontology of past and future objects."[26] In defending presentism we should thus ask is this assumption, however reasonable it might have been for Minkowski to make, one that will stand up to scrutiny?

We can graph any number of things without thinking that our ability to graph them shows they possess some unified structure. For example we regularly graph spatial location and temperature variance, population, political persuasion or any number of other things and yet it would be ridiculous to think that temperature or any of these others is a new dimension.[27] So why think that Minkowski spacetime has some ontological import these others lack? First, it was Einstein's aim to describe reality and in particular the structure of space that explained anomalies in the existing theories. Hence it is not at all surprising that anyone providing a geometry for that theory would expect that geometry to represent the same structure of reality. A second important feature that grounded this was that the existence of space was not in question and STR (in particular the Lorentz transformations) showed that space and time changed in a connected way as one considered observations made from different inertial frames. Many have argued that there were deep-seated verificationist leanings that were operative in Minkowski and others.[28] While this may be true it is nonetheless hard to ignore the empirical success of relativity theory. Even if one is not a verificationist the move from empirical success to ontological commitment provides at the minimum a *prima facie* justification for the ontological commitments made. Such justification however is not beyond question. Is the appeal of presentism an adequate justification for questioning the ontological assumptions made? Part of

26. Sider, *Four-Dimensionalism : An Ontology of Persistence and Time*, 44–45.

27. Bourne cites Mellor as giving a superb example of this by graphically representing the relationship between, hue, brightness and saturation in colors. Bourne, *A Future for Presentism*, 158.

28. See William Lane Craig, *God, Time, and Eternity : The Coherence of Theism II: Eternity* (Dordrecht; London: Kluwer Academic, 2001); and Bourne, *A Future for Presentism*.

the answer to that will be determined by what one must give up when they reject the assumptions. If one must give up completely on relativity theory to maintain presentism then the cost is too high; however, it is not immediately clear that one must be a realist about the unified four-dimensionalist manifold to get the empirical result that grounds the acceptance of relativity theory.

Before we begin a look at the range of the structures of spacetime that a presentist might accept it is worth covering a few reasons why we might be concerned about the eternalist, four-dimensionalist ontology generally affirmed by Minkowski spacetime. First, Minkowski spacetime is not unique, or we might say spacetime is not unique to relativity theory. While neither Newtonian nor neo-Newtonian theories were originally given in terms of a spacetime geometry, each could be cast in terms of spacetime. Neither type of theory, however, has independent reasons for affirming a unified spacetime manifold. While there might be some helpful additions by using such a manifold, nothing within either theory makes embracing spacetime particularly appealing. Furthermore even though either theory could be discussed using a spacetime geometry, we think both theories have been superseded by relativity. As noted above Sider pointed out that spatiotemporal theories are given usually using eternalist assumptions. We cannot connect the success of relativity theory with its eternalist assumptions without further argument.[29] Second, for the eternalist the concepts of change, motion and cause need modification.[30] How significant we should judge that modification to be is itself a matter of debate. Finally, there are differences between space and time that raise questions about the unified structure of spacetime. Time at the very least seems to have a progression to it that space lacks. Additionally that progression seems to have a unique direction. Minkowski himself in working out spacetime treats time as distinct from space. In determining a spacetime interval his equation is that the square of the interval is equal to the square of the speed of light times the square of the temporal change minus the sum of

29. I am not ruling out the possibility that it is the eternalist features superficially inherent in STR that account for its success. If that is true I am unaware of good reasons for thinking so. I am rather trying to show that there is no simple connection between the empirical success of relativity theory and its assumptions about the ontological structure of spacetime. This will be important in considering my closing criticisms.

30. Earl Brink Conee and Theodore Sider, *Riddles of Existence : A Guided Tour of Metaphysics* (Oxford: Clarendon, 2005) 52–56.

the square of the changes of the spatial changes (that is: $\Delta I2 = c2(\Delta t)2 - [\Delta x2 + \Delta y2 + \Delta z2]$). We note here that the temporal element is being treated differently than the spatial elements. The significance of this may not be obvious; however, it certainly appears to show a significant distinction. [31] Minkowski formulates this knowing Einstein's result for the relationship between temporal dilation and spatial contractions when inertial frame differences near the speed of light. While there is a connection it is an inverse relationship. John Gribbin notes, "This is why time cannot be regarded as simply a fourth dimension of space . . . When rulers shrink, time expands; when rulers expand time shrinks."[32] Gribbin's point is that the difference in the sign (positive or negative) between the spatial component and the temporal component is not merely to make the equation work, it has the consequence that we should view time and space as distinct and acting differently. Craig Bourne states the same point this way, ". . . this distinction itself should be taken to represent something objective. Special relativity thus treats time differently from space."[33] At the very least this gives us reasons to be concerned with the unity of spacetime as a basis for an eternalist's ontology. Finally, one issue from General Relativity Theory is worth mentioning.[34] Within the range of solutions to the field equations there are a number of "causally pathological spacetime" solutions.[35] That is there are solutions that are mathematically consistent but are rejected because of other characteristics that physicists deem to be unacceptable departures from what we believe about the causal structure of reality.[36] Sklar offers two examples. First, a spacetime might be mathematically

31. Bourne thinks this is the most compelling reason to rethink the putative ontological commitment of STR. Bourne, *A Future for Presentism*, 159.

32. John R. Gribbin, *Unveiling the Edge of Time : Black Holes, White Holes, Wormholes*, 1st ed. (New York: Harmony, 1992) 42.

33. Bourne, *A Future for Presentism*, 159.

34. Other problems given in the literature include: neo-Lorentz-Ives interpretation, Quantum gravity, Quantum entanglement.

35. I take this phrase from Lawrence Sklar, *Philosophy of Physics, Dimensions of Philosophy Series* (Boulder: Westview, 1992) 86.

36. There are problems with the standard interpretation of GTR even given causally acceptable solutions. One of the more commonly discussed is the Hole problem. Sklar give a brief summary of this argument stating, ". . . because space (or spacetime) is allegedly homogeneous and isotropic, the substantivalist view commits us to distinctions between possible worlds which are not real distinctions and is hence an illegitimate doctrine." Lawrence Sklar, *Philosophy and Spacetime Physics* (Berkeley: University of California Press, 1985) 11.

consistent but "causally pathological" if it contains closed loops where we might follow a causal path forward into the future yet still end up causing the event which originated the causal path we were following. Another similar pathological spacetime does not involve a causal loop, but nonetheless following a causal path returns one to a point in spacetime prior to the original event.[37] The point here is that there are interpretations of relativity that are capable of mathematical and graphical representation but are nonetheless rejected as possible representations of reality. The fact that Minkowski spacetime gives a graphic representation of STR need not be taken to imply that we must accept an eternalist ontology. Given these problems and, as I presented it above, the intuitive common sense appeal to presentism, it seems worth our while to consider the alternatives to embracing the ontological commitments of Minkowski's spacetime.

AN OUTLINE OF PROPOSED SOLUTIONS

There has been quite a bit written on how we handle the seemingly paradoxical conclusions of Minkowski spacetime.[38] Sider and Hinchliff each offer a categorical ordering of the range of possible responses. The first might be considered the radical option. It is radical because it rejects some of the conclusions to which STR is committed. Hinchliff states, "The view I am going to call 'surface presentism' reverses the direction of fit and tries to accommodate the special theory or a theory with its empirical consequences to a presentist picture."[39] He cites Prior as a 'hard-line' advocate of surface presentism. The relevance for our discussion is that this view rejects a realist interpretation of STR. STR gives us a description of how we would measure things but it does not reveal the structure of space or time (let alone spacetime). For example, one possible consequence Hinchliff cites is, "the speed of light will then be *measured* to be the same in all inertial frames, even though it is not."[40] This sort of response is a paradigmatic example of a "radical solution." There is no readily apparent scientific ground for thinking that some other interpretation of STR that

37. Sklar, *Philosophy of Physics*, 86.

38. For example, spatial contraction is a consequence of acceleration viewed from either reference frame. So in two non-inertial reference frames each will view the other as having undergone spatial contraction. Other paradoxes such as the twin paradox are also well-known.

39. Hinchliff, "A Defense of Presentism in a Relativistic Setting," 584.

40. Ibid., 585.

is internally consistent and empirically equivalent to realist interpretations of Minkowski is not true.[41] I think we should take such models seriously. They seem to face criticisms similar to the view I will eventually offer (although I hope mine is not as "radical"). While I think we should take them seriously a less radical solution is more appealing.

Sider considers five options.[42] The options that Sider considers divide between those that modify STR (hybrids 1–2) and those that modify presentism (hybrids 3–5). Those that modify STR select either a point or a plane of absolute simultaneity, while those that modify presentism accept some but not all of the regions of spacetime posited by Minkowski. His two options which preserve presentism's appeal by modifying STR each introduce some form of absolute simultaneity and thus are significantly radical departures from the standard interpretations of STR. Sider seems to use the introduction of a form of absolute simultaneity as a litmus test of an interpretation being a "radical departure" from the standard interpretation. I will follow him in this usage. Sider's criticism of the latter type of attempt (hybrids 3–5) is that the modification of presentism is too great. It might be worth noting that the modification which accepts the existence of whatever is present or in the past light cone (Sider's 3rd hybrid) is at least consistent with the concerns of open theism as I have laid them out above. Nonetheless there are significant problems with this view. Additionally, the selection between the options for what portion of spacetime is endorsed and what is denied appears to be *ad hoc*. If we are going to accept some of Minkowski spacetime as descriptive of an existent unified spacetime manifold, why would we not accept it all? Why would the past consist of a unified spacetime but the future not? I think we should agree with Sider here and consider this to be another limiting factor in deciding whether an attempt to unify presentism with STR is

41. In particular, by being empirically equivalent the "radical interpretations" such as surface-presentism, make themselves immune from strictly empirical critique. I don't mean to suggest by this that there are not legitimate philosophical concerns that we might have about such theories. Rather, I wish to highlight that the concerns are philosophical and hence ought to be weighed against other conceptual concerns that we might have with the realist interpretations of Minkowski spacetime when someone claims presentism is at odds with STR.

42. Sider, *Four-Dimensionalism : An Ontology of Persistence and Time*, 43–52. Please note my goal here is not to critique Siders' analysis, so I have kept my description to a minimum. I hope to lay out the radical sides to the dilemma that the presentist faces in assessing STR.

acceptable. Sider's conclusion is that no STR-presentism hybrid will work. Since he views other problems with presentism as significantly under-mining its appeal he is inclined to think that this lack of compatibility with STR is grounds enough to reject presentism in favor of eternalism. His work offers us some clear limits to operate within if we are to give a version of presentism that is not a radical departure from STR.

MY SOLUTION: RELATIONALISM

Sider argues that presentism is inconsistent with Minkowski spacetime because it requires an observer independent notion of simultaneity and within Minkowski spacetime such a notion is meaningless.[43] I want to argue that this is true only when you take a substantivalist approach to the spacetime manifold. I see no reason to think that Minkowski and others thought of the manifold in relationalist terms, so in this regard I am tak-ing a revisionist approach. Nonetheless, what I want to try to show it that it is at least possible to accept the result of STR that simultaneity is rela-tive to the inertial frame of the observer and that one need not embrace eternalism as a consequence. What I will propose would be consistent with eternalism if things have a four-dimentionalist structure; however, to necessitate eternalism one would have to provide an argument inde-pendent of STR for the claim that things have temporal extension.[44] The problem for presentism with relativity theory is not merely with the lack of simultaneity that STR brings but with the substantivalist treatment of the spacetime manifold. Sklar states it this way, "The issue here is not that of determinism, of whether or not the past and present events fix, by their law like connections to other events, what future events will, in fact, occur. The issue is rather the claim that if future happenings had present and past reality (if it was a fact now that I would buy ice cream tomorrow), then there could be no sense in which the future was open to possibility at all."[45] I want to put forward two things. First, I want to accept the relativ-ity of simultaneity and hence a denial of the absolute simultaneity of all events. As I attempt to outline below I intend this to be an epistemic and

43. Ibid., 42.

44. I don't mean to imply that no such arguments exist. My point is that given the alternative I hope to present one cannot get the criticism that Sider has leveled without further argument.

45. Sklar, *Philosophy of Physics*, 70.

an ontological claim. It is not merely that I cannot determine the correct answer, but that, given the definition of simultaneity in STR, there is no correct answer.[46] Second, I want to put forward that the past no longer exists and the future does not yet exist. When I say this what I want to deny is the ontological status of the spacetime manifold while upholding its empirical consequences including the denial of absolute simultaneity. In particular I argue it is possible to deny that reality has temporal extension without rejecting the consequences of STR.[47] If I do this right a physicist might conclude, well so what, it makes no empirical difference. Or, perhaps a physicist will show me that what I suggest is physically impossible. I hope not and I have done my best not to say things inconsistent with what I know about the mathematics of special or general relativity.

Given that the empirical claims of relativity theory are well-grounded there are four options for the structure of spacetime. First, we might continue to treat space and time as separate in their natures. To be sure there is a connection in their behavior but that connection might be accounted for in ways that do not necessitate their being unified into a single manifold. I take it this would constitute a more radical revisionist approach and as such I will not pursue it here. The second and third options are basically mirrors of each other. We can treat spacetime as possessing a unified nature and treat the manifold as a substance: the second option. Or as a third option, we can treat the unified manifold as relational, where spacetime is defined solely in terms of the relations that exist between things. Obviously the second option here is the way Minkowski intended his spacetime to be understood, but we have yet to see reasons why the third option must be ruled out. Finally, we can treat spacetime as partially relational and partially substantival. This option splits into two variants. (4a) The idea that spacetime is a manifold of temporal substance and spatial relation is part of the conceptual landscape here but I cannot find a good motivation for it. (4b) On the other hand the idea the spacetime manifold is a substantival space where temporal relations hold between

46. I wish to remain neutral on the question of whether there are other useful definitions of simultaneity.

47. I don't need to or want to argue for a relationalist view of spacetime. Instead I only need to argue that a relationalist view (at least of time) is possible. That is to say I want to argue that if one does adopt a relationalist view of spacetime one can accept the consequences of special and general relativity derived by mathematical physicists without accepting the philosophical/ontological consequence that denies the possibility of an open future.

things existing in that space has some promise for presentism. There are problems any way we go. I will thus remain neutral on the issue of whether space is substantival, but consider the possibility of temporal relationalism consistent with either 3 or 4b.

Common descriptions of spacetime often use metaphors like 'the fabric of spacetime' where spacetime is thought of as thing in itself. When treated in this way there seem to be good reasons to treat time as wholly real, that is no ontological distinction between past present and future, things as having temporal parts, and the present as an indexical concept. I think it is the use of this metaphor that has prevented many physicists and philosophers from considering possible ways to describe relativistic spacetime that do not treat time as being completely homogeneous with space. I think the way to do this is to treat time as relational. My basic approach to this is that I am more confident of presentism than I am of my commitment one way or the other to the nature of time as substantival or relational, hence if I can solve the problems raised by understanding time together with space by treating time relationally, this seems as good a reason as any to consider the notion that time is relational.

According to temporal relationalism times are nothing more than sequential relations of things.[48] Things exist and those things can stand in different relations to each other. The change in the thing or in its relationship with other things constitutes a temporal change. If there were no things there would be no time. Consider a possible world where there is one thing, a metaphysical simple. This thing exists alone and it has no parts, hence it is a simple. Because in that world there is and could be no change according to temporal relationalism in that world there is no change of time.[49] Now consider a world where there are two things, again each is a simple. In this world there can be both change and time although it is not necessitated. For example the two things could be moving apart. Although it is not immediately clear what the metric would be, or

48. We might wish to identify a time as something like 11:30pm June 1, 2009. As I am describing relationalism when we identify a time in this way we are identifying how things are sequentially, when compared to how they were 23.5 hours, 6 months and 2009 years ago. We could cash this out by reference to instantaneous world states; however, this adds a layer to the ontology that can obscure the point. I would want to argue that if world states exist they exist because there are things. In short both times and world states supervene on the existence and nature of things. The same might be said for states and possible states.

49. Whether there is time and it is a present of indefinable duration is controversial.

whether we could determine whether they were both moving or one was moving away from the other, we could have change to their relations and hence the relationalist would affirm a change in time as well.[50] Because of the restricted nature of this world there are limited ranges of states or relations for our two simples to stand in. In this world the present would be defined by the relation that existed between the simples. It is the state they are in relative to the range of possible states that they might stand in. In this world the present persists for as long as the two things remain in that state. The past is defined by all of the states that the two things have been in but are no longer. The future might be defined as either the states that the two things will be in or the range of possible states that the two things might go into. In other words time is defined by the relations of things. What is of importance to us is that there is no such thing as the present apart from the current relationship that exists between two or more things. There are things and things can be related to each other in different and changing ways but there is no further thing the present to which things are related.

What will temporal relationalism get us and to what will it commit us? The first thing this gets us is a causally well-ordered spacetime rooted in the nature of things themselves. Recall one of the concerns with relativity and spacetime raised above was that there were well-defined geometries that yield 'causally pathological spacetimes'. Minkowski avoided this by his structure of measuring a spacetime interval. The problem this raised was that it treated space and time differently. For relationalists the right causal ordering is not generated by rigging the system.[51] One of the things Minkowski was able to show was the fact that while we rejected simultaneity between inertial frames there is no inertial frame that one can go to from which your observations of my inertial frame will be causally reversed. Said another way, if in my inertial frame the ball hitting the window is what breaks the window, no matter how fast you pass by in

50. As before in this world the present might be extended; however, this is controversial and as long as the notion of an extended present is coherent, it is irrelevant to our main concerns.

51. No doubt some may object to my characterization of Minkowski as rigging his spacetime system. Perhaps this way of saying it is a bit harsh. My point is that Minkowski cannot appeal to something with his geometry that is the basis for the causal order, but rather he saw the need to build that temporal ordering in and was ingenious in doing so. On the other hand the relationalist has a basis for the causal ordering, namely the behavior of things which grounds the temporal succession.

your rocket ship (or perhaps you are on the planet and I am passing by) you will not see the window breaking before the ball gets there. How far the ball must travel to get there and how long it takes for it to get there will be judged to be different from each of our inertial frames but the order of causation will not be disturbed. In the end, both Minkowski spacetime (with its ontological commitments) and my temporally relational spacetime end with a causally well-ordered system, but Minkowski's comes from his designing that into the geometry, and relationalism's comes from the nature of the sequential ordering of things themselves.

To understand the problem for presentism we began with STR's commitment to the fixity of the speed of light. This was basic in Minkowski's spacetime. As we saw above it was also the basis for why the Lorentz transformations showed that not only would there be spatial difference between inertial frames, there would be temporal differences as well. The result was that according to STR judgments of simultaneity were always relative to an inertial frame. You simply cannot answer the question is A simultaneous to B without knowing which inertial frame you are using. Presentism seems to be in trouble here. If we treat spacetime as substantival there needs to be a temporal hyperplane to which the present refers. If the temporal hyperplane is itself defined by the inertial frame then for each different inertial frame there will be a different hyperplane. If we treat spacetime as relational instead of substantival the problem takes on a different light. The present is not a unique hyperplane even within an inertial frame. To define the present we need to define it relative to individuals. It is a relation between things. So for example, I am presently in this room, and I am presently typing "this word." These uses of present differ because I stand in different relations. I remain in the room but I am no longer typing those words. The relational presentist can affirm the relativity of simultaneity because of the relative nature of the relational present. Unlike substantivalism there is not a thing we are dividing up and trying to find some independent criteria for identifying one part as privileged. The relationalist affirms the existence of things that stand in changing relationship with other things.

Given my metaphysical commitments I think it is possible to have a world pretty similar to ours with a unique present, a privileged hyperplane of simultaneity. The present is defined by the relationships that hold between objects. If our world was a world in which no objects were accelerated in relationship to any other object there would be a unique present. So suppose there is a world in which there are two simples, and they are unaccelerated. In that world the present would be defined by the relationships that hold between the two objects. In that world because of the nature of the objects and their relations there would be a unique hyperplane of simultaneity.[52] If they were not at rest with respect to each other the present would be defined by their current relationship. In a world with three unaccelerated objects the present would be defined by the relationship that holds between all three of them. I think this is consistent with STR. As long as it is, it would only be the realist interpretation of Minkowski spacetime that could account for the eternalist view that the future exists. When I say I want to accept the ontological consequences of STR what I mean by this is that because our world involves objects that are accelerated there can be no single unique definition of the present. It is the nature of our world that makes a unique temporal hyperplane impossible. Here what constitutes a radical solution is to argue for the existence of a unique privileged hyperplane of simultaneity. That is the ontological commitment I want to try to avoid. On the standard understanding of presentism, there is a fact of the matter about what things are presently happening to an object.[53] I want to take seriously the rejection of this claim by STR and argue there is a way to understand presentism that does not conflict with it. Rather than accept the standard view that presentism entails that what exists is all and only what is temporally present, I want to argue that the relational presentists can accept the view that the present is defined by all and only what exists. This view does not entail eternalism, nor does it require that we define the present by a privileged hyperplane of simultaneity. But since the relationships between things, when they are accelerated (as they are in our universe), does not yield a unique answer to the question what is present, there is not a unique present. As noted above there could have been a unique present, but given the complexity of the distribution of things (in particular some things are accelerated), there is not a unique present. What exists is fundamental and as such not analyzable into something more basic, what is present is defined in terms of what exists, the existing things don't define a unique present. The very

52. It seems to me that if they were at rest with each other we would have an extended present. There would be nothing (internal to the world) to define the extent of the present.

53. This problem was raised by Dean Zimmerman in his comments.

existence and nature of the present is fixed by the things that exist and because those things are accelerated there is no unique present.

Before we ask whether this is too radical a departure from STR, we should look at whether it is too radical a departure from presentism. We wanted to affirm that what is past and future do not exist. I concluded my initial remarks about the nature of presentism stating that the eternalist think that everything's existence occurs at a time but that there is nothing special with reference to existence between one time and another, whereas the presentists think there is something unique about the present such that only presently existing things exist. In defining the present relationally we might modify that description in this way. The eternalist is affirming things and times that those things exist and in doing so denying there is any ontological privileged time. As a relational presentist I am affirming the existence of things and defining the present in terms of those things. Things exist and stand in relationships to other things, including the relation of being temporally present with another thing.[54] We might think that a consequence of presentism is that there will be a unique and correct answer to questions about what is and is not present. I think a relationalist can affirm presentism while denying that there is a unique and correct answer to questions of what is present because things can be accelerated. That is the things can be in differing inertial frames. No inertial frame is privileged. Because of this there is no single answer to questions of simultaneity. This is not merely an epistemological fact, that is, it is not merely that we cannot know the fact of simultaneity it is a deeper part of our reality. Someone traveling past the earth now at near light speed might say as they snap their fingers that their snap was simultaneous with my typing the first letter of the first word of the previous page; whereas I judge this action to have already taken place. As long as they know their relative speed and distance they will also be able to determine how it will seem different to me. What STR denies is a privileged frame for determining who is right. In the classic train example we get the following judgments. The person on the ground, we'll call him George, will think I view the lightning strikes as simultaneous, but the person on the train, we'll call her Tina will not. Tina on the train will think, I observe these lightening strikes as successive, but George will not. There is not a unique judgment

---

54. It is probably worth noting that while the existence of things is ontologically basic, what exists is epistemically inaccessible. Because of the limits of the speed of light I simply cannot know which things exist now.

nor is there a correct judgment. But this does not entail that there is an existing future or an existing past. George will note that the lightening strike that occurred at the rear of the train will not be observed by Tina our train traveler, for some time after he observes it. When it was present to him it was not yet present to her. Tina our train traveler will note when she does observe the lightening strike that it will already have been seen by George. We need not affirm that the future or the past exists. If we are to accept STR then we will also not affirm that either observer has the basis for affirming their experience was veridical and should act as the basis for correcting the observation of the other person.

How does this avoid problems that lead to the conclusion that the past, present and future are on an ontological par? The short answer is that there is no thing, "the future," which the relational presentist affirms exists. We might ask, what does Minkowski spacetime give us? One way to read it is that it gives us a future "history" of the world. A substantivalist about Minkowski spacetime or what I have referred to as a full-blown eternalist[55] thinks that the future exists in the same way as the present or past exists. The central thesis of this paper has been that we can embrace the empirical findings of STR without being full-blown eternalists. One way to assess what Minkowski spacetime gets us is a geometric representation of the consequences of the interconnectedness of space and time. It shows us what will happen to accelerated bodies and how it will affect measurements of time and space. The light cone we graph for a particle describes not how the particle will behave but what the range of possible behavior is for that particle. It tells us what causal interactions are possible without being committed to a particular actual future. It is this commitment to an actual future that presentists need to be concerned with[56] and if I am right here this commitment comes from an ontological commitment which is unwarranted by the empirical success of STR.

In fact the nature of STR as a theory is itself somewhat difficult to address given the later developments of GTR. In answering this question Brown states, "At its most fundamental SR is a theory that somewhere between a pure principle theory (like thermodynamics or Einstein's 1905

55. See footnote 5.

56. Sklar puts it, "The issue is rather the claim that if future happenings had present and past reality (if it was a fact now that I would buy ice cream tomorrow), then there could be no sense in which the future was open to possibility at all." Sklar, *Philosophy of Physics*, 70.

version of SR) and a fully constructive theory (like statistical mechanics)."[57] One of Brown's central theses is to rebut the idea of the determinative character of spacetime.[58] In presenting an assessment of the role of Minkowski spacetime in the full development of STR Brown concludes,

> At any rate, the nature of the big principle—what Minkowski called the world postulate—has often led commentators to remark that SR has the character of a "meta-theory," or that it has a "transcendental" flavour. It doesn't tell you how things interact; rather it tells you how any theory of interaction should behave.[59]

This assessment fits well with a relationalist reading of Minkowski. There seems to be no good reason to say we cannot embrace the conclusions of special relativity without embracing a substantival ontological stance.

ASSESSING THIS AS A REPLY TO THE CRITICISM

How well does this approach work? My central aim has been to respond to a certain sort of criticism namely that presentism should be rejected because it is inconsistent with the best interpretations of STR. Sider argued that the hybrid theories which sought to embrace both STR and presentism each gave up too much of one or the other theory. Two possibilities remained to reject presentism or to reject or radically revise STR. Rejecting or radically revising STR ran counter to the principle that a good philosophical theory will take into account what is given us by good or properly done science. We do not want to try to do philosophy in an intellectual vacuum. At least on the face of it I have not rejected STR. But perhaps I have been too revisionist. Our standard here should not rule out interpretations of STR that are not committed to eternalism.[60] But we have no clear standard for what would count as too radical. To some extent this judgment will be subjective. The most relevant issue in the criticisms seems to be the rejection of absolute simultaneity by the standard interpretation of STR. I have tried to avoid affirming absolute simultaneity in my discussion, but it may be that I am being too much of a revisionist elsewhere.

57. Harvey R. Brown, *Physical Relativity: Space-Time Structure from a Dynamical Perspective* (Oxford: Clarendon, 2005) 147.

58. Ibid., 24.

59. Ibid., 147.

60. To do so would beg the question at hand.

In answering this concern we need to identify what the relationalist account has kept. First it is able to keep the causal order of the physical. The standard interpretation of STR does not have a problem with this but it is a more general concern with GTR. We seem to get all of the important consequences of STR; however, many of the theories that are considered to be more radical are able to get the same empirical consequences as well. We don't get four-dimensionalism; however, not only is this a plus for presentist concerns, but it is difficult to see the motivation for a four-dimensionalist ontology apart from the ontological commitments of relativity theory. My approach is revisionary in that it is probably true that most physicists accept Minkowski spacetime as providing evidence of an eternalist ontology; furthermore, they are likely to be substantivalist about spacetime. But this is a philosophical commitment and not one entailed by the empirical results of the theory. Perhaps some will find it too revisionary, but it is hard to see how a non-question begging problematic standard can be given.

TWO FINAL PROBLEMS WITH MY PROPOSAL

I offer the above thesis only as a sketch of a reply to the issues of presentism's relationship to STR. I think there are several pressing philosophical concerns to be dealt with; however, my goal was to show that they were worth the effort. I take it that if a theory was fundamentally incompatible with such a key scientific theory as STR that it ought to be a philosophical non-starter. If it is a theory that is at least compatible with some non-radical interpretation of STR then the other philosophical concerns may be worth dealing with. There are two additional criticisms concerning my attempt to show the compatibility of presentism with STR; criticism of the connection between the two and not of presentism itself.

The first is that my approach is simply an instrumentalist approach.[61] In taking a relationalist view of time what I am actually doing is being an antirealist about spacetime and in continuing to affirm the empirical consequences of STR, I am treating it strictly as an instrument for generating empirical results and not something that tells us about the structure of reality. I think there is some substance to this claim; however, I would

---

61. This point was raised by Alan Rhoda in the presentation of a prior version of this paper. My instrumentalism may not be as obvious in the body of the paper as I have tried to make changes through out to enable me to best deal with his insightful comment.

like to show that even if I am being an instrumentalist my instrumental-ism has some significant differences to ordinary instrumentalism. As a set up for my reply I would like to point out that a critical issue assumed throughout the paper is that what might look like a strictly a scientific theory may have built into it metaphysical assumptions.[62] One of the val-ues that philosophy brings to the scientific endeavor is to uncover those assumptions and hold them up to philosophical scrutiny. While it can be difficult to distinguish between empirically grounded conclusions and those rooted in metaphysical assumptions,[63] the ontological commitments of Minkowski spacetime seem to be an obvious case of the intermingling of the two. If Minkowski spacetime is to be understood as asserting the existence of an eternalist universe, as a theoretical result that is empiri-cally established (that is a result of the evidence given by the theory), then it is wrong—that is, this is not an empirical result. The other option is that Minkowski's spacetime substantivalism is not strictly speaking a scientific theory, but a philosophical one. If we are to treat Minkowski spacetime as an empirical theory, that is limit the view to its empirical contents and empirically verifiable results, then the step from its empirical success to an eternalist universe is a philosophical move and needs to be defended on philosophical grounds.[64] I think this is the best way to understand the theory and as such when I reject the eternalist universe view commonly associated with Minkowski spacetime I see no grounds for the claim that in doing so I am putting forward views that are at odds with the best phys-ics. Perhaps when we do this we are at odds with the easiest philosophical implications of the best physics, but that, it seems to me is a very different claim to me and one that I do not see adequate grounds to accept.

62. Sklar's brief book on the philosophy of scientific theories elegantly makes this point. Lawrence Sklar, *Theory and Truth: Philosophical Critique within Foundational Science* (Oxford: Oxford University Press, 2000).

63. In his text Sklar argues that virtually all empirical conclusions from science are deeply intertwined with philosophical commitments and assumptions.

64. It has been pointed out that I seem to assume that the scientific and philosophical parts of a theory are discrete and can be separated. I do not mean to imply this nonethe-less there seem to be conceptual features of many scientific theories that extend beyond the empirically testable features of those theories. One of the primary reasons for taking STR seriously is that scientists have established may of its empirically testable claims. With any theory I think such support should be taken seriously while at the same time realizing that this success does not establish the conceptual elements of the theory. This is nothing more than a variation on the problem of the under determination of the data for a theory.

This may seem to be a defense of instrumentalism; however, I would rather defend the claim that, at worst, I am doing something only similar to typical instrumentalism and at best I am not being an instrumentalist at all. First, I think what I am doing is substantially different from being an instrumentalist. What we might call "classical instrumentalism," says something like this: the entities that the theory posits, but which are not empirically verifiable, need not be granted existential status. Rather we are merely supposing their existence in order to get the results. The fact that we get empirically verifiable results should not be taken as evidence for the existence of these non-empirical entities. In the "classical case" the theoretical entities in question are assumed in order to get the results. Given that Einstein was able to work out most of STR before Minkowski worked out the four vector spacetime there is something importantly different about this case. As I have argued for it above, the situation goes more like this: the theory works to get us a variety of valuable results— granted. The theory shows there is no point or plane of simultaneity that is not relative to some inertial frame and there is (and can be) no empirical ground to prefer one inertial frame to another—granted.[65] The theory shows there is a relationship between spatial contraction and temporal dilation—granted. This is taken to imply the result that space and time form a continuous whole, that is, eternalism—not granted. Here it is the metaphysical implication—the ontological structure of spacetime—that is at issue. This structure is not needed nor assumed in order to get the results, the way electrons are assumed. Instead the ontological status of the manifold is taken as an implication of the theory. Furthermore, I have argued that it is a philosophical implication as opposed to an empirical result and an unwarranted philosophical implication at that.[66] If this is correct then the charge of instrumentalism is misdirected.

It might be argued that while the facts given above do represent the historical development, this does not represent the thinking of physicist.[67] As physics is now taught the spacetime manifold operates far more like

65. Even this is now being disputed. See note 50. I here ignore these developments to give the stronger argument.

66. By unwarranted I do not mean to imply that I have shown it to be false. All I hope to have shown is that there are non-radical interpretations of STR that are consistent with some forms of presentism.

67. Not only might it be argued, but it was argued by Jeff Koperski in personal conversations on the matter.

electrons in atomic chemistry; the manifold is assumed in order to develop the results. If this is accurate two responses seem relevant. First, it is in cases of just this sort that instrumentalism seems most justified. When we know the results can be achieved without making the use of the theoretical entities (be they electrons or spacetime manifolds), but it is convenient to posit entities to enable us to more easily obtain the results as philosophers of science we should be asking whether instrumentalism is a rational approach to take. Second, in this case it still seems to me I am not a typical instrumentalist because I accept the results of STR as telling us something about the nature of spacetime. This was the point about trying not to offer a 'radical' solution. I am rejecting some of the conclusions that have been offered as going along with STR, but I am not arguing that the theory tells us little or nothing about reality or that it merely describes how things will appear to us under certain conditions. Hence even if what I am doing can be construed as similar to instrumentalist interpretation of other physical theories, I think it should not be thought of as being 'radical' in the same way that instrumentalist theories are often thought of as radical. In fact, I don't think this view should be thought of as radical at all. If it is radical it should be viewed as a radical metaphysical hypothesis; however, I think it is the more intuitive view and as such the view that should be held unless there are significant grounds for its rejection.

The final problem is what we will call the Copernican analogy problem. The criticism goes something like this: eternalism is to STR as the heliocentric universe was to Copernicus' planetary model. His model didn't just make it easier to calculate planetary movement, that ease indicated something about the actual motion and distribution of the heavenly bodies. By analogy the eternalism of Minkowski spacetime doesn't merely make relativity calculations more accessible, but in doing so it is indicating something about the actual nature of the spacetime manifold. Sure you can get pretty good results with a rightly modified geocentric model, but why would you want to? And sure you can get by as you have outlined above, but again why would you want to? You are sticking to an outdated metaphysic while trying to keep up with science. Perhaps this is right. But there are some important things going on here. For example, the contribution the geometry makes when interpreted as giving the causal possibilities of past and future interactions can easily be embraced as telling us the empirical constraints of a theory. This can be done without also embracing eternalism or the four-dimensionalism of full-blooded eternalism. So I am not rejecting the connection between the theory and the world in quite the same way as someone holding on to the geocentric universe. Furthermore, eternalism it seems to me is a longer philosophical stretch with less valuable results then the heliocentric move was. The claim that the earth orbited the sun was not empirically testable at the time but it was at the very least theoretically possible to test. Eternalism on the other hand has no indication that it has this feature. Second, like the heliocentric model it may well be that in time more adjustments to the model can be made which strengthen its claim to be descriptive and not merely pedagogically valuable. The current trajectory of eternalism's relationship to relativity theory would indicate otherwise. The implications from quantum mechanics and from the promising interpretations of GTR, indicate at best the ontological status of the spacetime manifold as given in STR is a useful tool and at worst it leads to wrong conclusions.[68] At this time now then both the Copernican criticism and the general claim that presentism is undermined by relativity theory are not adequate grounds to reject presentism.

68. I refer here to quantum gravity, quantum entanglement, the hole argument and to neo-Lorentzian interpretations of GTR which require the existence of absolute simultaneity.

6

Open Theism and the Metaphysics of the Space-Time Manifold[1]

DEAN ZIMMERMAN

INTRODUCTION

IN THIS PAPER, I sketch the contours of recent metaphysical debates about the nature of time, and show that Open Theists are committed to taking sides in this debate; they ought to accept some version of what are called "tensed theories" or "A-theories" of time. I also claim that the best version of the A-theory of time is presentism. I then consider how an Open Theist should respond to one of the most frequently cited objections to presentism: that it is inconsistent with a successful scientific theory, namely, Relativity. The version of Relativity most often mentioned in criticisms of presentism is Special Relativity (henceforth, "SR"—to be distinguished from General Relativity, henceforth, "GR"). On the face of it, SR implies that simultaneity is relative to inertial frames of reference. But presentists cannot easily admit that what is *present* could be a relative matter. Since A-theorists must hold that some events are all present together if and only if they are simultaneous with one another, presentists would seem to be committed to absolute simultaneity, and therefore to

1. This paper includes some passages from "Presentism and the Space-Time Manifold," in *The Oxford Handbook of Time*, ed. Craig Callender (Oxford: Oxford University Press, 2010); and "The A-Theory of Time, Presentism, and Open Theism," in *Science and Religion in Dialogue*, ed. by Melville Stewart (Malden, MA: Blackwell, 2010). The incorporated material is reprinted by kind permission of the publishers.

the overthrow of a scientific theory on metaphysical grounds—always a dangerous maneuver.

I shall try to show that the argument against presentism from SR is not nearly as strong as critics claim. Part of the problem is supposed to be that a presentist could not attribute Minkowskian metrical structure to space-time—the metric ascribed to the manifold by SR. I find a critic and a defender of presentism—Craig Callender and William Lane Craig, respectively—both arguing that, in circumstances otherwise favoring SR, the presentist ought rather to be a Lorentzian about space-time structure. On their view, a presentist must posit a Newtonian space-time in which the contractions of rods and slowing of clocks prevents our discovering the facts about absolute sizes and periods. William Lane Craig's argument depends upon an assumption Open Theists must accept: namely, that God is in time, sustaining the universe from moment to moment, aware of what events are truly present. I argue that neither Callender nor Craig has shown that a presentist Open Theist could not accept SR. But I also raise doubts about the significance of arguments against presentism based on SR, given the fact that SR proves to be only approximately true of our space-time.

A-THEORY VS. B-THEORY

It is a sign of McTaggart's stature that even one of his worst arguments includes enough insightful analysis to make it the natural starting point for almost all subsequent discussion of the topic. He gave the name "A-series" to "that series of positions which runs from the far past through the near past to the present, and then from the present through the near future to the far future, or conversely"; and the name "B-series" to "[t]he series of positions which runs from earlier to later, or conversely."[2] McTaggart's labels have stuck, and been put to further use. The "determinations" (his word), or properties, *being past*, *being present*, and *being future* are generally called the "A-properties." The relations of *being earlier than*, *being later than*, and *being simultaneous with*, are the "B-relations."

The deepest metaphysical divide among philosophers who argue about time falls between *A-theorists* and *B-theorists*. The former believe in

---

2. J. T. E. McTaggart, *The Nature of Existence: Vol. 2* (Cambridge: Cambridge University Press, 1927) sec. 306; and P. van Inwagen and D. Zimmerman, eds., *Metaphysics: The Big Questions*, 2nd ed. (Malden, MA: Blackwell, 2008) 68.

some sort of objective distinction between what is present, what is past, and what is future. Although A-theorists disagree about the exact nature of the differences among the three categories, they agree that the present is distinguished from past and future in a way that is not relative to any other temporal thing, such as a context of utterance, a time, or a frame of reference.[3] B-theorists deny the objectivity of any such a distinction.

Sometimes A-theorists are called "tensers" because they "take tense seriously"; while B-theorists are "detensers" who, by implication, don't (perhaps they laugh tense in the face). I think the most natural way to understand the claim that tense must be taken seriously is as the claim that the most fundamental truth-bearers correspond to tensed sentences— they are not the kinds of things that are eternally true or eternally false. And this is not the same as what I have called the A-theory, since one can hold the view while insisting that, really, all times are on the same footing, there is no particular one that is objectively special.

This remains true even when seriousness about tense is given a metaphysical reading in terms of propositions: Many think that the sentences we write down and utter are true or false in virtue of their relations to *propositions* that are true or false in some more basic sense. A proposition is something that can be expressed in many different ways; it can be believed by one person and disbelieved by another; and, at least in the case of a proposition that isn't about a particular sentence or thought, it would have existed and been either true or false even in the absence of all sentences or thoughts. This familiar conception of the ultimate bearers of truth and falsehood[4] can be conjoined with a tensed or a tenseless theory about the nature of the proposition. On a tensed construal, a proposition's being true is not typically a once-and-for-all thing. The sentence "I am

---

3. There are some friends of tense logic and tensed truth who are not A-theorists in my sense: namely, those who claim that the present *is* relative to a frame of reference. See, for example, H. Stein, "On Relativity Theory and Openness of the Future," *Philosophy of Science* 58 (1991) 147–67, and W. Godfrey-Smith, "Special Relativity and the Present," *Philosophical Studies* 36 (1979) 233–44. I am unclear, however, what is left of the thesis that the present is in any sense *metaphysically* privileged on such a view. Unless existence itself were to be relativized to observers or frames of reference (a doubtful proposition), two of the most widely held A-theories could not be held in conjunction with a relativization of the present—namely, "presentism" and "the growing block theory," described below.

4. It can be found in Bolzano, Frege, Church, Chisholm, and Plantinga, to name but a few.

bent" could now be used by me to express a true proposition; but the proposition in question hasn't always been true, and it won't continue to be true for very long. A tenseless account of propositions, on the other hand, takes them to be like statements made using tenseless verbs: they are not the kinds of thing that can be true for a while and then become false, or vice versa, merely because of the passage of time.

The competition between the tensed and tenseless approaches to the fundamental bearers of truth gives rise to a familiar dispute over the importance of "tense logic." Logic is (or at least includes) the attempt to describe the most general patterns of truth-preserving inference. If the things that are true and false can be true though they *have been false,* or are *about to become false,* then some of the patterns of inference logicians should be interested in will involve temporal notions. On the tensed conception of truths, it is a question of logic whether, for example, the proposition: It will be the case that I am bent, implies the proposition: It was the case that it will be the case that I am bent. Thus, relations like being true simultaneously, and being true earlier or later than, will turn out to be, at least in part, logical notions.[5] On the other hand, those who take truth-bearers to correspond to tenseless statements will regard this as a blunder: temporal relations are for science and (perhaps) metaphysics to explore; but they are not part of the subject matter of logic.[6]

I do not think that "taking tense seriously" in this sense has much metaphysical significance—at least not until some heavy-duty metaphysical assumptions are added. For one might insist that the source of the ineliminability of tensed propositions is simply the fact that much of what we believe is "perspectival," in the same way first person propositions are: Believing what I would express by saying "I am the one to blame" is different than believing what *anyone* could express by saying "Zimmerman is the one to blame" (I might believe the former but not the latter, because I have amnesia and do not remember my name). But it does not follow that I am special, different from everyone else. Similarly, one cannot derive that any time is special from the fact that there is a difference between knowing that it is raining *now,* and knowing that it is raining at such-and-such

5. See A. N. Prior, *Papers on Time and Tense,* ed. Per Hasle, Peter Ohrstrom, Torben Braüner, and Jack Copeland (Oxford: Oxford University Press, 2003) 7–19, "The Notion of the Present," *Studium Generale* 23 (1970) 245–48, and "Some Free Thinking About Time," in J. Copeland, ed., *Logic and Reality* (Oxford: Clarendon, 1996) 47–51.

6. G. Massey, "Temporal Logic! Why Bother?" *Noûs* 3 (1969) 17–32.

time (for any name or description of the time). One might instead simply conclude that some propositions are equivalent to properties of persons, or times. *Sub species aeternitatis,* there are merely a host of equally real people located at equally real times within the four-dimensional block of space-time.

Although taking tense seriously may not require an A-theory, A-theorists must be serious tensers. Without fundamental truth-bearers that can pass from true to false and back again, whatever objective feature an A-theorist associates with being present would be frozen in place!

I have claimed that seriousness about tense alone does not make one an A-theorist. One way to "beef up" seriousness about tense in order to reach a genuine A-theory of time would be to utilize an objective—i.e., not-relative-to-anything—truth-predicate, and to apply it to propositions that are only temporarily true. Let me sketch how this would go.[7] A serious-tenser treats the proposition that Zimmerman is sitting as a possible object of propositional attitudes, one that is true-relative-to some times but not others. If she also insists that, in addition to all these relative truth relations, it has the property of being just flat out *true*, she has managed to turn mere seriousness about tense into a genuine metaphysical doctrine about the nature of time. As shall appear, we Open Theists are committed to the objective truth of some temporarily true propositions, and so we qualify as A-theorists, no matter what else we might say about the differences between past, present, and future things and events.

PRESENTISM AMONG THE A-THEORIES

A-theorists offer a number of very different accounts of the objective distinctions they all posit between past, present, and future. Arthur Prior held a view that is sometimes called "presentism," the thesis that only what is present exists or is real, that "the present simply *is* the real considered in relation to two particular species of unreality, namely the past and the future."[8] I find this, in many ways, the most appealing of all the A-theories; as do Trenton Merricks, Ned Markosian, John Bigelow, Peter Ludlow, Tom Crisp, Bradley Monton, Craig Bourne, and others.

---

7. I explore these questions in more detail in D. Zimmerman, "The A-theory of Time, the B-theory of Time, and 'Taking Tense Seriously,'" *Dialectica* 59 (2005) 401–57.

8. A. N. Prior, "The Notion of the Present," *Studium Generale* 23 (1970) 245–48.

Other A-theorists offer non-presentist accounts of the distinction between past, present, and future. Perhaps the most popular alternative to presentism is the "growing block" view of time defended by C. D. Broad[9] and, more recently, in rather different forms, by Robert Adams[10] and Peter Forrest.[11] On their view, both past and present events exist, present events differing from past ones only in that there are (for the time being) no events later than them. Being present is, then, a matter of being among the latest things to have come into existence. For Broad, that is *all* there is to being present. Adams and Forrest, however, hold a more plausible view: that things and events change in important ways when they are no longer on the cutting edge. Pains, for instance, are no longer really happening when they are wholly in the past.

Still another sort of A-theory accepts the existence of past *and future* things and events. On such a view there is something special about what is present, some primitive property or perhaps more complicated feature that events have if and only if they are present; but future and past events and things are just as much a part of "the furniture of the world" as present events and things.

C. D. Broad introduced the concept of the "bull's-eye" to characterize this type of theory:

> We are naturally tempted to regard the history of the world as existing eternally in a certain order of events. Along this, and in a fixed direction, we imagine the characteristic of presentness as moving, somewhat like the spot of light from a policeman's bull's-eye traversing the fronts of the houses in a street. What is illuminated is the present, what has been illuminated is the past, and what has not yet been illuminated is the future.[12]

There is more than one way to understand the change in events as they become or cease to be present. McTaggart described a version

9. C. D. Broad, *Scientific Thought* (London: Routledge & Kegan Paul, 1923).

10. R. M. Adams, "Time and Thisness," in *Midwest Studies in Philosophy: Volume 11*, ed. P. French, T. Uehling, and H. Wettstein (Minneapolis: University of Minnesota, 1986) 315–29.

11. See P. Forrest, "The Real but Dead Past: A Reply to Braddon-Mitchell," *Analysis*, 64 (2004) 358–62; "General Facts, Physical Necessity, and the Metaphysics of Time," in Dean W. Zimmerman, ed., *Oxford Studies in Metaphysics, Volume 2* (Oxford: Oxford University Press, 2006) 137–52.

12. C. D. Broad, *Scientific Thought* (London: Routledge & Kegan Paul, 1923) 59.

of the view that takes the moving spotlight of "presentness" to be a property events gain or lose without undergoing any other significant changes. Quentin Smith accepts (and Timothy Williamson seems also to advocate)[13] a quite different kind of moving spotlight theory. Smith admits that past and future individuals and events, although no longer or not yet present, nonetheless exist.[14] But as Smith's things and events pass from being future to present to past, they change in more than just their "A-determinations"—i.e., their presentness, or their degree of pastness or futurity. Things and events are not located anywhere in space until they are present; when past, they again become nonspatial, though of course it remains true that they once occupied space. And presumably, many other empirically detectable properties come and go in this way—although exactly which properties are permanent and which come and go is a nice question.

Of the three options, most A-theorists seem to plump for presentism. In this essay, I shall take it that presentism is the best A-theory going, and explore the fortunes of the Open Theist who accepts it.

There are reasons to worry about whether presentism can accommodate all the truths we think there are about the past. Can the presentist make sense of such simple truths as the proposition that there have been three kings named "George," without becoming committed to the existence of past kings? Can the presentist make sense out of states of motion without becoming committed to the existence of past space-time points? These are fascinating questions that presentists are still trying to answer. By my lights, the prospects are not so bad.[15] Here, I shall set aside problems about whether the presentist can *express* every fact she should like to express; and consider what many take to be an even more serious objection: that presentism conflicts with SR.

TENSED AND TENSE-NEUTRAL NOTIONS OF EXISTENCE

But first, I must offer a brief digression on a very natural question about the nature of the dispute between presentists and non-presentists. One

13. T. Williamson, 'Existence and Contingency', *Proceedings of the Aristotelian Society*, Suppl. Vol. 73 (1999) 181–203.

14. See Q. Smith, *Language and Time* (New York: Oxford University Press, 1993) esp. ch. 5.

15. See D. Zimmerman, "Presentism and the Space-Time Manifold."

might well worry about how to understand the presentist's use of "There are . . ." and "exist" in her characteristic claims, such as: "There are no past or future objects or events; such things do not exist." "There is . . . ," "there are . . . ," "there exists," and "there exist" all contain verbs that may be used in tensed and tenseless ways. Noting this fact, some have grown skeptical about whether there can be any substantive disagreement between presentists and those who accept the existence of whatever will or did exist. The skeptic is drawn along this line of thought:

If the verbs in these phrases are genuinely present tense, then a true sentence commencing with one of these phrases expresses a true proposition only if the condition specified by the rest of the sentence is satisfied by something that is, or exists, *now*. And the debate between presentists and others is in danger of disappearing. Suppose the presentist says, "There are no dinosaurs," and someone else says, "There are dinosaurs." If the presentist is using a semantically present-tense "are" and the other person is not, they are simply talking past one another.

As I see it, the best thing for a presentist to do in these circumstances is to insist that there is a common meaning of "There exists," etc. shared by presentist and non-presentist alike, but one that is *not* analytically tied to present existence. And then she can claim that she and her rivals disagree about what exists in this sense. I have defended this sort of view myself; and one may find it also in Ian Hinckfuss, Ted Sider, and Tom Crisp.[16] The idea is that contexts can be created in which "There is" means something utterly unrestricted, and contains no tincture of tense about it. For instance, one might try to create such a context by saying, in the philosophy seminar room (or printing, in a philosophy book): "Yes, but what is there *really*, what exists in the broadest sense, ignoring all pragmatic restrictions to just things of interest to humans?"

Call such a use of "existence" *tense-neutral*. Given a common tense-neutral notion of existing, presentist and nonpresentist can use it for the univocal expression of their ontological differences. And there is some reason for confidence in the success of this approach; at least, if it fails, ontology probably collapses altogether. Compare attempts to deflate disputes about what there is in the modal or the imaginary or the fictional realms.

16. I. Hinckfuss, *The Existence of Space and Time* (Oxford: Clarendon, 1975); T. Sider, "Quantifiers and Temporal Ontology," *Mind* 115 (2006) 75–97; T. Crisp, "On Presentism and Triviality," in Dean W. Zimmerman, ed., *Oxford Studies in Metaphysics, Volume 1* (Oxford: Oxford University Press, 2004) 15–20.

David Lewis famously believed that every possible way that things could be—every "possible world"—is a concrete entity, just as concrete as our own. Meinong (or at least some "Meinongians," like the very early Russell) claim that there are Golden Mountains and unicorns; it's just that they fail to do some other special thing, called "existing." Peter van Inwagen and others believe that there is such a thing as the Hound of the Baskervilles and the apartment at 221b Baker Street. Many of us disagree with at least one of these philosophers! If the rejection of Lewis's extravagant ontology is to be more than just a trivial truth, "There are no concrete possible worlds besides this one" must have a "there are" in it that isn't equivalent in meaning to "there are, in the actual world . . ." If that were all it meant, then Lewis could happily agree with us. If, in "There are no merely imaginary objects," "there are" means simply "there are within the realm of the non-imaginary . . . ," then again Meinong need not object. Likewise, "There are no merely fictional entities" must have a "there are" that means something besides "there are, outside of fiction . . ." If these debates cannot be so easily deflated, it seems unfair to insist upon the deflation of presentism.

OPEN THEISM AND THE A-THEORY OF TIME

The A-theorist posits an *objective* distinction between past, present, and future; there is a fact of the matter about what is *really* happening, and what is merely past or future, and this fact is not merely relative to a time. In order to maintain such a position, the A-theorist must hold that some of the most fundamental truths are only temporarily true—on pain of "freezing" the present at a single moment. Thus the A-theorist is committed to propositions (or whatever the fundamental truth-bearers are) that can change their truth-values.

Although there are subtleties involved, the reverse is plausibly true as well: One is automatically an A-theorist if one grants that the most fundamental things that can be assessed for truth and falsity include things that change their truth-values. Philosophers' favorite candidates for the most fundamental true and false things are *propositions*: language- and mind-independent entities that can serve as the meanings of declarative sentences and the objects of "propositional attitudes" like belief and doubt. A philosopher who allows that a proposition can pass from flat-out true to flat-out false—not merely true-relative-to-such-and-such-time, and false-relative-to-some-later-time—would seem to pass muster as an

A-theorist, whatever else she might believe; her temporarily true propositions draw an objective distinction between past, present, and future.[17]

Commitment to propositions that change truth-value is, then, tantamount to acceptance of the A-theory, so long as it is coupled with the
thesis that the sense in which these propositions are true is *objective*—
they are not merely true relative to a time or utterance or other temporal
index. Some philosophers allow that there *are* propositions that change
their truth-value; but they also insist that such propositions are all on a
par with respect to truth, each being true relative to certain times and not
others—e.g., some of these changeable propositions are true-at-noon-on-
December-5-1918, others true-at-noon-on-May-12-2525, etc.[18] Although
such philosophers allow for propositions that change from true to false,
they also insist that, among the true propositions, there are *eternally* true
ones that describe the entire history of the world, including eternally true
propositions ascribing truth-at-various-times to the changeable propositions. And they deny that, among the propositions that change truth-
value, some are *objectively* true, *simpliciter*. These philosophers might be
called "B-theorists in sheep's clothing."

Are Open Theists automatically A-theorists? That depends upon
how many theses one wants to bundle together under the heading "Open
Theism." Peter van Inwagen, for example, is an important intermediate
figure.[19] Although he is not an A-theorist, he defends a doctrine that is
central to Open Theism:

> *The Unknowability of Future Free Actions*: God cannot create
> genuinely free creatures and also know what they will do ahead
> of time.

However, unlike most, if not all, of the "openly" (i.e., self-identifying)
Open Theist authors, van Inwagen believes that there is a fact of the matter about what any free creature will freely do—a fact that God cannot
know until the creature's choice has been made. Most of us who accept the
label "Open Theist," however, subscribe to the following doctrine:

17. For a lengthy meditation on this theme, see D. Zimmerman, "The A-theory of
Time, the B-theory of Time, and 'Taking Tense Seriously,'" *Dialectica* 59 (2005) 401–57.

18. D. Lewis, "Attitudes *De Dicto* and *De Se*," *Philosophical Review* 88 (1979) 513–43.

19. See P. van Inwagen, "What Does an Omniscient Being Know about the Future?" in
Oxford Studies in Philosophy of Religion 1 (2008) 216–30, Richard Swinburne is another
important Christian philosopher who takes a similar approach; see R. Swinburne, *The
Coherence of Theism* (Oxford: Clarendon, 1977) chapter 10.

Absolute Omniscience: If a proposition is true, then God knows it.[20]

And from these two doctrines, it follows that propositions that, as a matter of fact, accurately describe a creature's free choices, were not true before the choices were made.

If there were eternally true propositions describing the free actions I shall perform tomorrow, God would have to know them, given Absolute Omniscience. But that is impossible, given the Unknowability of Future Free Actions. The Open Theist, then, must deny that any complete description of the future is true, so long as that description includes future free actions on our part. Propositions affirming that I freely do one thing rather than another, at some future date, cannot now be true. But some of them will, eventually, be true. So the Open Theist is committed to the thesis that some propositions do in fact change in truth value. These propositions cannot merely be true relative to some times and not others. If that were the case, an eternally true, complete description of the world would be available "in the background," and God would have to know it. So Open Theists are certainly *not* B-theorists in sheep's clothing. They affirm propositions that change their truth-values objectively; and that is tantamount to acceptance of the A-theory.

If, as I claimed earlier, the best version of the A-theory is presentism, Open Theists should be presentists. The two views fit well together; for one thing, the Open Theist has available a response to what is (alleged to be) one of the stronger arguments against presentism—the "Truthmaker" objection—and it is a response not available to presentists unless they believe in a necessarily absolutely omniscient God.

PRESENTISM AND THE SPACE-TIME MANIFOLD

Objections to presentism based on SR make use of the notion of a space-time manifold. So I begin my discussion with a description of the kinds of manifold posited by different physical theories; and some remarks about how a presentist should conceive of these manifolds.

20. I am papering over puzzles about omniscience. For example, Patrick Grim uses Cantor's power set theorem to argue that there cannot be a set of all truths; and then worries that God's knowing every true proposition would require that there be such a thing. See P. Grim, "Logic and Limits of Knowledge and Truth," *Noûs* 22 (1988) 341–66; and, for a reply, see K. Simmons, "On an Argument Against Omniscience," *Noûs* 27 (1993) 22–33.

The controversies over substantivalism and relationalism about *space* that exercised philosophers like Leibniz and Clarke were transformed during the twentieth century into a debate about the proper attitude to take towards a higher dimensional entity, space-time. A space-time manifold is a set of minimal-sized "points"—locations at which something could happen or be located. Physics (among other sciences) needs mathematically precise descriptions of spatial and temporal distances between the locations of events—and perhaps even between the locations of events and locations where *nothing* happens, if such there be. One may conceive of these distance relations in space and time as an intricate web connecting the parts of a four-dimensional manifold—an entity in its own right, in addition to the matter and events that are located at its points. Newton's version of a four-dimensional manifold is probably best thought of as a single three-dimensional space persisting through an infinite series of moments. A point within the manifold needs four numbers, three to pick out an eternally existing spatial location in substantival space, and a fourth to indicate a location in time; but this four-dimensional manifold is a constructed entity, built partly out of a more fundamental, three-dimensional manifold. Later physical theories have made use of four-dimensional manifolds that do not fall neatly into a combination of a three-dimensional space and a series of times at which the space, and all its parts, exist. Newton's absolute sameness of place appeared unnecessary to many natural philosophers; in classical mechanics, what matters is only whether a laboratory or group of objects is moving inertially—that is, undergoing no acceleration or deceleration—and not whether they are moving relative to some supposed absolute standard. Galilean space-time does away with persisting points in a persisting Euclidean space; in this respect, it resembles the space-time of SR.

The easiest way to see the challenge posed by SR is to creep up on it, by first describing Newtonian and Galilean space-time manifolds, and then seeing how SR's manifold differs from them. Newton's space-time consists of a persisting, infinite, three-dimensional Euclidean space together with the series of times at which it exists. These days, Newtonian space-time is often described, somewhat anachronistically, as a four-dimensional manifold of points, in which an objective relation of same-place-at-a-different-time holds between the points of an infinite series of Euclidean three-dimensional spaces. The presentation of Newtonian absolute space and time as a theory about the metrical structure of a four-dimensional manifold is useful, because it allows for easy comparison of the Newtonian theory with its rivals, some of which can *only* be construed as theories about a four-dimensional manifold.[21] Newton's four-dimensional manifold of possible event-locations falls neatly into a series of infinite, Euclidean, three-dimensional spaces, one for each time. In each of these spaces-at-a-time, the events that do (or could) happen at various points in the space are (or would be) simultaneous with one another. If space-time were a four-dimensional salami, Newton's would be of a sort that comes pre-cut, divided up into a series of simultaneity slices.

Galilean space-time rejects Newton's persisting three-dimensional space; it is like a series of three-dimensional Euclidean spaces strung out in a fourth, temporal dimension, with no fact of the matter about which points in one of these spaces represent "the same place again" as points in other spaces. Like Newton's manifold, this one, if it were salami, would be pre-sliced; it falls apart naturally into three-dimensional regions at which events are, or would be, simultaneous. Despite the absence of a persisting space that could provide objective facts about sameness of place, the different spaces nevertheless have some interesting built-in relations. Certain paths through the series of spaces are special—they are the paths that could be taken by an object in inertial motion, undergoing no acceleration or deceleration. The fact that these paths are special is represented geometrically by construing them as straight lines in the fourth, "time-like" dimension of the Galilean manifold. A set of objects, all moving inertially and maintaining their distance relations, can serve as a standard for whether other objects are moving inertially or not; if the speed of another object is constant, relative to these objects, it, too, is moving inertially. More abstractly, a family of parallel paths in the fourth, non-spatial dimension represents a possible family of inertially moving bodies, and constitutes a "frame of reference." In Galilean space-time, all frames are created equal; in Newtonian space-time, one is special: the frame of reference of Newton's substantival space itself.

21. Really, on Newton's view, space is a three-dimensional thing with parts, each of which persists through time. One can talk, if one likes, about a four-dimensional manifold of point-like "possible locations of events," and say that a series of these things are related by "same location"; but this relation is not truly fundamental on his theory. The place-time points standing in this relation are only so related because they coincide with the same part of a persisting three-dimensional space.

SR, like Galilean space-time, makes a fundamental distinction between the possible inertial paths, which are represented as straight lines in a time-like direction, and time-like paths that could only be taken by objects undergoing acceleration. Like Galilean space-time, a parallel set of such lines constitutes a frame of reference; and no one frame is special, so there is no return to Newtonian absolute sameness of place. In addition to the straight inertial paths, Minkowski space-time (the manifold of SR) contains straight "light-like" paths, representing the lines along which light would propagate in a vacuum. The most important thing about SR's manifold, for present purposes, is the fact that—unlike Newtonian or Galilean space-time—it does not break down into a single series of three-dimensional, Euclidean spaces. There are spatially straight lines and three-dimensional, Euclidean spaces embedded in Minkowski space-time. But there is not just one set of them. Minkowski space-time is like salami that has not been sliced ahead of time into a single series of three-dimensional spaces. One could cut it at various angles, dividing it up into a different series of three-dimensional, Euclidean spaces each time—though these slices would of course overlap with the slices made at other angles. The space-time of GR, which I shall largely ignore, is like SR as one looks at smaller and smaller regions; but, on the large scale, it can be bent in all sorts of interesting ways, and indeed *must* be bent wherever there are objects with mass.

How should an A-theorist, and in particular a presentist, think about these manifolds? First of all, there is no harm in treating them as substantivalists do—as a kind of "cosmic jell-o" filling the spaces between objects and suffusing their insides as well. On the face of it, both SR and GR are theories about the structure of a manifold of space-time points, and the ways in which massive objects interact with this entity. As many philosophers of physics have argued, space-time, as described by current physics, certainly seems to have an intrinsic structure or "shape" of its own. This is especially true in GR, according to which this structure both affects and is affected by the particles inhabiting it. Since GR is much more likely to be true than SR, and therefore more likely to be the real source of any conflict between physics and presentism, I shall interpret both versions of Relativity in this "realist" or "substantival" fashion.[22]

22. In a survey of the current state of the substantival-relational dispute, Tim Maudlin concludes that, given GR, substantivalism—or something near enough to it—is inevitable, since "[t]he set of all spatiotemporal relations between occupied event locations

THE PRESENTIST'S VERSION OF MINKOWSKI SPACE-TIME

How should a presentist think about the space-time distance relations between points that underwrite the structure of the relativistic four-dimensional manifold? The relations that are most important for causal purposes are positive and null space-time distance. They underlie space-time's role in telling particles and photons "what to do next." Where will a photon go if it is located at a certain point (and in a vacuum)? The sets of points that are on light-like paths (points each of which is at zero space-time distance from the others) tell a photon located at one of them to "stay on this line, in future." Where will a particle go if it is located at a certain point and moving inertially? The relativistic structure of the manifold implies that some points constitute "straight lines" with *positive* distance relations; their standing in this relation means that they tell a particle located at one of them, and not acted upon by any forces, to "stay on this line, in future." One might say that the points at zero-distance are connected by a relation of "light-like accessibility"; and that the straight lines with positive distances among their points are connected by a relation of "inertial accessibility." It is less clear to me how a presentist should think about space-time distance relations holding between "space-like separated" points (distances represented as negative numbers in most presentations of Special Relativity). I see no obstacle, in principle, to a simple approach: they are spatial distances among sets of points that constitute three-dimensional spaces. One of the surprising upshots of Relativity, no matter one's metaphysics, is that an instantaneous point can be part of more than one instantaneous, three-dimensional space.

The A-theorist must add something to the Minkowskian manifold. According to us, there is an objective fact about what is happening at present. On the presentist version of the A-theory, what is happening at present includes everything that is real, everything that exists. Much of reality has just come into existence, and much of what exists will soon

---

cannot generally provide enough information to uniquely settle the geometry of the embedding spacetime" ("Buckets of Water and Waves of Space: Why Space-Time is Probably a Substance," *Philosophy of Science* 60 [1993] 199). The relationalist needs a "plenum" of entities—a field of some kind—upon which to hang GR's web of spatiotemporal relations; and the best candidate is hard to distinguish from the substantivalist's space-time. It is easier to be a relationalist about Newtonian and Minkowskian space-time (though not so easy to be a relationalist about Galilean space-time); but this seems of little relevance to the current debate, since SR seems certainly false, and GR is either true or at least much closer to the truth.

pass away utterly. If Minkowski space-time is a manifold consisting of the set of locations at which events could happen, the present is a sort of "wave of becoming" that moves through this manifold. The Open Theist believes that God knows where this wave of becoming is located. Since she naturally thinks that the A-theory has always been and will always be true, she must think that there has always been and will always be a fact of this sort (continuously changing, of course); and the Open Theist believes that God has always known and will always know where the wave is located. For somewhat complicated reasons, given the way causation is supposed to work in Minkowski space-time, the location of the wave right now must be an infinitesimally thin slice of the manifold.[23] So the A-theory requires that the manifold come with a built-in division into a series of "slices," each consisting of the three-dimensional universe-at-an-instant, and accurately described by a set of propositions true only at that instant. Since Open Theism requires that God knows these propositions successively, God's time is, in effect, the time of this privileged division of the manifold.

But should the A-theorist—especially the *presentist* A-theorist—accept the existence of "past and future space-time points"? Here, there are alternatives. One approach would be simply to acquiesce in their existence. I do not see that "admitting them into our ontology," as the saying goes, would be terribly costly. They are theoretical entities the existence of which is implied by a successful, but in many ways surprising and unintuitive, physical theory.

Presentists have other options, however. If one takes for granted the metric structure of Minkowskian space-time, surrogates for past points can easily be constructed out of the points in the present slice—whatever its shape. For each past point, there is a region in the present slice of the manifold that contains all and only the points on the slice that were inertially or light-like accessible from the past point; the region in question is the presently existing slice of the point's forward light-cone. In SR, these regions could be used as descriptive names for each formerly-filled, now non-existent space-time point—each such point has exactly one point-surrogate in the presently existing slice. So long as there is a well-grounded, presently obtaining fact about which collections of points constitute point-surrogates, the current geometry of the present slice will include

---

23. See D. Zimmerman, "Presentism and the Space-Time Manifold."

enough information to recover all the facts about which past space-time points constituted inertial and light-like paths. For every presently existing point *p* and every inertial or light-like path, a particle could have taken that leads up to *p*, there is a unique set of point-surrogates consisting of all and only the surrogates for points on that path. In Minkowskian space-time, that is all the metrical structure there is.

Another important question about an A-theorist's attitude to Minkowski space-time is this: What is the real nature of the dimension labeled "time-like"? The wave of becoming occupies different locations along this time-like dimension of the manifold at different times. If these locations really were separated by *time*, by temporal distances, then there would be two temporal dimensions—time and hyper-time.

Fortunately, there is no reason to treat the time-like dimension of the manifold as a genuinely temporal one. The manifold is a theoretical entity with a job to do. Close consideration of that job will reveal the nature of this fourth-dimension. The manifold is a space of possible event-locations, one dimension of which has a direction to it, the direction in which things will tend to go over time. The points along a line in that direction are not literally related by relations of earlier and later; they are related by inertial and light-like accessibility.

THE OBJECTION TO PRESENTISM BASED ON SR

Hilary Putnam, Ted Sider, and others have claimed that presentism is inconsistent with SR, and that this constitutes a conclusive refutation of presentism.[24] Based on conflict with SR, Putnam concludes that "the problem of the reality and the determinateness of future events is solved . . . by physics and not by philosophy."[25] According to Sider, the argument that SR and presentism are inconsistent "is often (justifiably, I think) considered to be the fatal blow to presentism."[26] In the remainder of this paper, I respond to their claims on behalf of the presentist Open Theist.

Putnam (rightly, by my lights) attributes to "the man on the street" a combination of views that amounts to presentism: "All (and only) things

24. See H. Putnam, "Time and Physical Geometry," *Journal of Philosophy* 64 (1967); T. Sider, *Four-Dimensionalism* (New York: Oxford University Press, 2001) 42–52; Mellor endorses the objection, although he does not regard it as his main argument against the A-theory, D. H. Mellor, *Real Time II* (London: Routledge, 1998) 55–57.

25. H. Putnam, "Time and Physical Geometry," *Journal of Philosophy* 64 (1967) 247.

26. T. Sider, *Four-Dimensionalism* (New York: Oxford University Press, 2001) 42.

that exist *now* are real"—and he insists that, by "real," we ordinary people-in-the-street do not mean something merely relative, so that what is real-to-me might not be real-to-you; we mean to be talking about a transitive, symmetric, and reflexive equivalence relation, one that holds between events currently happening to us and at least some other events happening elsewhere, to other things—including events happening to things in motion relative to us.[27] He then assumes that this equivalence relation must by "definable in a 'tenseless' way in terms of the fundamental notions of physics." But the metric of a Minkowskian space-time does not include a relation that fits the bill—one that will carve the manifold into equivalence classes of co-present points in a way that does not look "accidental (physically speaking)."[28] "Simultaneity relative to coordinate system *x*," for some arbitrarily chosen inertial frame of reference, will provide an equivalence relation, alright; but there are infinitely many coordinate systems to choose from, and nothing physically special about just one of them. No other relations look any more promising.[29] So Putnam concludes that presentism is inconsistent with SR, and alleges that this inconsistency proves presentism's falsehood.

Sider offers an argument that is similar to Putnam's, at least in its overall thrust. After running through all the ways a presentist might try to define the shape of the present in terms of the manifold's Minkowskian geometry, Sider concludes that the presentist has little alternative but to suppose that the present effects a foliation that is "arbitrary"—that is, one not "distinguished by the intrinsic geometry of Minkowski spacetime."[30] But positing such a thing is "scientifically revisionary"; if presentists take this route, "[a] physical theory of time other than special relativity must be constructed."[31]

I have responded to this line of argument in more detail elsewhere. Putnam and Sider seem to be claiming that presentism would require that SR be overturned; that presentism is inconsistent with SR for the same

27. Putnam, "Time and Physical Geometry," 240–41; Putnam does not, in his argument, emphasize the need for symmetry in the "real-for" relation; but, as Saunders points out, Putnam pretty clearly does, and should, assume its symmetry S. Saunders, S. "How Relativity Contradicts Presentism," *Philosophy of Science* 67 (2002) 282.

28. H. Putnam, "Time and Physical Geometry," *Journal of Philosophy* 64 (1967) 241.

29. Ibid., 242–43.

30. T. Sider, *Four-Dimensionalism* (New York: Oxford University Press, 2001) 47.

31. Ibid., 52.

kind of reason that classical or Newtonian mechanics is inconsistent with SR. To see whether their claim is justified, one needs some sense of what such inconsistency amount. Not just any supposition that privileges a foliation qualifies as rejection of SR. After all, different distributions of matter will privilege different foliations; but merely positing material contents within a Minkowskian manifold would not be thought inconsistent with SR. There is a criterion for inconsistency with SR that actually seems to be used by physicists and philosophers of physics when they consider, for example, whether various versions of quantum theory can be made consistent with SR; and it is roughly this: A theory is inconsistent with SR if it includes laws that appeal to structural features of the manifold that go beyond the Minkowskian metric. Must the A-theorist's wave of becoming introduce such structure? Suppose the universe were, to all appearances, a Minkowskian manifold; but the material contents of the manifold select a foliation in some way—e.g., there is a unique center-of-mass frame, which effects a foliation—and the wave of becoming successively occupies those slices because the distribution of matter distinguishes them. I argue that such a world represents a way for SR and the A-theory to be true together. Philosophers of physics generally admit that, if the special foliation needed by some interpretations of quantum theory could be tied to physically privileged foliation of this sort, quantum theory would be rendered consistent with SR; the presentist should be able to say the same.

To reach a hypothesis about the physical world that cannot be rendered compatible with the A-theory, one must stipulate not only that the manifold is Minkowskian, but also that: either no physical phenomenon distinguishes a foliation; or, if some does, it is not lawfully tied to the wave of becoming. But even in the absence of a physically privileged foliation to provide "rails" upon which the wave of becoming could run, there remains the possibility of laws governing its motion that do not advert to non-Minkowskian structure. Consider a metaphysical law of A-theoretic evolution of the following sort: the present must coincide with the planes of simultaneity of *some* frame of reference; but *which one* is not a matter of natural law, but a matter settled by contingent facts about the initial conditions of the universe. In that case, the *laws* governing the present would not single out any frame as special, and space-time's built-in structure would not be telling the wave of becoming where it has to go. The manifold's frames of reference constitute a perfectly democratic plurality; the deciding vote is cast not by spacetime, but by contingent facts about where in the manifold the universe happens to begin. I discuss this hypothesis in more detail elsewhere, insisting that it amounts, at most, to a borderline case of adding lawfully relevant, intrinsic structure to space-time.

PRESENTISTS AND LORENTZIAN SPACE-TIME

I have, abstractly, defended the possibility of laws governing the wave of becoming that do not violate SR's prohibition on intrinsically privileged frames of reference or other added space-time structure. But a prominent critic and a prominent defender of the A-theory have claimed that it is difficult or impossible to maintain the A-theory together with a Minkowskian theory of space-time. These authors seem to think that adding presentism, in particular, creates pressure to give up SR in favor of a neo-Lorentzian approach to the structure of space-time.

The dialectic here is a little tricky. Neither the critic nor the defender of the A-theory seem committed to the *truth* of SR, or to the empirical adequacy of neo-Lorentzian physical theories in our universe. So their claims require some subtle interpretation. Here is what I take to be the most charitable reading: *Even if*, contrary to fact, SR had turned out to be empirically adequate, meshing nicely with other physical theories; the A-theorist should *nevertheless* have rejected it in favor of a neo-Lorentzian account of space-time. The critic of presentism, Craig Callender, sees this as a serious strike against the view; the defender, William Lane Craig, argues that neo-Lorentzianism is attractive in its own right, and so regards commitment to it as an unproblematic consequence of the A-theory. How either of these claims should strike us, given the skepticism all parties seem to share concerning the empirical adequacy of SR, is a little mysterious. Presumably, Callender thinks that it is a strike against the A-theory that it *should* have led its defenders to adopt a physical theory with theoretical deficits *in these hypothetical circumstances*. And William Lane Craig apparently thinks that it is important, for the viability of the A-theory, that there would be no cost involved in being neo-Lorentzian, *in these hypothetical circumstances*. I am not sure I agree with either of these assumptions. But let that pass.

Would adding a presentist's privileged foliation to a space-time with Minkowskian metrical structure result in an unstable view, forcing presentists to reject Relativity in favor of a theory of motion like Lorentz's—a theory according to which the manifold of space-time has Newtonian metrical structure and there are forces that are "hidden" from us in a strangely conspiratorial way? If this is what presentism requires, it would be deeply revisionary, relative to an evidential situation that otherwise favored SR.

I disagree with their shared conviction that an A-theorist, in these hypothetical evidential circumstances, would have good reason to reject SR in favor of a neo-Lorentzian approach to space-time. Lorentz rejects the structure that Relativity posits, along with the explanations of motion made possible by that structure; and the presentist need not go so far as that. Here, by way of background, is a "potted" version of the development of Lorentz's view.

Lorentz knew that, when a flash of light is generated at a certain location, it spreads through space in a way that does not depend upon the speed of its source. Contrast a flash of light to a bomb. If a bomb explodes while moving rapidly toward me, sending shrapnel in all directions, the bits coming toward me will have a higher velocity than the bits moving away from me. The shrapnel from a stationary bomb exploding at the same place would, on the other hand, have the same velocity in all directions. But a flash of light from a moving bulb and a similar flash from a stationary bulb would not differ in this way. Each flash would spread out from the point of origin in the same way—rather like the waves from a pebble dropped or thrown in still water, which spread out at the same speed in every direction, no matter which direction the pebble was moving when it struck the surface. Now, in the case of the pebbles and waves, only people in boats that are stationary relative to the water will find that all the waves are moving at a constant rate away from their point of origin. Those in a stationary boat north of the place where the pebble was dropped will find the north-going wave front coming towards them just as quickly as the south-going wave front is moving away from them. But compare such a boat with one that is moving from the north toward the source of the waves, and that has the same velocity, relative to the water, as the waves themselves. People in this boat will find the north-going waves striking their bow more rapidly; and they will find that the south-going waves directly opposite them are stationary relative to their boat—the south-going waves and the south-going boat maintain a constant distance.

Prior to the formulation of Special Relativity, scientists naturally assumed that light and objects in motion would behave much like waves and boats. There would be just one state of motion that a laboratory could be in that would allow its instruments to measure the rate of propagation of light as being the same in all directions. If light were a wave propagated through a medium of some sort, the objects in such a laboratory would be stationary relative to that medium. The measuring devices in other laboratories, in motion relative to the *truly* stationary laboratory, were expected to measure the speed of light as higher in some directions than others. The objects in the stationary laboratory—together with any other objects, anywhere in the universe, that were stationary relative to them— should constitute a privileged frame of reference. If a thing were in the same position at different times, relative to *these* objects, then it would have a special status. In this way, the behavior of light was expected to privilege just one relation of "same-place-at-a-different-time"; and space-time would come with the sort of built-in structure that Newton posited.

Surprisingly, as a matter of empirical fact, it turns out that light appears to propagate at a constant rate in all directions, no matter one's state of motion. What could this mean? Lorentz believed that the appearance must be misleading; and he supposed it was caused by fluctuations in the sizes of measuring devices and in the behavior of clocks when they are in motion relative to objects in the privileged frame—the set of objects relative to which the speed of light is truly constant in all directions. So why is it that the equipment in a laboratory moving rapidly (relative to the privileged frame of reference) toward some light source does not measure the speed of light as faster than the equipment in a laboratory at rest in the privileged frame? Lorentz's hypothesis was that the clocks in the moving laboratory have slowed down and the distances among the parts of its instruments have shrunk. The clocks and instruments in the stationary laboratory do not undergo these effects. Light from the source really is moving toward one of the laboratories at a higher speed, but there is no way to tell which lab it is; the contractions and time dilations seem precisely designed to conceal this information.

Special Relativity provides a very different style of explanation for the apparent constancy of the speed of light in all frames of reference, and the contractions and time dilations that seem to occur within an inertial frame in motion relative to one's own. Special Relativity, like Newtonian physics, makes ineliminable reference to a manifold with a built-in structure that plays a big role in explaining why objects move as they do. The structure they attribute to the manifold is, however, very different from that of Newtonian space-time. The structure of the Newtonian manifold, as I described it earlier in four-dimensional terms, is based upon three fundamental types of relations among points: (i) spatial distance relations within each momentary three-dimensional space, (ii) temporal distance relations between the points in different spaces, and (iii) a "same-place-at-a-different-time" relation between points in different momentary spaces. Special Relativity bases the structure of space-time upon a very different relation of "space-time distance"—one that leaves no room for (iii), and makes separable spatial and temporal distances between points seem second-rate, at least in the order of physical explanation.

In Minkowskian space-time, points can be separated by positive, negative, and null space-time distances. The meanings of these measurable quantities are closely tied to the explanations of motion that Relativity affords. Here are some of those connections.

Relations of space-time distance give a sense to "straight lines" in the manifold: a straight line in the space is the shortest distance between two points. What is Relativity saying about points when it says they lie along a straight line and stand in positive distance relations? Such a line has a "time-like" direction; and it corresponds to the possible path of a particle that is neither accelerating nor decelerating—an object in a state of "inertial motion". What does it mean to say that points within the manifold are at zero distance from one another? Not that they are "the same place" or "the same point." It means that they correspond to points along a path that light would take in a vacuum. What does it mean to say that points are on a straight line and standing in negative space-time distance relations? In that case, the line is "space-like"; it corresponds to a straight line in a three-dimensional region of the manifold—a region that looks like the-universe-at-an-instant.

Lorentz's theory and SR differ in the kinds of explanation they give for various phenomena. Suppose you are moving rapidly away from me; and suppose we are both moving inertially, and are isolated from outside influences. The trajectory you will appear to me to take in the future is, according to Lorentz, a function of your past velocity relative to the privileged frame and my past velocity relative to that frame, plus whatever forces are responsible for shrinking objects and slowing clocks (and other processes) in things that are in motion relative to the privileged frame. SR, on the other hand, explains our motion in terms of the straightness of our space-time paths and their places within the manifold, not in terms of our velocities relative to a privileged frame of reference. As unaccelerated objects, we have been traveling on "straight lines" in space-time; in the absence of forces, we will go on to occupy points along the same lines; and these lines are sharply divergent. Here, the structure of space-time (its straight lines and angles) is doing all the work of explaining why the objects do what they do. (If there were other forces at work, if we or the other object were undergoing acceleration or deceleration, more factors would come into play.) Movement of particles along geodesics, and of light along light-like paths, is assigned to the realm of the "kinematical" rather than the "dynamical"; these phenomena "are kinematical in the sense that the moving system is just exhibiting default spatio-temporal behavior."[32] The Lorentzian explanation, on the other hand, appeals both to the metrical structure of space-time (not the relativistic structure based on space-time distances, but Newtonian structure based on more familiar spatial and temporal relations) and to forces that produce spatial contractions and temporal dilations.

Lorentz's theory and Special Relativity would seem, then, to provide radically different kinds of explanations for some of the observed facts. They appeal to different kinds of structure within the space-time manifold; and Lorentz must posit various forces and effects not needed within Special Relativity.

For many reasons, Lorentzian theories are currently highly unpopular (to put it mildly). If the A-theory implied that space-time does not have anything like the structure SR uses to explain states of motion, but must instead have the Newtonian structure of Lorentz's space-time, the A-theory would be in serious danger of refutation by physics—*if* we were in an evidential situation which otherwise favored SR. Relativistic explanations of the motions of objects have many theoretical advantages over Lorentzian explanations (though Lorentz's actual theory is able to make the same observable predictions, by making suitable assumptions about the way everything is affected by motion relative to the absolute rest of the privileged frame).

The most objectionable feature of neo-Lorentzian theories is not that they posit some real contractions and time dilations, and other merely apparent contractions and time dilations. Rather, it is their inability to give the kinds of explanations of these relativistic effects that are available

32. M. Janssen, "Drawing the line between kinematics and dynamics in special relativity," unpublished manuscript (2009) 58.

within SR. Acceptance of a manifold with the structure of SR allows one to lump a certain class of motions together as the "default" states of motion for photons and for massive objects. When something moves along one of these straight lines of light-like or inertial accessibility, no dynamical explanation is needed—no forces need come into play, the explanation can be entirely kinematical. Apparent contractions and dilations follow from the structure itself. Lacking this structure, the neo-Lorentzian must offer explanations of the appearance of mutual contractions and dilations, while *being* forced to affirm that only some of them are real. This requires forces at work to hide the real frame.

The presentist who accepts SR is not in this position. Consider an analogy: a fanciful thought experiment involving physically inefficacious telepathy. Suppose that electrons are conscious; but that their consciousness has nothing to do with their states of motion, and has no physical effects. Mental changes do not change an electron's physical states, and changes in its physical states do not *directly* affect its conscious states—though the distance relations among electrons are relevant to their ability to communicate telepathically. These conscious electrons live in a manifold with the metrical structure described by SR, but can transmit thoughts at faster than light speed. However, it takes longer to communicate with electrons that are further away. There is one way of slicing the electrons' manifold that explains the speed of telepathy. If the laws governing telepathy are tied to a built-in structural feature of space-time itself, this phenomenon would be inconsistent with SR by the usual standards. If these laws were instead tied to some foliation privileged by the contingent material contents of space-time—for example, if the foliation associated with the center of mass of the universe somehow determined which electrons could telepathically affect which other electrons—then adding electron telepathy would not immediately violate SR. But, in either case, the "telepathically privileged foliation" has no effects upon the states of motion of the particles inhabiting this manifold. The space-time structure posited by SR can—and should—remain in place, doing its normal job in explanations of the electrons' motions.

Superluminal telepathy would not constitute a revolution in the theory of motion, so long as the metrical structure of space-time remains just as SR says. Neither would there need to be a revolution in the theory of motion, along neo-Lorentzian lines, if there were an A-theoretically privileged foliation.

Here is proof that the presentist could hardly be *forced* to become a Lorentzian simply by adding a preferred foliation. Lorentz's immobile, universal ether provided an absolute relation of sameness of place over time, effectively turning Galilean space-time into Newtonian space-time again. The ether serves as a privileged inertial frame; and the only way presentism could affect a return to Newtonian space-time would be by privileging an inertial frame—i.e., successively occupying the optical simultaneity slices of some inertial frame. But it need not do so. An argument can be given for the conclusion that the present must take the shape of a thin slice of the manifold, and that the series of co-present slices must constitute a foliation.[33] But I know of no argument concerning the shape of the A-theorist's present that requires that the events in a single slice must be optically simultaneous; for all the presentist cares, the foliation could consist of "nonstandard simultaneity slices," hypersurfaces that are not flat, three-dimensional, Euclidean spaces; they would not correspond to the planes of simultaneity associated with a particular inertial path through space-time. If the hypersurfaces were sufficiently irregular, the shortest path between two points on a slice might never consist entirely of points within the slice. In that case, no single inertial frame would be privileged. Adding a foliation that does not select an inertial frame to play the role of absolute Newtonian space could not constitute a return to Lorentz.

CALLENDAR AND CRAIG

The sense in which a presentist can accept SR can be illustrated by considering one of Craig Callender's arguments against the A-theory. Callender has two options to offer the A-theorist, should she happen to discover that she lives in what otherwise appears to be a Minkowskian world: (i) "[O]ne could adopt the empirically adequate Lorentzian interpretation", thereby rejecting SR on metaphysical grounds and returning to a Newtonian manifold that posits absolute space and absolute time. (ii) "Alternatively, we might keep the Minkowski metric but add more structure to spacetime. We might add a foliation, i.e., a preferred stacking of spacelike hy-

---

33. An argument I give elsewhere; see D. Zimmerman, "Presentism and the Space-Time Manifold."

persurfaces that divides the spacetime manifold. Becoming, then, could occur with respect to this preferred stacking".[34]

Callendar would like to saddle the A-theorist with the first option: "by far the best way for the tenser to respond to Putnam *at al.* is to adopt the Lorentz 1915 interpretation of time dilation and Fitzgerald contraction."[35] He does not, however, explain *why* he thinks the A-theorist should take this route, rather than taking his option (ii). And when, later on, he faults the A-theorist for having to retreat to Lorentz,[36] one begins to suspect that Callender's second alternative was the better of the two all along.

What does Callender think would be so bad about a Lorentzian approach to the physics of space-time? In Lorentz's Newtonian space-time, the Fitzgerald contraction looks like the work of forces shrinking objects in the direction of motion when they move rapidly relative to the ether, while their clocks slow down as well; from the point of view of such rapidly moving objects, objects at rest in the ether will look to be contracted and clocks to be temporally dilated, although this would be an illusion. As Callender sees it, the Lorentzian "introduces unexplained coincidences: why do those rods and clocks keep contracting and dilating, respectively? As a kinematical effect in Minkowski space-time, Minkowski space-time is a common cause of this behavior, which is otherwise brute in the Lorentzian framework."[37] It is simpler and more elegant to be able to regard the Lorentz invariance of laws governing many different kinds of forces as stemming from the same source, namely the structure of space-time.

But this the presentist can do, so long as she accepts the fundamentality of the Minkowskian metrical structure of her manifold. Its structural features—the straightness and space-time lengths of light-like and inertial paths, in particular—provide the kinematical background upon which dynamical theories can be erected. True, the presentist gives these structural properties a metaphysical gloss somewhat different from that of the ordinary B-theorist. But that need not amount to rejection of SR.

34. C. Callender, "Shedding Light on Time," *Philosophy of Science* (supplement) 67 (2000) S595–96.

35. C. Callender, "Finding 'Real' Time in Quantum Mechanics," in *Einstein, Relativity and Absolute Simultaneity,* ed. Williams Lane Craig and Quentin Smith, 52 (New York: Routledge, 2008).

36. Ibid., 67.

37. Ibid.

The presentist has the means to talk about every past space-time point, to ascribe properties to sets of them that satisfy the Minkowskian metrical description, and to construe this metrical structure as relevant to the motion of particles through the manifold in a way that certainly *sounds* just like the kind of relevance a B-theorist would ascribe to the properties of his Minkowskian manifold. Whatever differences there are between the way presentist and B-theorist understand the ontology of the manifold and the nature of the relations between points that give it metrical structure, I do not think they should be called scientific differences. It would be a stretch to insist that the laws of physics can only be interpreted as laws about the relations within a B-theorist's block; and that the trajectories in the A-theorist's manifold are clearly *not* what physicists are interested in describing.[38]

It is instructive to consider the case of grafting a preferred foliation onto an otherwise Minkowskian space-time for other reasons. Some interpretations of quantum theory require an objective, universe-wide relation of simultaneity that generates a foliation of the manifold. How radically would this alter one's physics? Here is Maudlin's assessment: "This would not demand the elimination of any relativistic structure, but would undercut the relativistic democracy of frames."[39] By not eliminating the manifold's structure—such as the facts about which time-like paths are straight and which are curved—the quantum theorist who takes this route would not be robbed of the explanatory resources of the Minkowskian manifold.

> . . . [N]o positive part of the relativistic account of space-time is being *rejected*: rather, in addition to the Lorentzian metric, a new structure is being *added*. Because of this, there is a straightforward sense in which no successful relativistic account of any physical phenomenon need be lost or revised: if something can be accounted for without the foliation, then one need not mention it. So there is no danger that existing adequate relativistic accounts of phenomena will somehow be lost: *in this sense, the content of relativity is not being rejected at all* [my italics].[40]

38. Here, I am responding to an interesting objection raised by William Lane Craig, in correspondence.

39. T. Maudlin, *Quantum Non-Locality and Relativity*, 2nd ed. (Malden, MA: Blackwell, 2002) 202.

40. T. Maudlin, "Non-Local Correlations in Quantum Theory: How the Trick Might Be Done," in *Einstein, Relativity and Absolute Simultaneity*, ed. Williams Lane Craig and Quentin Smith, 160 (New York: Routledge, 2008).

A presentist who takes her manifold, with its intrinsic structure, seriously can legitimately claim that, in an otherwise Minkowskian world, her added foliation would be no worse than the quantum theorist's; it would not rob her theory of the explanatory resources provided by SR.

William Lane Craig seems to agree with me that the A-theory does not, all by itself, prove to be inconsistent with SR, requiring a return to Lorentz. But when God's existence is added to the A-theory, an argument against SR emerges.

> It seems that God's existence in A-theoretic, metaphysical time and His real relation to the world would imply that a Lorentz-Poincaré theory of relativity is correct after all. For God in the "now" of metaphysical time would know which events in the universe are now being created by Him and are therefore absolutely simultaneous with each other and with His "now."[41]

Here is Craig's argument to illustrate "the difference God's existence makes for our conceptions of time and space:"[42]

1. God exists.
2. A tensed theory of time [i.e., a version of the A-theory] is correct.
3. If God exists and a tensed theory of time is correct, then God is in time.
4. If God is in time, then a privileged reference frame exists.
5. If a privileged reference frame exists, then a Lorentz-Poincaré theory of relativity is correct.[43]

If 5 is to be true, "reference frame" in 4 must mean "inertial frame." (Craig also believes that, in General Relativity, the presence of a kind of "cosmic time" provides a natural "frame" that corresponds to God's experience of time; but it is not an inertial frame, and privileging it would not amount to a return to a Lorentzian space-time with absolute sameness of position.) I have questioned 4, by supposing that the A-theorist's privileged foliation (and thus God's time) need not privilege an inertial reference frame, under the assumption of SR. Craig's argument for 4 is contained in this passage:

41. W. L. Craig, *Time and the Metaphysics of Relativity* (Dordrecht: Kluwer, 2001a) 173.

42. Ibid., 171.

43. W. L. Craig, *God, Time, and Eternity* (Dordrecht: Kluwer, 2001) 165.

The truth of (4) is based on God's privileged status; the events which He knows to be occurring now can be associated with some hypothetical reference frame which is preferred precisely because it is God's frame. In speaking of God's frame, I mean merely that it is the reference frame on whose associated hyper-plane of simultaneity at the time of any event on the world line of a hypothetical observer at rest in that frame lie those events which God in the "now" of metaphysical time knows He is then creating. Now it needs to be understood that we are speaking here in the context of SR, which posits a flat spacetime. . . . A discussion of God's relation to time within the context of GR may be reserved for the sequel; our present concern is with the flat spacetime of SR. Within this context, the events which God knows He is now causing all lie on a three-dimensional hyper-plane which is associated with some inertial frame.[44]

Here, Craig simply takes it for granted that the "now" of metaphysical time—the slice of the manifold in which God is directly creating new events—is a hyperplane associated with a particular inertial frame. He does not consider the possibility that it be a nonstandard simultaneity slice. (I have not found any further arguments for 4 in Craig's numerous books and articles about God and time.) If the A-theoretic foliation of a Minkowskian space-time consisted in a series of nonstandard slices, the privileging of the series could not be thought to restore Lorentz's absolute space-time.

Furthermore, even if God's frame did correspond to an inertial frame, that would not be incompatible with the manifold's having Minkowskian metrical structure; with explanations of motion being given in terms of that structure rather than in terms of the quite different Lorentzian scheme of absolute space, in which motion relative to absolute space causes spatial contraction and time dilation. The answer to Craig is the same as the answer to Callendar: the presentist can insist upon the fundamentality of the Minkowskian metrical structure of her manifold, and deny that it contains a Newtonian persisting space. The Minkowskian structural features—the straightness and space-time lengths of light-like and inertial paths, in particular—provide the kinematical background upon which dynamical theories are to be erected. The location of the A-theoretically privileged slicing is supposed to be a contingent matter; where it falls is a further interesting fact beyond the Minkowskian metric;

44. Ibid., 165–66.

but the latter can play its role in explaining the shapes of the paths taken by particles, no matter where the A-theorist's present may lie.

Choice of a single frame by the wave of becoming does give one set of distance relations among objects a special status, metaphysically; and Craig might see that as a vindication of Lorentz. But the presentist is able to explain the Fitzgerald contraction as "a kinematical effect in Minkowski space-time," and to regard a Minkowskian manifold as "common cause" of all frame-relative spatial contractions and time dilations, whether or not they are relative to God's frame. If the presentist insists that the Minkowskian metrical structure of her manifold is the real subject matter of SR, the presentist is in the same position as Maudlin's quantum theorist with a quantum-theoretically privileged foliation: the "old" Minkowskian explanations of various phenomena do not become inapplicable, merely because some additional structure has been posited.

CONCLUSION

Accepting the A-theory implies that there is something special about one way of slicing the manifold. Fortunately, the additional temporal structure does not automatically lead to a Lorentzian theory of space-time. The A-theorist need not deny that the metrical facts based on relativistic space-time distances are fundamental features of the manifold, and fundamental to explaining why particles and photons move as they do. The A-theorist must, however, deny that they constitute all the facts about spatiotemporal structure; there is, according to presentists and other A-theorists, a privileged foliation corresponding to the series of co-present time-slices.

Lorentz's theory is sometimes faulted simply for positing something we cannot discover by means of experiment. We A-theorists had better get used to that accusation, since it will dog us no matter what theory of space-time we adopt; that is the sort of argument to which I responded in the previous section. But I take it that the real costliness of Lorentz's view—for the A-theorist, at least—is its need to posit forces at work in some frames but not others. It is simpler and more elegant to be able to regard the Lorentz invariance of laws governing many different kinds of forces as due to a common origin, namely the structure of space-time.[45]

---

45. The advantages of such an explanation are defended in C. Callender, "Finding 'Real' Time in Quantum Mechanics," in *Einstein, Relativity and Absolute Simultaneity*, ed.

The presentist who adds a foliation to the manifold in which events occur, while affirming its fundamentally Minkowskian metrical structure, retains the right to draw the line between kinematics and dynamics exactly where it belongs on orthodox versions of SR; and this provides a sense in which "the content of Relativity is not being rejected at all"—to borrow Maudlin's description of the parallel case of the added quantum-theoretically privileged foliation.

Most criticisms of presentism based upon physics appeal to SR. This is somewhat odd, since SR is admittedly only approximately true; and, according to its successor, GR, the Special theory only gives an accurate description of a certain kind of empty space-time. Because its falsehood is granted, the cost of conflict with SR is not obvious. There is some justification for continuing to pit presentism against SR. The details of SR are more easily grasped and more familiar to philosophers; and the geometry of a space-time consistent with GR is similar to that of SR (approximating Minkowskian structure to an arbitrary degree around each point). It is an interesting exercise in hypothetical philosophico-theological cosmology to examine the ways in which the God of Open Theism might fit into a Minkowskian space-time. Solving this problem may suggest solutions to the question how such a God might interact with manifolds we take to be closer to our own; and an answer to the question is good to have in one's back pocket, on the off-chance that unforeseen scientific advances might call for a return to a uniform geometry more similar to SR than to GR. Still, the Open Theist should be more concerned with *live* theories.

Elsewhere, I argue for the compatibility of presentism and GR;[46] and I do not believe that adding God to the presentist's picture makes a significant difference to the defense of their compatibility. In the same place, I also point out that certain interpretations of quantum theory add their own privileged foliation, one that would *have* to coincide with the presentist's—at least, the two foliations must coincide, given the plausible A-theorist assumption that, if an event has already happened, it cannot be causally dependent upon events that are happening now. But all speculations about ways to combine presentism and extant physical theories should, at this point, expect to be provisional—halfway houses on the

---

Williams Lane Craig and Quentin Smith, 50–72 (New York: Routledge, 2008); Y. Balashov and M. Janssen, "Presentism and Relativity," *The British Journal for the Philosophy of Science* 54 (2003) 327–46.

46. D. Zimmerman, "Presentism and the Space-Time Manifold."

path to something more stable. Physicists have reached no consensus on the question: how are quantum theory and GR to be reconciled? When and if they do, we Open Theists, in virtue of our commitment to the A-theory, may well have some work to do reconciling the resulting theory with belief in a privileged present. In the meantime, the relative ease with which presentism—even theistic presentism—can be combined with SR encourages the hope that, when scientists do finally converge upon a uniquely appropriate manifold for quantum gravity, it will pose no further problems of principle.

Open Theism and Religious Life

7

Prayer and Open Theism

A Participatory, Co-Creator Model

ROBIN COLLINS

INTRODUCTION

THIS PAPER IS AN attempt to work out an adequate non-process, open-theist account of the efficacy of petitionary prayer that is generally compatible with the way petitionary prayer is portrayed in the Christian scriptures, particularly its stress on faith and persistence as a typical requirement for efficacious prayer. I will call this account the "co-creator model." Throughout the paper, I will assume that petitionary prayer is in some cases efficacious in bringing about, or at least "making a difference," in some way beyond ordinary psychological and physical means.[1] Thus, for the purposes of this paper, I am rejecting what could be called the purely "consciousness raising" account of petitionary prayer, where the efficacy of petitionary prayer is reduced to transforming us both spiritually and psychologically. Although prayer certainly does have these effects, the Christian scriptures portray the effects of petionary prayer as going far beyond "consciousness raising."

1. By ordinary psychological and physical means, I mean those means that would be allowed by the following two assumptions: (1) all causation between the mind and the physical world is via the brain; and (2) the brain only influences the rest of the body, and the physical world, via causal or lawlike connections recognized in the physical sciences.

Further, I will assume that the efficacy of petitionary prayer in some way involves God's special action. Some models of the efficacy of petitionary prayer, which have gained some recent popularity, see prayer as working via a paranormal influence on the one for whom we pray. I call such models "naturalistic models" of prayer since God plays no direct role. This view is advocated by such writers as medical doctor Larry Dossey in *Healing Words*.[2] In this model, prayer works in a similar way to the well-known *placebo* affect, except it works non-locally. In the well-documented placebo effect, the belief that we will get well often helps us get well, though how it does this is not well understood. Thus, one's beliefs are able to affect directly one's own body. This much is accepted by medical science, as is testified by the standard use of double-blind testing of new drugs by the medical community in which neither the patient nor the researchers know which individuals received a placebo and which received the drug. The claim of those who advocate the naturalistic understanding of prayer is that this ability directly to affect the outcome of an illness, or other aspects of the world, through our thoughts, beliefs, and intentions extends far beyond our own body.

Much could be said in favor of this view of prayer. First, it has some initial plausibility, being simply an extension of the mysterious placebo effect beyond the confines of our own body. Second, advocates of this view claim that it is backed by purportedly rigorous scientific studies in which human intentions do seem to affect the outcome of the growth of certain organisms, such as bacteria in a Petri dish,[3] though recent large-scale studies have failed to confirm that petitionary prayer for other humans is effective.[4] Third, it has some support from scripture. There are many pas-

---

2. Larry Dossey, *Healing Words: The Power of Prayer and the Practice of Medicine* (New York: HarperOne, 1995).

3. Ibid.

4. The failure to produce any evidence for the power of intercessory prayer in the most methodologically rigorous recent prayer studies, such as the mammoth STEP project (Study of the Therapeutic Effects of Intercessory Prayer) involving people praying for groups of cardiac patients (H. Benson et. al. "Study of the Therapeutic Effects of Intercessory Prayer (STEP) in Cardiac Bypass Patients: a Multicenter Randomized Trial of Uncertainty and Certainty of Receiving Intercessory Prayer," *American Heart Journal* 151.4 [2006] 934–42), does not offer significant evidence against the co-creator model. One reason is that there was no way for controlling for prayers offered by loved ones that were not part of the groups recruited to do the praying. Another was that the prayers were offered by people who lacked personal connections with the patients, thus making it doubtful whether they met the criteria for effective prayer in the co-creator model—e.g., co-working with the will of God.

sages in which Jesus tells someone that their faith has made them whole, such as what Jesus says to the woman with the issue of blood in Mark 5:34: "Daughter, *your faith* has made you well; go in peace, and be healed of your disease." Such passages suggest that faith has an intrinsic power to bring about the healing. (Also see Luke 18:42, Luke 8:50, Mark 9:23, and Mark 11:23.) Fourth, it explains purported cases of healing in other non-theistic religions, such as Buddhism, in which the no appeal is made to a deity for healing. Finally, a theist could make sense of the responsiveness of the universe to our prayers by claiming that God created the universe to be responsive to humans at some subtle level beyond our current scientific understandings, just as God created the universe in such a way that we could discover its underlying structure.[5]

Despite its strengths, for those who take scripture seriously the naturalistic understanding does not seem adequate. In scripture, prayer is typically portrayed as being offered to God, with God "answering" our prayer by acting on our behalf. In the naturalistic understanding, however, God is left completely out of the picture, except perhaps for being the one who designed and sustains the system by which our prayers can have this sort of influence. To correct these problems, one could combine this naturalistic model with a model in which God is directly involved in the answering of our prayers. This is what I will propose in what I call the "co-creator" model of petitioner prayer below.

As a matter or terminology, I will say that God "answered" a prayer or that it is efficacious only if something sufficiently similar to the state of affairs that is explicitly prayed for occurs. I recognize, however, that many people would want to say that God answers a prayer even if no state of affairs resembling the one requested occurs: e.g., some people would claim that God has answered a prayer to heal a certain person of cancer even if the person dies of the cancer; they would say that God answered the prayer but not in the way requested.

5. At present, science is incapable of determining whether such effects actually occur. Thus, one's likelihood for the existence of such interconnections will be determined by whether such connections contribute to the overall value of reality; if they do, then since God is perfectly good, we have reasons to believe such connections exist since their value would give a God to create a reality that included them. Further, at least at the microscopic level, quantum mechanics also provides a precedent for this form of holistic, top-down causality, since in many quantum systems the behavior of wholes is partially determined by something transcending the parts and their interrelationships. Even though quantum mechanics implies non-locality at the microscopic level, it is important to stress that it does not necessarily imply non-locality for the everyday world; I believe it does, however, considerably raise the plausibility of such non-local effects at the everyday level.

Before going into my own account, I will motivate it by considering the nature of petitionary prayer under theological determinist, Molinist, and typical open theist accounts. For purposes of illustration, throughout the paper we will use a fictitious case of a person Jane who prays to be healed of cancer on 1/1/2000 and is healed on 1/2/2000.

THREE CLASSICAL MODELS OF PRAYER

Theological Determinist Model

Under theological determinism, God both predestines Jane to pray and decides either to heal or not to heal Jane. Thus, under theological determinism, Jane's prayer does not itself influence God. Indeed, this conclusion is in keeping with the overall theological position traditionally adopted by those who advocate theological determinism, namely that God is so sovereign that he cannot be affected in any way by his creatures.[6] As the famous reformed theologian Jonathan Edwards wrote, "God is sometimes represented *as if* he were moved and persuaded by the prayers of his people; yet it is not to be thought that God is properly moved or made willing by our prayers;"[7] instead, God bestows mercy *"as though* he were prevailed upon by prayer."[8] Thomas Aquinas says similar things, holding that prayer neither affects God nor helps bring about the prayed for event. Rather, Aquinas claims, there is some good—such as recognition of our dependence on God—by asking things of God: ". . . we pray not that we may change the Divine disposition, but that we may impetrate that which God has disposed to be fulfilled by our prayers in other words 'that by asking, men may deserve to receive what Almighty God from eternity has disposed to give,' as Gregory says."[9] Of course, under theological determinism, Jane's actions can influence other events, even though all of Jane's actions are ultimately the result of God's decrees. For example, God could

6. Although God is neither male nor female, to avoid unnecessary awkwardness, in this paper I follow convention use the male pronoun to refer to God. I acknowledge the problems with this convention, however, since it can subtlety reinforce the false idea that God is male, along with the related symbolic understandings of the divine.

7. Jonathan Edwards, *The Works of President Edwards: In Ten Volumes*, vol. VI. (New York: G. & C. & H. Carvill, 1830) 321.

8. Ibid.

9. Thomas Aquinas, "Summa Theologica," in *Calvin Colleges Ethereal Library of Christian Classics*, trans. Mark Browning (http://www.ccel.org/ccel/aquinas/summa.html, 1997) 2.83.2.

predestine Jane to help her friend Bill find a job, which in turn could result in Bill's getting a job. Even though God ultimately predestined Jane to act in the way she did, it would still be true that Jane's actions were partly responsible for Bill's obtaining a job. Put differently, Jane was the instrument God used to bring about John's getting a job. In contrast, in the case of Jane's prayer, it does not make sense to think of God's using Jane as an instrument to influence God's own decision to heal Jane, since that decision was already made prior to Jane's existence. Rather, from all eternity, God had decided both that Jane would pray and that he would heal Jane, and hence under this view Jane's prayer could not be said to have had any influence on God's healing her.

Finally, even though Jane's prayer in no way brought about her healing, the following counterfactual still might be true: if Jane had not prayed, then she would not have been healed.[10] The truth of this counterfactual, however, does not negate our claim that Jane's prayer our no difference in whether or not she would be healed. To see this, consider an example of a storm that produces rain in a certain area. Basic meteorology tells us that when a major storm arrives, the barometric pressure falls. Thus, the storm is what philosophers call the common cause of both the rain and the barometric pressure falling, just as under theological determinism God is the common cause of both the prayer and its answer. Given that, there was no other possibility of rain (except for the storm), the following counterfactual would be true: if the barometric pressure had not fallen, it would not have rained. Yet no one would say that the barometric pressure's falling brought about the rain, or that it made a difference in whether or not it rained. This case is relevantly analogous to the case of prayer under theological determinism. God is the common cause (or determinate) of both Jane's healing and Jane's praying, and thus Jane's praying can no more be said to make a difference in whether Jane was healed than the barometric pressure's falling can be said to make a difference in whether it rained.

Thus, it might seem, advocates of theological determinism will either have to deny that prayer makes a difference with regard to whether the prayed for event occurs or advocate a naturalistic model of petionary prayer. There is one further alternative, however: they could say that prayer,

---

10. This counterfactual might be true because the following counterfactual concerning God's free choice might be true: if God had decided not to cause Jane to pray, then God would have decided not to heal Jane.

like other actions, creates the appropriate conditions in us, others, and even other aspects of the world, for God to act, even though the prayers do not influence God. Further, the prayer could create these conditions not only through normal channels, but via some sort of special causal power. Thus, they could offer a theological determinist version of the co-creator model elaborated below. Indeed, the well-known Bible commentator and theological determinist Matthew Henry could be understood as offering just such an understanding of how petitionary prayer could be efficacious in the person praying receiving mercy from God. Says Henry, "It is true, nothing we can say can have any influence upon him, or move him to show us mercy, but it may have an influence upon ourselves, and help to *put us into a frame fit to receive mercy.*"[11] So, as will become clearer below, the co-creator model does not itself require open theism, though it fits better with open theism's emphasis on the cooperative and interpersonal interaction between God and humans.

Molinist Model

In defending a Molinist perspective on petitionary prayer, Thomas Flint, probably the leading philosopher defending Molinism, considers the case of Peter prayer for the healing of the lame man in Acts 3:1–10. First, Flint agrees that Peter's prayer cannot causally influence God's decision whether to heal the lame man. Says Flint:

> God's knowledge of how Peter and others would freely act will be based upon his middle knowledge of how Peter and others would freely act in various circumstances, not upon his free knowledge as to how they will act. Since his middle knowledge is not caused by Peter's action, and since God's decision to cure the lame man in the wake of Peter's prayer is part of the one all-encompassing creative decision that God makes, Peter's act of prayer neither causes God to know anything about Peter nor effects any change in God's intentions.[12]

Flint then goes on to say that prayer can still make a difference, stating that "from a Molinist perspective, Peter's prayer can be thought of as making a

11. Matthew Henry, *Daily Communion with God: Christianity No Sect; The Sabbath; The Promises of God; The Worth of the Soul; A Church in the House* (New York: Robert Carter, 1848) 77.

12. Thomas Flint, *Divine Providence: A Molinist Account* (New York: Cornell University Press, 1998) 226.

difference even if we don't think of that prayer as having any causal effect upon God, or as leading to any real change in God."[13] According to Flint, a necessary and sufficient condition for Peter's prayer to make a difference is that his prayer was a free act and if he had not prayed, then God would not have healed the lame man.[14] If these conditions are satisfied, this means that "Peter had counterfactual power over A [God's healing the lame man], power which he exercised by praying."[15] Such power implies that Peter's prayer made a difference.

Despite Flint's claim, I must confess that I have difficulty seeing how this model does significantly better than a non-co-creator version of theological determinism concerning the issue of whether our prayers make a difference. To see the problem, we begin by noting that Flint's reasons for thinking Peter's prayer made a difference are based on this notion of its having counterfactual power over A. This, however, simply means that (i) if Peter had not prayed, then A would not have occurred, and (ii) Peter's prayer was not causally determined by God or anything else—that is, it is free in the Molinist sense.[16] Since (i)—that is, counterfactual dependence—is satisfied in the case of theological determinism and yet we showed that prayer does not make a difference under that view, (i) is not sufficient for prayer making a difference.[17] Thus, the claim that prayer makes a difference rests on (ii) being satisfied in addition to counterfactual dependence. It is difficult to see, however, how the addition of (ii) is relevant to prayer making a difference. In every *agreed upon case* in which we would want to say that an event A makes a difference to whether another even B occurs, the additional component to counterfactual dependence of B on A is that A causally contributes to B. This at least provides a powerful case for counterfactual dependence conjoined with causal contribution being a sufficient condition for "making a difference,"

13. Ibid.

14. Ibid., 227.

15. Ibid.

16. According to Flint, for the Molinist a person is free if they are not determined by events not under not under the agent's control.

17. Some might question whether counterfactual dependence actually obtained in the example of determinism we used in the last section. For an uncontroversial example, consider a case in which God decreed that Peter pray. Logic demands that truth of the following counterfactual: if Peter had not prayed, then God would not have decreed that he prayed. Yet, clearly, Peter's prayer did not make a difference to what God decreed.

and for causal contribution itself being a necessary condition. Further, it provides a powerful case for what could be called the "causal contribution" account of making a difference—that is, the account according to which the property denoted by "making a difference" is simply causal contribution combined with counterfactual dependence (or perhaps even causal contribution alone). In light of this, simply to assert that in the case of prayer (i) and (ii) are sufficient for making a difference seems very *ad hoc*. In order to make his account plausible, therefore, Flint would need to provide some further argument. For example, he could attempt to argue that as ordinarily used the phrase "makes a difference" really picks out some property that entails (a) the necessity of causal contribution in all ordinary, agreed upon cases but not in the case of prayer, and (b) the necessity of libertarian freedom in the case of prayer (and certain other actions resulting from God's middle knowledge) but not in other ordinary, agreed upon cases.[18] As far as I know, neither Flint nor any other person has provided such an account. Of course, Flint could simply stipulate that what he means by "making a difference" is that conditions (i) and (ii) are satisfied, but then the phrase "making a difference" becomes empty, losing all connection with our ordinary use of the term.

Open Theism and the Apex Model

Open theists often claim that their view of God provides a better account of petitionary prayer as it is portrayed in scripture than that of theological determinism or Molinism since it allows our prayers to affect God, which thereby allows the prayer to causally contribute to the occurrence of the prayed for event. Merely saying this, however, does not go beyond what Rick Ostrander[19] refers to as the popular *apex* model of prayer. This model views the action of prayer as forming an apex involving the human being's praying and the condition prayed for at the bottom of the apex, with God at the top: that is, a prayer (P) affects God (G), who in turn decides whether to answer (A) the prayer. For the case in which prayer is efficacious, we can symbolically represent this as P→G→A.

18. That libertarian freedom is typically not a necessary condition is clear from ordinary cases: e.g., one can make a difference in a poor person's life—such as by giving the person money—even if one's actions are determined.

19. Rick Ostrander, *The Life of Prayer in a World of Science: Protestants, Prayer, and American Culture, 1870–1930* (Oxford: Oxford University Press, 2000) 132.

The way in which P affects God is crucial to whether this model affirms the relationality between humans and God that is a primary motive of open theism. One way in which P could affect God is by providing God with knowledge of the truth values of certain propositions. For example, our praying might cause God to come to know that we prayed. Then using this knowledge, God might decide whether to answer our prayer by some set of criteria. A critical question here is whether these criteria promote relationality. Suppose, for instance, that God decides whether or not to answer a prayer based solely on some set of moral criteria— e.g., by weighing the probable potential good involved in answering the prayer as compared to not answering the prayer, along with some other relevant moral criteria. Deciding in this way, however, seems to undercut the desired relational aspect of prayer by making God seem analogous to cosmic computer, or a "great administrator," that simply decides based on a fixed set of moral criteria. This problem is particularly pronounced given the view of many open theists that God has made complete contingency plans for all eternity—e.g., God has already decided what action to take for every possible set of creaturely free choices; if this is correct, then God's answer to our prayer merely involves executing a preexisting contingency plan once God knows the relevant facts about what free creatures have decided to do.

In order for the apex model to affirm relationality, therefore, it will have to postulate that prayer affects God in some way other than God's gaining propositional knowledge. Further, it will want to avoid making God simply a link in a causal chain from P to A, since among other things, this would negate relationality. (God becomes like a candy machine dispenser, but less reliable!). So, how could we conceive of P's affecting God so as to include relationality in our model? William Hasker has suggested to me the analogy of our asking for a friend's help, which typically helps create relationality. The dynamic of asking involves at least two components: (i) an informative component, in which we let our friend know that we need help; and (ii) a relational component, in which we *invite* our friend into an aspect of our lives. Clearly, (i) does not exist in the case of God, but (ii) can. So, one might think that the purpose of prayer is invite God to act in our lives, or in the case of intercessory prayer, to act in other people's lives. And, perhaps God has restricted God's self to act in this way to make room for some joint human-divine action in the world.

In her widely discussed essay on petitionary prayer,[20] Eleonore Stump advocates a model similar to this, though not within an open theist framework. According to Stump, if God were simply to meet all our needs or desires without our specifically requesting this of God, God would become like an "overbearing parent" that constantly meddled in her child's life without the child requesting it. This parent-child analogy can be highly misleading at this point, however, unless it is specified that the child is an adult. In the case of a very young child, it is the responsibility of the parent to act unilaterally in the child's life with regard to anything that significantly involves the child's welfare. As more separation develops between the child and parent, then being invited before acting becomes much more important; and finally, in the case of friends, it becomes crucial except in rare circumstances.

A major question immediately arises for Stump's account with regard to unanswered prayer. One reason Stump gives for unanswered prayer is that if God answered every request, then it would result in "overwhelming spoiling":[21] the person would then treat God like "cosmic candy machine" that responded to every need and desire. One criticism often raised of Stump's reasoning here is that even prayers for the most basic needs that allow us to function at all—such as relief from debilitating depression—are not granted. Not only would any good parent—or an all-powerful friend—meet such basic needs, but meeting them would certainly not result in any overwhelming spoiling.

Of course, one could go beyond Stump's proposal and argue that since God sees the whole picture—all the potential consequences of granting and not granting a prayer—there could be other reasons why God does not answer some prayers. Although this is certainly true, such a response does not explicitly take into account the consistent New Testament teaching that persistence and faith are typically required for efficacious prayer. The book of James, for instance, states that "if any of you is lacking in wisdom, ask God, who gives to all generously and ungrudgingly, and it will be given you. But ask in faith, never doubting, for the one who doubts is like a wave of the sea, driven and tossed by the wind; for the doubter, being double-minded and unstable in every way, must not expect to receive anything from the Lord" (James 1:5–7, NRSV). This passage makes

20. Eleonore Stump, "Petitionary Prayer," *American Philosophical Quarterly* XVI (April 1979) 81–91.

21. Ibid., 143.

clear that it is God's desire to give us wisdom, but only on the condition that we ask God in faith. This same requirement of faith and persistence is stressed over and over again by Jesus (e.g., Mark 9:23, Mark 11:23 stress faith and Luke 11:5–8 and 18:1–8 stress persistence.) Of course, we must take into account that when the gospels record Jesus as making seemingly exaggerated claims such as that whatever one asks for in faith she will receive (e.g., Mark 11:24), he might be engaging in Middle-Eastern hyperbole, which was a common way of speaking at the time. Nonetheless, this does not negate the overall emphasis of the New Testament on faith and persistence for effectual prayer. Further, the claim that such passages only apply to very advanced Christians, not the ordinary Christian—a speculation advanced by C. S. Lewis[22]—seems to me to be a position one should take only as a last resort, when all other theologically plausible ways of understanding these passages fail. Any Christian model of prayer that hopes to be faithful to the Biblical witness, therefore, must address why faith and persistence are stressed in the New Testament as typically being key requirements for efficacious prayer. This is what we will attempt to do in our co-creator model.

THE BASIC CO-CREATOR MODEL

The basic idea behind the co-creator model is that for those cases in which petitionary prayer is efficacious, humans and God work together to help bring about the states of affairs for which we pray. Further, it claims, God has so restrained God's self that typically he cannot (without violating his own constraints) act without our joint effort. *The reason God has restrained God's self in this way is to provide space for us to act on our own, and truly contribute to other people's lives and the direction and development of the world.* As should be clear from our discussion of theological determinism, the co-creator model does not require the truth of open theism, but it fits better with open theism's stress on the importance of mutual divine-human relationality. Further, it is important to note that the co-creator model denies a key assumption typically made by philosophers who defend or argue against the efficacy of petitionary prayer: namely, the assumption that insofar as prayer makes a difference in whether an event occurs, it does so by making a difference in God's decision as to whether

22. C. S. Lewis, *Letters to Malcolm: Chiefly on Prayer* (Fort Washington, PA: Harvest, 2002) 60–61.

to bring about the event. This assumption, for example, underlies Scott Davison's recent arguments that the current philosophical defenses of the value of petitionary prayer fail.[23, 24]

The co-creator model starts with the assumption that our prayers directly affect (that is, affect without being mediated by special acts of God) those things or persons for whom we pray, a position also asserted by the naturalistic model discussed above. Put differently, the universe is constructed in some deep and subtle way to be responsive to human intentions, just as the body is responsive to our thoughts, as in the case of the placebo effect. It goes beyond the purely naturalistic model, however, by claiming that the Holy Spirit works within us not only to initiate our prayers, but to amplify their causal efficacy by cohering with our own intentions in analogy to how a laser beam gains its power by various individual light waves cohering together. As mentioned when we discussed the naturalistic model, many scriptures suggest that our prayers offered in faith have such a direct effect, such as Luke 18:42, Luke 8:50, Mark 5:24, Mark 9:23, and Mark 11:23; further, it seems to be presupposed in

23. Scott Davison, "Petitionary Prayer," *The Oxford Handbook of Philosophical Theology*, eds. Thomas Flint and Michael Rea (Oxford: Oxford University Press, 2009).

24. Ideas similar to the co-creator model were prominent among "evangelical liberals" in the early part of the Twentieth Century (see Rick Ostrander, *The Life of Prayer in a World of Science: Protestants, Prayer, and American Culture, 1870–1930* [Oxford: Oxford University Press, 2000] 131–35). As far as I know, however, these ideas were never developed and were largely motivated by an antipathy towards supernatural intervention, something I do not share. A related view to mine is also presented by process theologians and philosophers, such as Suchocki (Marjorie Hewitt Suchocki, *Theological Reflections on Prayer: In God's Presence* [Atlanta: Chalice, 1996]), and Philip Clements-Jewery, *Intercessory Prayer: Modern Theology, Biblical Teaching and Philosophical Thought* (London: Ashgate, 2005) 144–47. Unlike process thinkers, I assume that God is omnipotent. Finally, Lewis presents, but does not develop, the idea that for those very advanced Christians that can pray in faith, their prayer is effectual because they become God's fellow-workers. As Lewis says, "the fellow-worker, the companion or (dare we say?) the colleague of God is so united with Him at certain moments that something of the divine foreknowledge enters his mind. Hence his faith is the 'evidence'—that is, the evidentness, the obviousness—of things not seen" (C. S. Lewis, *Letters to Malcolm: Chiefly on Prayer* [Fort Washington, PA: Harvest, 2002] 61). Lewis seems unable to apply this view to the average Christian, or adequately develop it, since he accepts the impassibility of God and complete divine foreknowledge (Lewis, *Letters to Malcolm: Chiefly on Prayer*, 48), which leads him to think of faith as sharing in God's foreknowledge of what God is going to bring about (i.e., the "answered" prayer) and does not allow for any real way for us to be us to be co-creators since God becomes the sole cause of whether the prayer is answered.

1 Cor 13:2 where the Apostle Paul says "if I have all faith, so as to remove mountains, but do not have love, I am nothing."

Another hypothesis is that persistent, faithful prayer creates "openings" for God or his emissaries to act in the world and that bad intentions and unbelief create barriers, where these openings and barriers are to be understood as resulting from God's self-imposed constraints on how he will act in the world. The idea of prayer creating openings is suggested by the story in Daniel 10: 12–14, in which it took twenty-one days for the angel to deliver the message to Daniel because of resistance from the "Prince of the Kingdom of Persia"; the passage suggests that Daniel's persistent prayer and fasting (for twenty-one days) helped provide the opening for the message to get through. (See section on unanswered prayer below for additional discussion.) On the other hand, this idea that unbelief can block God's power is suggested by Mark 6:5–6, which indirectly portrays unbelief as inhibiting Jesus from doing mighty deeds in Nazareth: "He could do no mighty deed of power there [in Nazareth], except that he laid hands on a few sick people and healed them. And he was amazed at their unbelief" (Mark 6:5–6, NRSV).

Although this model claims that prayer in some way affects God, the way it affects God should not to be thought of in a mechanical way, as a sort of mental/spiritual technology of accomplishing our ends. Rather, out of abiding in Christ, and establishing a close relationship with God, comes the persistence and faith needed for effective prayer. Specifically, the faith needed for effective prayer is best thought of as being the "faith of Christ or God" (see below) and as related to the "groanings of the Holy Spirit within us" (Rom 8:26–27). In this process of participating in the "faith of Christ," we do not simply submit to God, but we act as full agents in personal interaction with God. This sort of prayer involves much more than simply "saying one's prayers," or making an explicit request, though this might be part of one's prayer life. It involves being in communion with God and dynamically working with the Holy Spirit in everything one does; this in turn involves a whole way of life and orientation to the world, such as a sensitivity to the God given potentiality of things and people (particularly what God has called them to be) and a sensitivity to God's overall movement in the world.

QUESTIONS AND FURTHER EXPLORATIONS OF THE MODEL

Faith, Grace, and Personal Effort

A key part of the co-creator model revolves around how we are to understand faith. Besides the aspect of trust and loyalty, several other aspects of this faith are particularly worth noting. First, the type of faith involved in prayer, I suggest, involves *envisioning* as yet unrealized possibilities, something closely connected with *hope*. One finds this sort of faith in the Old Testament prophets, who envisioned a time of peace in which the lion would lie down with the lamb, and in the great people of faith listed in Hebrews chapter 11. This aspect of faith is central to any sort of creative activity, and is crucial to everyday life: for example, raising a child involves envisioning what the child could be. Our ability to envision the future in this way is one thing that appears to separate us from the animals, which only seem to live in the present. It is a truly extraordinary human capacity, a gift of God, that is central to what we are as creatures that are actively involved in and help bring about the temporal unfolding of the world. Indeed, it is central to almost all aspects of life.

Helping us envision a future of the kingdom of God is perhaps the primary way in which God works through human beings, and brings about his purposes in the world. For example, God could arguably be thought of as giving each person a general sense or vision of what his or her specific purpose in life is. Indeed, helping provide the people with a vision might be one reason that prophets were so important in the Old Testament.

Second, I suggest, faith is closely connected with *Love*. This aspect of faith is directed toward other people and involves discerning and affirming the unrealized potentials of oneself and other people for becoming whom God created them to be—e.g., beings in caring, creative intersubjective relationship with God and others. Arguably, this sort of faith is at the heart of love of other people, which, I suggest, crucially involves valuing them for who God created them to be. This is also linked with the Christian call to be the salt of the earth. Besides being a preservative, salt is also used to bring out flavors in food—e.g., unsalted bread tastes flat. Accordingly, part of being the "salt of the earth" is to help one's self and others realize their true potential. Indeed, the two aspects of faith listed above show that faith, hope, and love form a triad that mutually support one another. As it says in 1 Cor 13:13, "And now faith, hope, and love abide, these three; and the greatest of these is love."

Third, I suggest, Christian faith is better thought of as something that comes from God, not something we generate; all we can do is be receptive and provide the conditions for it to occur. Indeed, arguably, almost all of those scriptures typically translated "have faith *in* Christ" or "have faith *in* God" are better translated as "have the faith *of* Christ" or "have the faith *of* God." For example, making this substitution in the NRSV, Galatians 2:16 reads, "Yet we know that a person is justified not by the works of the law but through the faith *of* Jesus Christ"; Galatians 2:20 reads "it is no longer I who live, but Christ who lives in me. And the life I live, I live in the flesh I live by the faith *of* the son of God"; Phil 3:8–9 reads "for his sake I have suffered the loss of all things, and regard them as rubbish, in order that I may gain Christ and be found in him not having a righteousness of my own that comes from the law but one that comes through the faith *of* Christ"; Finally Mark 11:22 reads "Jesus answered them, have the faith *of* God. Truly I tell you, if you say to this mountain be 'be taken up and thrown into the sea,' and if you do not doubt in your heart but, believe that what you say will come to pass, it will be done for you."[25]

Having the faith of Christ is a matter of grace, of being in close communion and alignment with Christ. Thus, once we notice this, the apparent conflict between grace and the requirement of faith and persistence is largely solved, along with the idea that effectual prayer needs to be in accordance with God's will. One must be aligned with God's will to have this sort of faith. Further, praying in this way furthers, instead of hinders, one's relationship with God. In this understanding, God co-creates with us through the faith of Christ operating in us, where one of the primary

25. The footnotes to the NRSV Bible present this alternative "of" translation. At least for the passages in the book of Galatians, this alternative understanding is also elaborated in much more detail by Duke University Biblical scholar Richard Hays (Richard Hays, *The Faith of Jesus Christ: The Narrative Substructure of Galatians 3:1—4:11*, 2nd ed. [Grand Rapids: Eerdmans, 2002]) and has currently gained considerable ground in the field of Biblical Studies.

The faith of God idea also fits well with a theory of Atonement I have developed elsewhere (Robin Collins, "Girard and Atonement: An Incarnational Theory of Mimetic Participation," in *Violence Renounced: Rene Girard, Biblical Studies, and Peacemaking*, Studies in Peace and Scripture 4, ed. Willard Swartley [Herald/Pandora, 2000] 132–56), which I call the Incarnational theory. According to this theory, on the Cross, Jesus acted in full faith, hope, and love while experiencing the depths of the human life situation of vulnerability, uncertainty, unjust persecution, and alienation from God and others. This in turn created a fully divine and while fully human forms of faith, hope, and love in Christ; salvation, in turn, results from progressively participating in this faith, hope, and love that exists in Christ.

aspects of this faith of Christ involves envisioning in hope and love a new, yet to be realized reality.

This idea of having the faith of Christ also nicely coincides with the emphasis in scripture of God's working *incarnationally* through us in prayer: our prayers themselves are joint acts of God and us. For example, Rom 8:22, 26 says: "We know that the whole creation has been groaning with labor pains until now; and not only the creation, but we ourselves who have the first fruits of the Spirit, groan inwardly while we wait for adoption, the redemption of our bodies. . . . *Likewise the Spirit helps us in our weakness; for we do not know how to pray as we ought, but the Spirit intercedes with sighs to deep for words. . . .*" Further, in Phil 2:12–13 Paul says that God generally works in and through human beings to further the kingdom of God in us and others: "Work out your own salvation with fear and trembling; for it is God who is at work in you, enabling you both to will and to work for his good pleasure." Thus, these scriptures suggest that God typically works within us by co-operating with human faith, will, and activity, not by omnipotent fiat.

Consequently, effective petitionary prayer presupposes the prayer of communion with God and "abiding in Christ." Only by doing this can we align our intentions and will with God and hence be true co-creators with him. As John 15:7 says, "If you abide in me, and my words abide in you, ask whatever you wish, and it will be done for you." Also, I suggest, effective prayer requires an attitude of openness to events—not trying to control things. As John 3:7–8 says, "Do not be astonished at what I said to you, 'you must be born from above [or anew].' *The wind blows where it chooses, and you hear the sound of it, but you do not know where it comes from or where it goes. So it is with everyone born of the Spirit.*"

Even though having faith is a matter of God's working in us, nonetheless it is the case that if one believes (as taught by Jesus, James, and Paul) that persistence and faith are generally required for efficacious prayer, then one must hold that sometimes prayer is not efficacious because we lacked faith or did not persist. Indeed, according to Matthew's Gospel, when the disciples asked Jesus why they could not drive out the demon in the demon possessed boy he said, "Because of your little faith. For truly I tell you, if you have faith the size of a mustard seed, you will say to this mountain, 'Move from here to there,' and it will move; and nothing will be impossible for you" (Matt 17:20–21, NRSV). But this should not lead us to think effectual prayer is a matter of us working harder, by our own efforts.

As stressed above, the kind of faith and persistence needed for effectual prayer only comes from a dynamic interaction with God—it is the faith *of* Christ. Thus, the best we can do is to "abide in Christ" and stay in that dynamic interaction. So, it is not a matter of working hard as much as it is of being open to God's working in us through the Holy Spirit.

Related to this last concern is the worry that acceptance of this model would lead to blaming the sick person, or those interceding for them, for not being healed. Several responses can be offered to concern. First, anyone who would blame someone for not having enough faith or persistence could as well be blamed for not being loving enough or having enough faith to intercede effectively for the sick person. Second, the co-creator model does not claim that it is always in accordance with God's will that a sick person be made well—e.g., Paul's thorn in the flesh is usually taken as a counterexample to this idea.

Third, even in those cases in which it is true that if one had only prayed longer, or had more faith, the prayer would have been granted, it does not follow that it is appropriate to blame ourselves for not praying with enough faith or with enough persistence.[26] To see this, consider the following analogy. If one had one's car checked over every week, one would greatly reduce the risk of having an accident because of a mechanical failure. But, if someone were to get into an accident because of a mechanical failure of her automobile, we would not blame the person for not having her car inspected the week before. Why not? Because it is not reasonable for one to have her car examined every week given all the other important activities to which one must attend. One is only to blame if one is negligent—that is, when one does not take reasonable precautions, such as having one's car inspected once a year. Similarly, at most, one could only be to blame for not having enough persistence and faith if one prayed with much less persistence or faith than could reasonably be expected in the circumstances. Even then, however, blame should not be our response, but rather compassion expressed both in

---

26. I speak here of "enough" faith and persistence. But, one might object, don't the gospels report Jesus as saying that one only needs the "faith of a mustard seed," the smallest seed of the field? One reply is that what makes the mustard seed analogy significant in this context is that mustard seeds can sprout and grow into very large bushes. So, what Jesus might be implying is that if you combine a mustard seeds worth of faith with the water and soil of persistence it will grow to become a powerful force for the kingdom of God.

our praying for the person and in helping the person to pray with more persistence and faith.

Moreover, we must always recognize that even though what we specifically pray for might not happen, often God uses even apparent failure to bring about a greater good. Even in cases in which an illness ends in death, tremendous spiritual and personal growth can take place both for the sick person and the one who takes care of him or her. Finally, we never know the obstacles in the spiritual realm that a person is facing: these obstacles could provide one reason a person's prayer appears to be unanswered even though she exercised more than normal faith and persistence. We will explore the idea of spiritual obstacles more in the next section.

The Problem of Unanswered Prayer

Any view in which prayer is considered to be sometimes efficacious raises the issue of unanswered (or non-efficacious) prayer. Why do some prayers fail to be efficacious? Simply to say that these prayers were not in accordance with God's will is an inadequate answer, since it seems clear that many non-efficacious prayers are for things that the New Testament says are God's will. For example, as mentioned previously, the first chapter of the book of James makes clear that God wants us to have wisdom, and yet many pray for wisdom and nonetheless seem largely to lack it. Or, as another example, God does not want us to continue falling prey to a besetting sin, yet many have prayed to overcome such sins—such as alcoholism—and still fall prey to it.

Several answers could be given for unanswered prayer from within the co-creator model, besides superficially saying that the person did not have enough faith or persistence. First, typically prayer is only effective insofar as we are operating as co-creators with Christ. That is, generally speaking, we must be "abiding in Christ," "tuned into" the will of God, and having the faith *of* Christ. One clarification should be made regarding this, however. Being tuned into the will of God does not mean that we are not independent agents, which would defeat the entire understanding of the co-creator model. Many passages in scripture suggest that God wants humans to be separate agents, not merely doing whatever they think God wants without question. For instance, in many places in scripture humans are commended or rewarded for questioning what appears to be God's will, such as the case of Abraham (Gen 18:23–33), Moses (Exod 32:9–14), Hezekiah (Isa 38:1–5) and the Canaanite woman (Matt 15:23–28).

A second reason for unanswered prayers is the existence of "obstacles" in the spiritual realm that prevent a prayer from being efficacious, in analogy to how such obstacles exist in the everyday realm—e.g., to starting a new business. Such an obstacle is portrayed in Daniel chapter 10:12–14, where the angel tells Daniel "the prince of the kingdom of Persia opposed me for twenty-one days. So, Michael, one of the chief princes, came to help me, and I left him there with the prince of the kingdom of Persia. . . ." Some of these obstacles are bigger than others are, and so require more persistence in prayer. If the obstacle is small, then one might receive the answer right away. If the obstacle is larger, more persistence is required to remove the obstacle. For example, presumably if Daniel quit praying for wisdom after two days (instead of the twenty-one it took him to receive an answer), he would have never received what he prayed for. In the case of Daniel, for example, we could postulate a dynamic interaction between humans and angels—they not only aid us, but we aid, empower, or energize them through our prayers, thereby helping them overcome the obstacles. This speculation fits well with relational theologies in general and is certainly a plausible way of reading the spiritual import of these passages from Daniel.

Another reason for unanswered prayer is that often we do not have the strength, or the conditions are not right, for an obstacle to be removed. This means we must be sensitive to the Holy Spirit regarding what to pray for, and what to focus our energies on in prayer. An analogy in the "natural" realm is that successful people know where to invest their energies and money. They are able to perceive "openings" and know which obstacles to avoid, and which they have a chance of overcoming.

The claim that spiritual obstacles provide at least one reason prayers seem to fail is further attested to by several other places in scripture. In Matt 17:20–21, for example, Jesus tells his disciples that the reason they could not cast out the demon from the demon-possessed boy was "because of your little faith." At least according to some ancient manuscripts, Jesus then goes on to say that "this kind does not come out except by much prayer and fasting," indicating that the obstacle is particularly significant in this case. In Eph 6:10–20, the Apostle Paul tells us that our struggle is not against enemies of flesh and blood but "against the authorities, against the cosmic powers of this present darkness, against the spiritual forces of evil in heavenly places" (NRSV, verse 12); In 1 Corinthians 10:3 Paul also suggests the existence of these spiritual obstacles when he declares that "we do not wage war according to human standards; for the weapons of our warfare are not merely human, but they have divine power to destroy strongholds." Finally, as mentioned above, the gospel of Mark tells us that because of the people's unbelief, in his hometown of Nazareth Jesus "could do no deed of power there, except that he laid his hand on a few sick people and cured them" (Mark 6:5, NRSV)—suggesting that the people's unbelief created an obstacle to the exercise of his power.

One way of understanding these obstacles and spiritual forces of evil is provided by Walter Wink's extensive and important study of the New Testament's use of these terms. Wink claims that phrases such as "the cosmic powers of present darkness" primarily refer to those *spiritual* and *invisible* forces and patterns corresponding to the internal dimensions of human existence, culture, and institutions; according to Wink, these exert great influence and control over human behavior. Further, Wink claims that this spiritual or invisible dimension is inextricably part of the nature of human culture and institutions, but not reducible to its outer manifestations. In the same way that the free choices of each individual affect our culture (though culture is something that transcends the sum of individuals), Wink claims that human sin has perverted these powers from their true calling, as given in Col 1:16. Wink links this perversion with the Fall, which Wink sees as referring to the "sedimentation of thousands of years of human choices for evil." [27] According to Wink, the redemption we have in Christ in turn has broken the hold these powers have over our life, and further enables us to help redeem them to their true purpose. (See, e.g., Col 1:13, 20.)[28]

Although I believe the above account goes a long ways toward accounting for why some prayers are not efficacious even though they seem to be definitely in accordance with the will of God as revealed in scrip-

27. Walter Wink, *Engaging the Powers: Discernment and Resistance in a World of Domination* (Minneapolis: Fortress, 1992) 69.

28. For a general account of Wink's idea, see his highly acclaimed *Engaging the Powers*. For a more exegetical treatment of relevant New Testament passages, see his *Naming the Powers: The Language of Power in the New Testament* (Minneapolis: Fortress, 1984).

For a detailed account of original sin and that develops Wink's idea in the context of evolutionary theory, see Robin Collins, "Evolution and Original Sin," in *Perspectives on an Evolving Creation*, ed. Keith Miller (Grand Rapids: Eerdmans, 2003).

ture, why a specific prayer is not efficacious will often remain a mystery. The above discussion only presents a general picture of why some prayers might not be efficacious. Hopefully, this will keep us from blaming ourselves or getting angry at God for non-efficacious prayers, yet at the same time motivate us to develop a life lived in communion with God and in prayer which exemplifies both faith and persistence.

Why God Requires Prayer

In the co-creator model, prayer becomes a way that we can contribute to the well-being of others and ourselves in a way that transcends our normal bodily powers and in a way that explicitly involves God. Hence, under this model, it makes sense that God would make what happens in the world partly depend on prayer for the same reason God allows the welfare of others to depend on everyday external actions. The difference is that prayer both explicitly involves God and is accessible to everyone, even those who have no skills or are disabled. Further, prayer allows for the involvement of beings beyond the physical realm, such as angels.

This brings us to the question of why God has created a world in which humans are dependent on one another. One reason, I suggest, is that this dependence allows eternal connections of appreciation and intimacy to develop between humans and even between humans and other beings, such as angels. Elsewhere, I have developed this idea into what I call the "connection building theodicy."[29] For example, if you self-sacrificially help me during my time of suffering, then it will always be the case that you were there for me when I needed you. Thus, given that I am not an ingrate—which I certainly would not be in the heavenly state—I will eventually come to appreciate what you have done for me in this earthly life. Thus, there will be an ongoing, eternal connection of appreciation between you and me that arguably is of great, if not infinite, value since it lasts forever. Further, given that you have contributed to my life in a deep way, what you have done will in some way become a deep part of my life, and hence who I am; this will also form an intrinsically valuable, eternal connection of intimacy between you and me.

The connection building theodicy can explain why prayer requires persistence: if prayer required little effort or persistence on our part, then there would be little appreciation from others for helping them via our

29. "The Connection Building Theodicy." Unpublished Essay.

prayers, since so little effort would have been required. (Other views that place great value on virtuous actions can offer similar explanations). Finally, God's co-creating with us builds connections of intimacy between God and us: if God simply acted with his omnipotent power, without working in and through us (and in cooperation with us), there would be much less intimacy developed. We see this from a human analogy: few things have the potential for developing deep intimate bonds between people as true, cooperative engagement in common projects—as ideally happens in marriage.

The connection building theodicy also can explain why God often uses the agency of angels when "answering" prayer instead of "answering" prayers directly. (See, for example, Dan 10:12–14 and Acts 5:17.) By working and struggling on our behalf—as Michael and the other angel are recorded as doing in Daniel 10:10–21—connections of appreciation can form between humans and angels: when all is brought to light, we will eternally appreciate the angles for expending great effort on our behalf.

The Nature of Asking

The above analysis still leaves unanswered the question of why God requires that we *ask* him instead of creating the world in such a way that our faith and intentions non-locally affect the world, as in the naturalistic model of prayer discussed in the introductory section. Under the naturalistic model, God could still be involved in the process by supplying us the faith, grace, and guidance concerning what to pray. So, why is asking of particular importance? To answer this question, we first must consider what "asking" God involves. In the human case, asking can be analyzed into at least three elements: (i) desiring that something be done and that the person asked be involved in the process of bringing about the event; (ii) informing the person asked of one's desire; and, (iii) believing that asking will help bring about the other's involvement. An example of a case in which all three elements are present is that of a wife asking her husband to help with jacking up the car by saying "John, I would like you to help me jack the car up."

Applying this analysis to human's asking God, the informative element expressed by (ii) drops out; further, (iii) would need to be modified to something like that of having the belief that the desires expressed in (i) will positively affect whether God will be involved. Given that (ii) drops out, and (iii) is modified in the way suggested, arguably the essence of asking God becomes: (i*) an intentional, voluntarily sustained desire that something be done and that God be involved in bringing it about; and (ii*), the accompanying belief that having this desire makes a positive difference in whether or not God is involved.[1]

A human analogy will help illustrate why (i*) and (ii*) can plausibly be thought to capture the essence of asking God. Suppose that the husband in the above example gained perfect telepathic powers that gave him complete knowledge of anything his wife wanted for him to do for or with her, including the strength of her desire and whether it was intentional or something that just spontaneously popped into her head. Given these powers, it is likely that verbalizations of the requests would cease, no longer serving any function; even silent verbalizations—such as the wife "directing" the thought "John, would you help me with X" toward her husband—would likely cease. To modify a saying from Jesus, her husband would know what she desired of him before she "asked" him. Nonetheless, the need for the relevant, intentional desires would still remain.

This way of viewing the nature of asking, I believe, helps to counter the common temptation to think that prayer is pointless: at least part of this temptation, I suggest, arises from the failure to properly re-conceptualize what asking involves when the normal informative component of asking is removed as it is the case of an omniscient agent. If one continues to think of "asking" as primarily in terms of a vocalization or sub-vocalization (directed toward God) of certain desires, then the clear purpose that such vocalization has in the human case—that of informing the other of one's desires—is lost; without a new account of the reasons for this type of asking, inevitably it will seem purposeless. In contrast, the reasons for having the desires given by (i*) do appear to carry over from

---

1. Praying *in faith*, however, will involve various aspects of faith discussed above in addition to the desires involved in (i*) and (ii*). Further, I suggest that typically prayer involves a double movement that might need to be repeatedly enacted: that of first desiring the outcome and that God be involved, and then giving the results over to God. Finally, it should be noted, prayer need not involve any trying to make the event occur through our will or intentions; this is true even though we might believe that the desire given by (i*) has a positive influence, since such a belief is different from willing, or intending, for something to happen—e.g., it is different from willing to move my arm or exerting discipline to finish this essay. Finally, I suggest that this sort of prayer involves a double movement that might need to be repeatedly enacted: that of first desiring the outcome and that God be involved, and then giving the results over to God.

the human case, as can be seen by the perfect telepathic husband example given above.[1]

This account of what it means to ask God also helps clarify the value of asking God, since one of its essential components is a desire for God to be involved in bringing about the desired event. Such a desire will involve a continual openness towards God's work in one's life and in bringing about the desired outcome, which will often be accompanied by recognition of our dependence on God for the event occurring, such as our dependence on having the "faith of Christ" discussed earlier. Thus, since God could be said constantly to be asking, and depending on, humans to help bring about his will in the world, this desire for God to be involved will help create a synergistic relation of *mutual* give and take, and co-creation, between God and humans. This, I suggest, is of great value.

Besides the reasons given earlier for the importance of persistence in prayer, this view of what is involved in asking God—desiring that the event occur and that God be involved with us in bringing about the event—makes the need for persistence as a general condition for effectual prayer seem a natural requirement: by being persistent we demonstrate

---

1. Of course, one could claim that God requires vocalization or sub-vocalization of what one desires in order to count as petitionary prayer. There are several problems with this claim. First, given that in the normal human case vocalization serves an informative role that does not apply in the case of asking God, this claim would need independent support: one cannot just appeal to what "asking" involves in the human case. Second, it is difficult to see why God would require this, especially persistent and continual vocalization. It is much easier to see why the desires mentioned in (i*) would be required since having these desires is organically connected with God's co-working with us. Although vocalization or sub-vocalization might be helpful for some people, for others (such as me) it can be detrimental by reinforcing a false conscious or subconscious perception of God as not knowing what we desire before we vocalize it; or in the case of persistent prayer, a perception that we have to remind God of our desires since he might have forgotten or neglected them. These perceptions can persist even though we intellectually know they are false. (This objection, of course, assumes that we should try to make our perceptions and practices accord with what we believe God to be like.)

Third, thinking that persistent prayer requires persistent vocalization will inevitably often pit prayer against applying natural means to bring about the prayed for outcome, since often one cannot both fully engage in this type of prayer and fully use all the natural means at one's disposal, leading one to neglect one of the activities. As pointed out in the main text below, however, understanding petitionary in terms of (i*) and (ii**) makes one's use of these natural means part of prayer. Finally, persistent vocalizations run the risk of becoming vain repetitions. As Jesus says in Matthew 6:7–8, "But when ye pray, use not vain repetitions, as the heathen do: for they think that they shall be heard for their much speaking. Be not ye therefore like unto them: for your Father knoweth what things ye have need of, before ye ask him" (KJV).

and enact our commitment to the kingdom of God and God's involvement in our life, which in turn keeps us from treating God as puppet of our every whim. Finally, given this understanding of what it means to ask, praying for an event to occur (such as a healing) is not only consistent with using every means at our disposal (such as medical treatments) to bring about the event, but in fact demands that we do this since doing this demonstrates (and even constitutes) the seriousness of our commitment: as the book of James says, "faith without works is dead" (James 2:17, 2:20, 2:26). What turns this desire and commitment into prayer is our additional desire and expectation that God will be involved, along with the belief that our desires themselves will make a difference.

CONCLUSION

In this essay, I developed a model of petitionary prayer that both assumes that prayer makes a difference that goes beyond normal psychological and physical causation and at the same time incorporates the teachings of the New Testament regarding the importance of faith and persistence for efficacious prayer. Further, I attempted to do this in a way that was consistent with larger theological constraints—such as that effectual prayer is not a matter of self effort, but of grace; that prayer should promote an appropriate human-divine relationship; and that prayer is of great value. I argued that standard theological determinist and Molinist conceptions of prayer did not meet these criteria, specifically that of prayer making a difference; further, I argued that although open theism clearly allows for prayer to make a difference, an account is still needed that makes sense of the requirement of faith and persistence in prayer while at the same time being consistent with prayer promoting interpersonal relationality between God and humans. To meet these criteria, I developed what I called the "co-creator" model. This model incorporates what I called the "naturalistic" model, in which prayer is claimed to have a direct causal affect on whether the prayed for event occurs; unlike the naturalistic model, however, it also claims that God is involved as a co-worker with us in helping bring about the prayed for event. Along the way, we noted that although the co-creator model is consistent with theological determinism and Molinism, it is more consonant with the theological emphases of open theism on the importance of a dynamic interpersonal relationship between God and humans.[2]

2. I thank William Hasker, Jeffrey Koperski, David Basinger, Alan Rhoda, and David Schenk for commenting on an earlier version of this paper.

Index